Frederick Aflalo

Sea-fish

An account of the methods of angling as practised on the English coast

Frederick Aflalo

Sea-fish

An account of the methods of angling as practised on the English coast

ISBN/EAN: 9783337124038

Printed in Europe, USA, Canada, Australia, Japan

Cover: Foto ©Lupo / pixelio.de

More available books at **www.hansebooks.com**

SEA-FISH

AN ACCOUNT OF THE METHODS OF ANGLING
AS PRACTISED ON THE ENGLISH COAST, WITH
NOTES ON THE CAPTURE OF THE MORE SPORTING
FISHES IN CONTINENTAL, SOUTH AFRICAN, AND
AUSTRALIAN WATERS

BY

F. G. AFLALO

(WITH CONTRIBUTIONS BY VARIOUS HANDS)

ILLUSTRATED

London: LAWRENCE AND BULLEN, Ltd.
16 HENRIETTA STREET, COVENT GARDEN

MDCCCXCVIII

PREFACE

IN the following pages will be found some account of coast-fishing under modern conditions. Few sports have grown so rapidly in popularity; and one result of the recent increase of sea-anglers has been a tendency, on the part of both makers and amateurs, to adapt fishing tackle to the special requirements of salt water to an extent not dreamed of a few years back. Of these improvements, not a few of which have appeared during the two years that have elapsed since the publication of the last work on sea-fishing, the author has endeavoured to take note in the second chapter. It may be objected that not one-fifth of the fishes included in the British list are mentioned in this book; but sea-fishing as a sport is a question of *methods*, many kinds of fish being captured by each style.

The direction, however, in which writers on the sport can best serve their readers is undoubtedly that of local information; for it is here, in the shifting of the fish from one ground to another, in the erection of new piers and the destruction of old, that the greatest changes take place. A paternoster or leger, made up and baited as recommended by Mr. Wilcocks in his *Sea Fisherman*, would, *in the right place*, take fish as well to-day as thirty years ago; but so quickly do local conditions change, so capricious in their movements are the fish, that even Mr. Wilcocks might gladly accept the latest "marks" from the veriest novice.

The primary importance of up-to-date and accurate information about the seaside localities most visited by amateurs, those more particularly within easy reach of town, has not been lost sight of in the present manual, but is the subject of numerous references, not alone in the Appendix—to which many well-known amateur sea-fishermen, mostly resident at the coast, and therefore in touch with all the latest news, have been so good as to contribute—but also throughout the book.

The Editors have to acknowledge the kindly collaboration in the Appendix, the help of the Editor of the *Fishing Gazette* (R. B. Marston, Esq.), and of the Angling Editor of the *Field* ("Red-spinner"), in giving the names of several sea-fishing correspondents ; and the assistance of Messrs. Allcock and Bartleet (Redditch), Cummins (Bishop Auckland), Farlow and Hancock (London), Hardy Brothers (Alnwick), and Hearder (Plymouth), in the matter of tackle illustrations. For three of the Eastman Kodak reproductions the author is indebted to Harold Frederic, Esq.

F. G. A.
H. M.

CONTENTS

	PAGE
INTRODUCTORY	1

CHAPTER I.
NATURAL HISTORY NOTES ON THE CHIEF SEA-FISH, AND BAITS 12

CHAPTER II.
SEA-RODS, REELS, AND VARIOUS TACKLES 42

CHAPTER III.
HAND-LINING 79

CHAPTER IV.
SHORE-FISHING 93

CHAPTER V.
FISHING FROM PIERS AND HARBOURS 102

CHAPTER VI.
BOAT-FISHING 144

APPENDIX.
INTRODUCTORY.—ON "MARKS," WITH ALPHABETICAL LIST OF FISHING STATIONS, WITH NOTES BY VARIOUS CONTRIBUTORS 203

INDEX 251

LIST OF FULL-PAGE ILLUSTRATIONS

THE BASS	. . . .	*Frontispiece*		
,,	BREAM	*to face page*		12
,,	COD	,,	,,	20
,,	DORY	,,	,,	30
,,	GARFISH	,,	,,	38
,,	MACKEREL	,,	,,	60
,,	GREY MULLET	,,	,,	66
,,	RED MULLET	,,	,,	75
,,	PLAICE	,,	,,	90
,,	POLLACK	,,	,,	150
,,	TURBOT	,,	,,	180
,,	WHITING	,,	,,	196

LIST OF ILLUSTRATIONS

	PAGE
PILCHARDS ON THE PORT BOW! (*From a Kodak snap by Harold Frederic*)	11
DEATH OF THE BLUE SHARK (*From a Kodak snap by Harold Frederic*)	41
SHORT ROD	45
"FARNE" ROD	45
"WEEGER" FITTINGS	47
SNAKE RING	48
PULLEY END RING	49
"BICKERDYKE" END RING	49
TOP RING	49
BRASS HEAD RING	49
VULCANITE WINCH (OPTIONAL CHECK)	51
AUTOMATIC WINCH	52
FIVE GENERAL HOOKS (ACTUAL SIZE)	55
REVOLVING BOOM	56
SEA-PATERNOSTERS	57
PATERNOSTER ATTACHMENTS	58
CHOPSTICK	60
"SPIN-BROWN" TACKLE	61
PLUMMETING LEAD	62
GEEN'S LEAD	63
PIPE LEAD	63
SENSITIVE PIPE LEAD	63
BOAT-SHAPED LEAD	63
JARDINE'S LEAD	63
BABY	65
EEL AND BABY	65

LIST OF ILLUSTRATIONS

	PAGE
SPINNER AND BANDS	65
RUBBER-EEL	65
SOLESKIN AND BABY	65
CREEL	68
THE "GRESHAM" BAG	69
LANDING-NET	71
GAFF-HOOK (WITH SCREW CAP) FOR LASHING	72
GAG	73
PIKE-SCISSORS	73
DISGORGER	74
"PRIEST"	75
FISHERMAN'S KNIFE	75
LINE DRIER (CLOSED)	77
LINE DRIER (OPEN)	77
CORNISH SHEARING-LEAD	84
REVOLVING HAND-WINDER	86
POLLACK REEL	87
AUTOMATIC STRIKER	88
INTERCHANGEABLE LEADS	89
"MAHTEB" SPROOL	90
A CONGER HOLE	92
COURGE	119
"PIER WONDER"	131
PIER PATERNOSTER	141
CLEARING RING	142
A BASS POOL ON THE ARUN (*From a photograph by J. White, Littlehampton*)	143
PLANO-CONVEX MINNOW	151
POLLACK FLY	151
RUBBER-EEL AND SPINNER	151
CANE OUTRIGGER	157
CORK BUOY	158
PATENT ANCHOR	170
DIVING BELL FOR GROUND BAIT	177
CONICAL LEAD	188
NEW ADJUSTABLE LEAD	194
WHITING TACKLE	197
WHIFFING FOR MACKEREL (*From a Kodak snap by the Author*)	201
SARCELLE'S "MOGADOR" BAIT	225

SEA-FISH.

INTRODUCTORY.

"HAPPY England!" exclaims Goldsmith in his *Animated Nature*, "where the sea furnishes an abundant and luxurious repast, and the fresh waters an innocent and harmless pastime."

Times are changed indeed! Not alone are many of the said inland waters fished out, others become private property, others again depleted by lime and coal-tar; but even the sea, its harvest gathered without restraint by the trawl, has within the last twenty years been invaded by many in search of that same "innocent and harmless pastime," which is increasingly hard to find inland at a moderate cost, and of which the following pages treat in some of its modern aspects.

It is not easy, even for an enthusiast, to say anything new in praise of sea-fishing. Four B.S.A.S. dinners, with their accompanying orations, have exhausted the subject,—the healthfulness of the sport, its cheapness, the variety and excellence of the fish, and the constant charm of uncertainty as to whether the result of an outing may be a blank, a boatload of fish, or a capsize.

One aspect of sea-fishing has, however, been curiously overlooked; and that is its artistic possibilities. The river and lake have had their idylls; and it is hard to write nowadays of the fly-fisher's birds and beasts, his companions of the waterside, without going over old ground. The haunts of the sea-angler, which are not, by the way, necessarily restricted to draughty piers or evil-smelling harbours, are, however, still without their bard. I am not, least of all in the present little handbook, offering myself for the post; I merely want to raise my voice against the prevalent notion that there is nothing in modern sea-fishing over and above the mere hooking and unhooking of fish; and that the elements of scenery and bird life, so great a factor in the enjoyment of a quiet day beside the trout-stream, are altogether wanting at the coast.

The perpetual motion of the sea, the glare of the sun and the turmoil of passing steamers, are, let us grant, foreign to that feeling of perfect rest so suggestive of the river's bank. The gull is without doubt less beautiful than the dipper or kingfisher, less tuneful than the nightingale or sedge-warbler; the rolling of the porpoise lacks the grace of the otter's splash; nor are there many who would prefer the sight of some fishy cormorant drying its wings on a slippery rock to that of the lean grey heron motionless in the shallows. It would be foolish to insist that the typical beauties of river and lake find their match on the sea-shore. Yet there is a grandeur about the open sea which, not more than half realised by those who traverse it in the security of modern steamships, comes home daily to the sportsman who spends his time miles from land in a mere cockleshell of a boat, with no other company than that of rorquals twice the length of his craft, sharks, seals and unsuspicious sea-fowl, many of which scarcely touch earth from one year to another.

At times, the very delight of sea-fishing is in its loneliness, especially down off the rugged Australian coast, where every other fish is snapped from the incoming hook by sharks that could, if so minded, crunch the boat with a flick of their powerful tail as if it were so much matchwood.

To the river-side angler, whose most memorable adventure is perchance with an inquisitive cow, or an equally inquisitive keeper, this hankering after the company of sharks may come as a shock; but the presence of danger—not indeed ignored, but mastered—must carry with it a feeling of satisfaction unknown where danger is not. Equally pleasant memories in their way are the skilful handling of the tiller in a sudden squall, the delicate rounding of an ugly rock, while yet keeping the trailing hooks clear of the lobster-pots on the other quarter, or the judgment called for in launching and beaching in a heavy ground-swell; and if I say that they have no equivalent on the average river, I shall not, I think, be far wide of the mark. Danger and difficulty in moderation are conditions of sport, and the sea offers plenty of both.

Another hitherto neglected point that tells in favour of sea-fishing is its cosmopolitan range. I do not mean to say that it is advisable to hang out a line anywhere in mid-ocean and expect a great catch; for there is often a strong combination of depth, currents, and, in the wake of ships at any rate, sharks against the fisherman.

On the contrary, it is essential to hit the exact grounds frequented by the fish. The sea-angler soon recognises the fact that, beneath the water, as on land, there are considerable tracts, mostly of sand or mud, uninhabited, the fish crowding to the spots where the conditions of life are easier. This is found to hold equally good of fishing within a mile of the coast or hundreds of miles from land. At the same time, so great is the abundance of fish in the sea and so fierce are their appetites, that a paternoster, or other suitable tackle of the kinds described in the following pages, baited with fresh meat or fish, will usually take fish of some kind in any deep water. I have taken fish in this manner in various parts of the Channel, Mediterranean and Indian Ocean, in the Suez Canal, in the Gulf of Aden and in the shallower water off the north coast of Java.

Cosmopolitan range of sea-fishing

It is important at the same time to bear in mind the need of precise acquaintance with the fishing-grounds, concerning which much information will be found in the Appendix.

If those who have its interests at heart will only develop it along the right lines, advocating methods not distasteful to the angler who has served his apprenticeship in fresh water, and attractive to those who have never handled rod or line before, there is little doubt that the sport of sea-fishing, of such recent origin that there was until 1893 no society representing it, has a great future.

One of the greatest attractions of this sport is perhaps the close acquaintance entailed with the sea. The very colour of the sea becomes revealed to the angler to an extent not vouchsafed to other landsmen. Instead of talking of the "blue" sea, he knows that, save when very deep or far from land, it is more often pea-green or sandy-brown. He knows that its waters are at times deeply suffused with the spores of red or olive weeds, and that then is his best chance of a good haul of mackerel. He knows too the far less welcome "broodiness," so common at certain seasons on the coast of south Devon, when the sea is of a dirty yellow and the fish refuse all manner of bait. He is not unmindful of the significance of the phosphorescent "briming" of warm summer nights when the sea is "on fire." And he may perchance have fished off Pentewan, or other Cornish clay works, where the water is, especially after rain, of the colour known to thirsty schoolboys as "sky-blue." So far from injuring the fish, this has the effect of darkening the bed of the sea in that part; the small fry gather in the half darkness for protection; thither they are followed by the large mackerel, and these are in their turn pursued by the fishermen. Not only, then, does the amateur who properly studies his subject find the actual colour of the water directly affecting the weight of his catch, but its thickness is taken into consideration when deciding on the particular bait for the day's fishing. Thus, at Deal, it is usual to try the sprat bait for cod when the water is clear, the lugworm when it is thick. The distinction is merely that between those baits that are found by sight and those others that are traced by scent.

Colour of the sea

The tides are a most important factor in the sport of sea-fishing, and the angler should always,

Tides

more particularly when interested in pier-fishing, be in possession of a correct tide-table (N.B. Those sold at seaside libraries are not invariably correct) for each month. A very few piers, Bournemouth among them, are fitted with a tidal gauge and indicator; and few of the visitors who may have noticed the clock-like arrangement beneath the bandstand on the last-named pier have any idea what a very sensitive recorder it is, with its floats and balances, the line traced by the pen showing at a glance—to those, at any rate, who know the secret—the exact state of the tide for the time being. The rise and fall varies much on different parts of the coast, being as a rule greater at the more exposed ports than in receding bays, as instances of which I may quote Hastings[1] and Bournemouth. At the former, there is at low spring tides nearly half a mile of uncovered sand and shingle between high and low water mark; whereas at the latter, the rise and fall is a matter of a few feet only. Spring tides are those which occur at the new and full moon, the rise and fall being then considerably greater than at the neap tides, which occur in the moon's first and third quarters. It is generally accepted that the fishing is best at the former, when the additional speed of the currents sets so much more fish food on the move; but glancing through a few of the more recent entries in my diaries, I am disposed to give the preference to the quieter conditions obtaining during the slacker neap tides. Indeed, so strong are the spring tides, especially on the third and

---

[1] On the west Sussex coast, the fall of tides is still greater, the average difference on the Littlehampton quays at high and low water being not far short of 15 feet, and, at spring tides with strong N.W. wind, as much as 18 feet.

fourth days after new and full moon, that fishing is only possible for an hour or so, just after high and low water, and then only close inshore. During the neap tides, on the other hand, it is possible to fish uninterruptedly during the greater part of the day, so that, even if the fish are not feeding quite so ravenously, the total catch is usually better. The remarkable "second tides" at Bournemouth are referred to on a later page.

On a par with tides in the powers that rule the sea-angler's fortunes are the winds; indeed, they are, if anything, of greater importance. *Wind*

We may at once set aside the east wind as "impossible." A few small pout, or a dog-fish, may, it is true, be caught during a spell from that quarter; but in the main, the old rhyme has in it all the elements of truth, and I believe the exceptions in favour of easterly wind are even less frequent at sea than on river or lake.[1] The ideal breeze—only it must be no more than a *breeze*—for south-coast fishing is from the south, just enough to fan the water into the lightest of ripples. It is well to keep an eye on it when abroad in very small craft, as, although the south wind itself has not the habit with us of developing into a "buster," as it does on parts of the Australian coast, it has, nevertheless, an awkward knack of veering suddenly and without warning to the south-west, in which quarter it increases with such amazing velocity that it is possible for a very ugly sea to get up all unnoticed in the course of ten minutes. It is, therefore, a mistake, at all events when out on a strange part of the coast, to make fast any of the sheets, even in the calmest of weather, the smallest mizen

[1] Curiously enough, east wind is best for both bass and mackerel under the lee of Chapel Point, Mevagissey.

only being left up to keep the boat head to the wind.

The north wind has, of course, the effect, being then a land breeze, of calming the Channel grounds; but I do not like it for all that, for it seems to drive the fish out of the bays into deeper water, in addition to which it has the undesirable effect of making the inshore water both clear as crystal and cold as spring water,—a combination fatal to sport.

The north-west wind, however, is on the whole about the best that Channel fishermen can wish for, as it brings no rain, and at the same time keeps the sea calm without making the water either cold or too clear. Moreover, it very rarely goes to the south, as the wind shifts as a rule with the sun, not in the opposite direction.

The sea breezes have the effect of stirring up the bottom and thickening the water, but this is accomplished in far less time by a few hours of heavy rain.

Of the effect of thunder on sea-fishing, which **Thunder** has been much written about, I regret to have no interesting data to quote. My diaries are absolutely conflicting on the subject, for they show under these conditions almost as many bad days as good; the general opinion among the fishermen—and I give it without comment for what it is worth—is that the fish bite well during "thunder weather," especially pouts. On the other hand, I have had many blank days when the thunder only threatened without actually rolling.

In concluding these few introductory remarks, **Table fish** I would say a word on a subject which I confess to having somewhat at heart. The sea-angler will soon make acquaintance with a number of excellent table fish, among them the dory and garfish, which, having tried at first out of mere curiosity, he will not be long in welcoming as a change from the more hackneyed sole and turbot, the latter too often cooked in the abominable "portion," in which form it retains about the same amount of nutriment that one would expect to get out of a piece of boiled flannel. The colonials and foreigners who recently visited our capital, and who must from time to time have heard much of the British fishing industry, may have experienced more than one rude shock as regards the poor choice of fish both at the restaurant and on the private table. It is not improbable that the new recruit to the sport of sea-fishing may learn to appreciate the taste of a large number of fish of the very existence of which he had no previous suspicion. Some, as the pollack, coal-fish, and wrasses, he will not try more than once; but others, as the grotesque couple above mentioned, will, if properly cooked, be to his jaded palate a delight. Nay, he may even hook a red mullet or two—I have not done so in the course of fifteen years of steady sea fishing, but am beginning to regard this as exceptional bad luck—and there is no finer mouthful of animal food in the sea or out of it. At the same time, I cannot seriously include under the heading of "edible" sea fish the eighty-eight species so described by Professor McIntosh in his recent interesting work on our food-fishes; or even, for the matter of that, Mr. Cunningham's seventy. Both these estimates are surely over-generous, and thirty kinds of British sea-fish are in all probability as many as most of us would care to try.

One word with reference to the imperative need of eating only the freshest of fish. This is capable of exaggeration. Mackerel and, in summer weather, silver whiting should, it is true, be eaten as soon as possible after they are caught. Few, however, of our other edible sea-fish, be they cod, pout, or flat fish, should be cooked until a dozen hours or thereabouts after they are dead, by which time *rigor mortis* will have set in, and the flesh is far firmer and more fit for the cook.

<small>Fresh fish</small>

In concluding these introductory remarks, I offer a hint or two on the subject of the best clothing for sea-fishing. The sport is not as exacting as most in this respect. For sea-fishing it is customary to use up all one's old clothes; and indeed, what with the sea-water, the bait and the fish, this is about as destructive to clothing as any other occupation. It should at the same time be remembered that it involves a great deal of exposure,—to heat in the summer, to cold in autumn, or at nights,—and provision should be made accordingly.

<small>Clothing</small>

The chief danger of the sun, both direct and reflected by the water, is to the eyes and the back of the neck. I usually protect these in hot weather by a pair of tinted glasses and a pugaree respectively; but one day at the beginning of the present summer I forgot, or had not yet started, my usual precautions, and the result, aggravated no doubt by a long swim as soon as I got back to the beach, was a touch of the sun, that brought back a sickness and dizziness that I had not known since one very hot day in Ceylon. The remedy for this (and it is a useful one to bear in mind) is to take a weak dose of chloroform and water, lie down for an hour in a cool, dark room, and then dose the liver well. The notion that commonly prevails to the effect that it is necessary to visit the tropics in order to know sun-stroke is both false and dangerous.

INTRODUCTORY

Another contingency that should be borne in mind when choosing one's "get up" for a day's sea-fishing far from the coast is the possibility of an upset. The limbs, the feet more particularly, should in no way be hampered, and the boots, or shoes, should be so loosely fastened, if at all, that a very slight effort will rid the feet of them. Personally, I do most of my summer boat-fishing bare-footed.

PILCHARDS ON THE PORT BOW!
[*From a Kodak snap by Harold Frederic.*]

CHAPTER I.

NATURAL HISTORY NOTES ON THE CHIEF SEA-FISH, AND BAITS.

WITHOUT urging for one moment the necessity of reading deeply of the anatomy of sea-fish—the exact number of their fin-rays or of the scales along the lateral line, the nature of their pyloric appendages and air-bladder, and all the rest of it—I am nevertheless certain that the angler who is at pains to acquaint himself with certain matters in their life-history will reap the rewards of his study. Sport of any form is in a measure inseparable from natural history; and if this holds true of shooting or hunting, it surely applies with additional force to fishing, which calls for some knowledge of the individual tastes of the fish, of the depth, time of year and hour of the day at which they are most likely to take the natural or artificial bait. In addition to the utility of such knowledge, we must not lose sight of the interest it lends the day's fishing. There are "sportsmen" of course who cannot be "bored" with the habits of the fish, whose sole enjoyment consists in being conveyed to the grounds and having their hooks baited and their fish unhooked by the boatman. For these

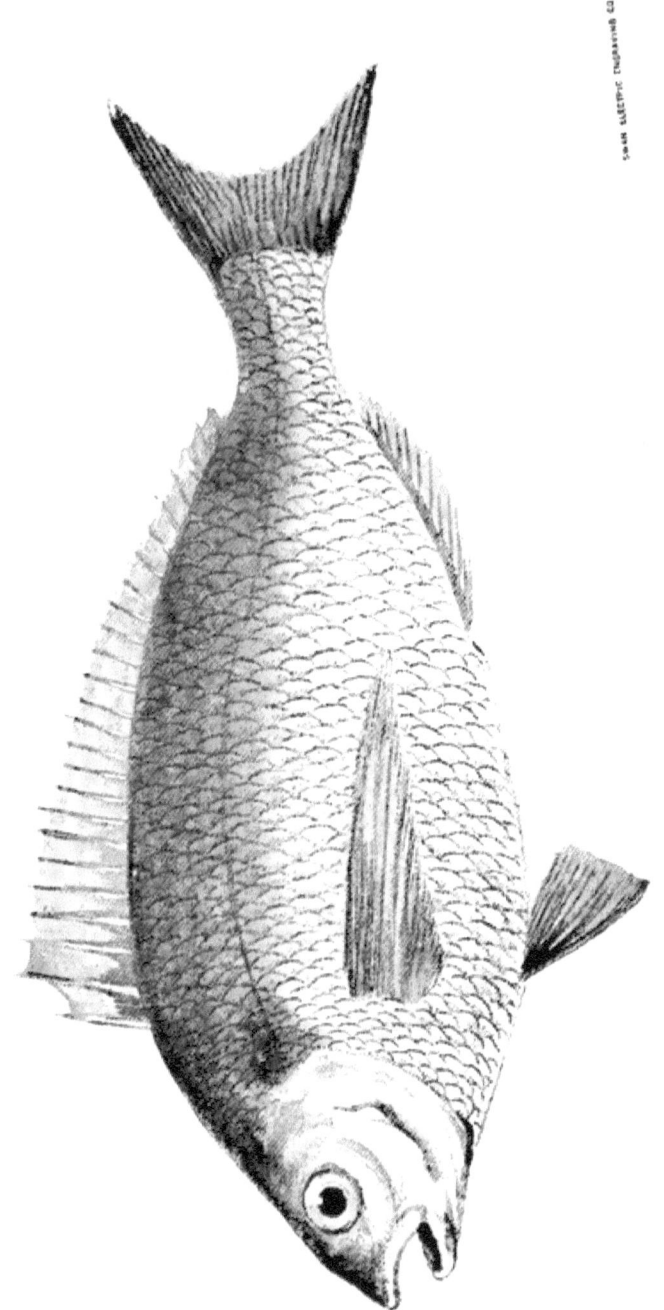

SEA BREAM.

gentlemen the "natural history" of a fish is limited to one item, its fitness for the table. They are not, however, in the majority, and their views need no consideration.

The fishes named, save incidentally, in the following pages number about a score, and include members of both great sub-classes, the bony and the cartilaginous fishes. In a sporting, and not zoological, handbook like the present, there is no objection to separating closely allied forms for the sake of the convenience gained by giving the fish and baits in alphabetic order. As an instance, the flounder and plaice are by this arrangement separated by a number of species not even remotely allied to them.

Atherine, see *Sand Smelt*.

Bass

This sea-perch is, save for table purposes, the finest fish of our coast, and its pursuit is at one time or other the chief aim, at once the pleasure and pain, of the angler. At a later stage, he accepts philosophically the truth that there can only be about a thousand of these fish left in the Channel, and that very good sport may be had with pollack, mackerel and cod, of which the numbers are the same as ever. For all its lineage—and it ranks higher far than the so-called "king of fishes"—the bass is a very foul feeder; and I take this tardy opportunity of retracting, what eight years ago I believed to be perfectly true, that the baits for bass should be absolutely fresh. On the contrary, it has since been demonstrated to me, both by the lobster-pot and the hook, that, in the absence of *live* bait, a stale or "high" bait is as a rule more tempting to the bass. Generally preferring the neighbourhood of estuaries, and even wandering some miles up rivers,[1] this is among the fish that perform regular journeys to and from the deep water, hugging the coast from the middle of June until the end of August, on some parts of the coast rather later. Through the greater part of its sojourn in the shallow water, the bass feeds, especially on fine mornings and evenings, close to the surface, where it may often be found by following the movements of the gulls that co-operate in the destruction of "mackerel midge" and sand-eels. After a spell of rough weather, however, bass are found just behind the broken water, routing up the sand, and are therefore taken in such spots with a bait pitched into the surf. The feature in the bass that most concerns the angler is the presence of eight or nine sharp spines in the first dorsal fin, which he should carefully avoid; indeed, the bass is altogether one of the most prickly of fish, and it is advisable to stun it, and hold it in a cloth, before attempting to remove the hook. To these few particulars of the fish that bear directly on its capture the present remarks may be restricted.

It is commonly thought, by those who have no special reason to think at all about the matter, that Blue shark sharks belong exclusively to tropical climes; and the assurance that there are many species of shark in the English Channel, examples of many hundreds of pounds being netted on the south-west coast, would be, covertly at any rate, classed with the memoirs of Mandeville and

---

[1] Bass are caught with rod and line fully a mile above Arundel on high spring tides. As long as the water tastes salt (a simple test), they will take the bait, a live dace or roach.

Munchausen. Such is, however, the fact ; and my own rod has accounted for a good many small blue sharks down in Cornwall, pigmies of twenty and thirty pounds, but quite enough to demoralise your top joint. The boldness of these small sharks is amazing. On one occasion this summer, a couple of blue sharks were swimming around my boat only a foot or two beneath the surface, and we persuaded the smaller to seize a pilchard on a conger hook. An attempt to gaff it failed, the gaff striking the shark, but coming away. The brute seized the bait again, however, and was then gaffed and killed. Mr. Frederic's kodak snap of its capture is reproduced on a later page. Of its kind, and viewed apart from the foolish prejudice that attaches to these useful scavengers, the blue shark is a handsome fish, its form tapering gracefully, and the contrast between the steely blue of the back and the silvery white of the belly giving it a striking appearance both in and out of the water. Its most objectionable feature from the angler's point of view, apart from its untiring raids on the lines, is the sickly smell of its blood, an odour as of bilge-water, which it shares with many others of its family. Care should therefore be taken not to spill any of the blood on the boards of the boat ; for the odour clings to the wood for days, and is very trying to any one inclined to resent such influences when on the water. The shark is killed, if possible, over the side, a blow on the shovel-shaped snout being effective if properly delivered, and is then slung over the stern, a bight of line being passed over its tail. It makes excellent bait for the crab-pots, and should always be kept for the crabbers ashore, who often have the good taste to remember such trifling services. Many a time, after giving one or two sharks to Cornishmen, I have found an unexpected crab or lobster on my breakfast plate. I am not sure whether one would find such delicacy nearer town; but I hope so.

Few would think of fishing specially for sharks, though I do recollect one sportsman with whom they were a perfect hobby—he would kill a score or so a week—but they often fasten themselves unasked on the pollack-lines, and then the angler soon learns a curious habit of all the tribe,—that of swimming to the surface and endeavouring to shake the hook out, a habit also noticed in the garfish. It is important to bear this in mind, especially when playing a shark on the rod, as the slackening of the line would lead any one ignorant of their ways to suppose that the fish had broken away, whereas this is just the moment to be in readiness for a sudden rush.

Bream In the sea-bream we have a very different type of fish from the bream and bream-flat of our inland waters, a perch-like form with sharp dorsal fin, a lover of clear deep water, found, not in the mud, but among the rocks.

Sea-bream are gregarious and frequent certain grounds, the whereabouts of which can only, save by chance, be learnt with local help. They feed freely as a rule, and within a few feet of the rocks in which they live. These often lie in deep water several miles from the coast, necessitating the use of the hand-line. It is necessary to strike at once, and care should be taken, as with the bass, not to handle the sharp spines on the back. The red and black sea-breams, the former known when full grown as "schnapper," furnish between them most of the sport obtained in Australian waters; but, our own bream are not by any means so highly thought of, either for sport or the table.[1]

The young of the red bream, known as chad, differs in so many points from the adult that it might be another species. It is mentioned here rather on account of the excellent pollack-bait that can be made from a strip of its very tough skin. So far as its capture goes, it is one of those fish that need no invitation, but comes round the boat in certain weathers in its hundreds, nibbling to rags the pilchard bait meant for pollack. Then is the time to put out a smaller hook, baited with a strip of pilchard; secure a chad or two, and bait the pollack-hooks with a slab from the side (the entire length of a small chad being none too much for the purpose). The other chads are unable to spoil so tough a bait, and the pollack relish it as much as they do the more oily, but less showy, pilchard. In the intermediate stage, weighing about ¾lb., this fish is known in Cornish dialect as a ballard.

Chad

In this member of the cod family, which in habits bears strong resemblance to the pollack, we find a small barbule present on the lower jaw, and a more abrupt division between the dark green of the back and the white of the belly. This is the "saithe" of the Scotch fishermen, and is caught, like the pollack, on surface-lines.

Coal-fish

[1] I caught a 2 lb. example of the Spanish bream this August at Mevagissey (whence Day obtained his example), a beautiful and rare visitor to our coasts.

Cockle A bait in favour with many, but one with which I am bound to admit I have not had wonderful results, the cockle, is too well known to need many words. What is less generally known perhaps is that cockles are able to leap on the wet sand, and that, if placed on the sand near the water's edge, they will at once make straight for the sea. Small as is our species, it has American relatives, specimens of which have been dredged weighing as much as three-quarters of a ton, their scientific name denoting that it would take three bites to finish them!

Cod Type of a large and important family, that also includes such sporting fish as the pollack and whiting, the cod is for the most part a fish of deep water, though a number approach the coasts in winter, usually between October and Christmas, and are then angled for, especially at Deal. This fish is found more particularly, though not exclusively, in cold seas, and has the family beard, the young, or "codlings," being spotted. It is caught on our shores weighing 50 lbs.; but the amateur will not in all probability meet with any of more than half that weight. Though found indifferently on the sand or among the rocks, the edge of a reef is found to be the best ground for inshore cod.

Conger Conger-fishing is not every man's pastime, for it entails a good deal of roughing it, night-fishing among the rest. The conger, the female of which grows to a length of 8 ft., commonly 5 ft., and a weight of near 100 lbs., is a scaleless eel, distinguished from the river-eel by the continuous black-edged dorsal fin and the projecting lower jaw. Its colour varies according to the depth of water and the nature of the ground from which it is taken, fishermen even distinguishing two "kinds," black and white conger. The belly is invariably white. Essentially a rock-fish, the conger is rarely taken on the sand, save at the edge of a reef. It feeds chiefly at night, and has a preference for fresh baits, indeed in many parts the angler who has only yesterday's mackerel or herring might as well take a book. Squid, however, an excellent bait for this fish, may be used on the second day, even on the third in moderately cool weather. The conger is particularly fond of small rockling, a bait less known than it deserves, though I put on half a 3-bearded rockling that I had just caught one evening this summer on the Durley Rocks, Bournemouth, and the conger, of which there were plenty on the feed, would not touch it.

Crab

There are many kinds of crab (see also *Hermit Crab*), but the one with which the sea-fisherman is most concerned is the common green crab at the particular season when it is casting its shell, a periodical moulting which these crustaceans undergo in common with reptiles. It is when in the soft condition involved in this change that the crab hides instinctively in the crannies of rocks out of reach of the fish, bass and rays among them, against which its shell no longer protects it, and it therefore makes a good bait.

Of the three or four worms used by the sea-fisherman, none is perhaps finer, as none is certainly less known, than that nereid which conceals itself in the convoluted end of the whelk-shell occupied by a hermit crab, and which, for want of a better English name, I have called "crab-worm," just as the fisherman know the hermit as the "crab-whelk." There is usually an implied mutual advantage in these natural partnerships, or commensalisms; but, although it is easy to understand that the worm gains at least shelter and probably some scraps of food, it is by no means obvious what profit accrues to the crab. It is surprising how long a worm will coil itself in the extreme corner of the shell; it is a fragile creature, and must be removed very carefully and without any rupture, else it is useless as bait. It is almost impossible to keep these worms alive for any time once they are removed from their natural asylum, damp weed, darkness and a cool temperature being essential; therefore it is best to take crab and all in the boat, breaking each shell as the worm is required. There is not, of course, a worm in every shell, but there are on the average perhaps a score to fifty crabs.

<small>Crab-worm</small>

This curious creature, which carries its eight feet on its head, is, together with that other octopod the squid, much used in conger-fishing. It must first be cleaned of the ink-like fluid with which it thickens the water when evading its enemies or stalking its prey. Curiosity is fatal to both these cephalopods; they may be speared by the light of a torch, or, a more usual way of taking them, caught on bare hooks jigged beneath a piece of china. I have caught them on three cod-hooks lashed in a triangle, when, off the Cornish coast,

<small>Cuttle</small>

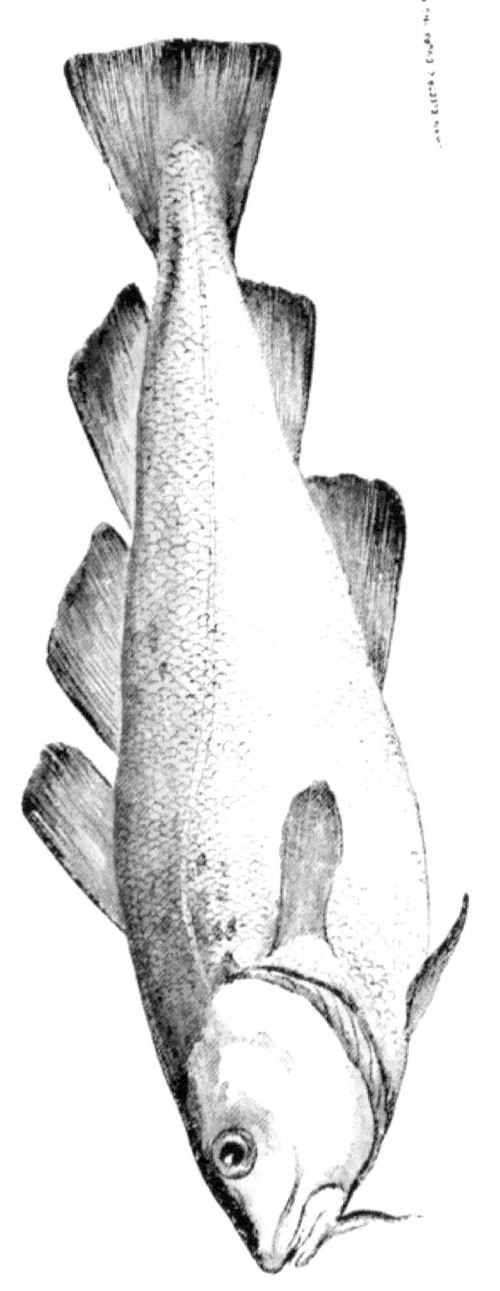

COD.

they sucked every bait off the hooks intended for pollack. The curious backward jerk, caused by the expulsion of water from the mouth, is unmistakable ; but these animals never by any chance get hooked, unless on a triangle. The best way of getting cuttle is usually from the trawlers ; it is nearly always possible, for instance, to pick up a couple from the boats anchored each morning in summer off the Hastings fish-market.

There are at least two kinds of dab ; one, the long rough dab, related to the great halibut, the other of the same genus as the plaice. It is this latter, the sand-dab, that the angler is most likely to catch; indeed, it is one of our commonest resident fish. The popular idea that a dab is only a young plaice is of course quite incorrect, the plaice being always easy of distinction by reason of its red spots. Always, like most of the flat-fish, a dweller in the sand, the dab usually feeds on or near the ground, though I have known of isolated cases in which it took a spinner near the surface. Both this and the larger dab have very rough skin, and the sand-dab is also found in brackish water. *Dab*

The dog-fish of the Channel are five or six in number, but it will suffice for the purpose of the present notes to distinguish the spur-dog and rowhound (or rough hound), the nurse being mentioned below. The spur-dog is a black and white fish, which, growing to a length of over 3 feet, is particularly objectionable on account of the sharp spike—hence its name of piked, or picked, dog—in front of each back fin. Like all *Dog-fish* the shark tribe, this fish heads straight for the surface on feeling the hook. The rowhound, the wet skin of which has the extraordinary property of bleaching other fish in the same basket, is also taken to a length of 3 or 4 feet, and is covered with numerous reddish spots. It is less savage in its behaviour than the last, but so common as to be a serious trouble at times.

Dory The dory, more familiarly "John Dory," is one of the most delicious eating, and also one of the ugliest, fish in our waters. It lies in ambush in the shadow of rocks and piles, rushing out at intervals to gorge itself with sand-eels or other small fish, and the best way to catch it is on a drift-line baited with a whole smelt or launce. The action of a dory in the water—I know of no pier where there is a better chance of watching them than that at Bournemouth—is more graceful than the appearance of this fish on the table would lead one to suppose, the long filaments on the dorsal fin waving like fronds of weed, and possibly helping to deceive the fish.

Eel The eel of our rivers may seem out of place in a work on the sport of sea-fishing; and I do not know indeed that I should have mentioned it at all but for the fact that the common eel—we have but one freshwater species in these islands, the so-called *species* being only the fish of different sex and age—goes down to the sea to breed, the young eels, or "elvers," re-ascending the river, their parents dying, so far as is known, after the first spawning. Not only then do eels begin and end their existence in the sea, but they may also be taken there

by those who have any fancy for so sordid a game;
and I have seen hundreds hooked off the eastmost
breakwater at Hastings,—eels that had descended
the little river at Rye, and worked westward along
the rocky gullies that fringe that portion of the
Sussex foreshore.

In the flounder, too, we have a fish that, in the
light of modern angling perhaps, belongs **Flounder**
more strictly to the fresh-water fish, but it
is mentioned here for the sake of giving the points
in which it differs from the other flat-fish taken in
salt water,—the presence of rough tubercles along
the base of the fin-rays. It is occasionally taken
with tumours on the back, which, according to
Cunningham, the fishermen believe to be its eggs.
It breeds in salt water only. Mr. Wheeley gave
some useful hints on catching flounders in the
preceding volume of the *Angler's Library*.

In the "greenbone," as it is often called from
the colour of its bones, we have a type in **Garfish**
many respects unique among our fish, with
its snipe-like bill, and the hardest roof to its mouth
that ever living creature had. The singular habit
of this fish, leaping to the surface when hooked,
and endeavouring in such manner to shake out
the hook, has been alluded to above. The angler
who has the fortune to hook a garfish on his
mackerel-gear, the most frequent way of taking
them, will further notice that it has an unmistakable and not wholly pleasant smell. In spite
of which, however, as well as of the colour of
its bones that has prejudiced so many against it,
the garfish is better eating than most fish caught

in our seas, and why it should never find its way to the restaurant is a marvel.

The gurnard is cited by many as another instance of an unprepossessing fish with much to recommend it for the table; but I must confess to a decided dislike of its flesh, which I have always found so woolly as to defy even the most cunning stuffing. The gurnards, which in our seas amount to half a dozen species, are characterised by brilliant colouring for the most part, and have appendages resembling barbules, or feelers, in reality the free rays of the pectoral fins, on which they crawl, as it were, over the rocks. They are slow swimmers, generally taking a stationary bait, but occasionally seizing a spinner that moves sufficiently slowly and at considerable depth.

<small>Gurnards</small>

[The *Haddock* is not a very usual catch with the amateur; but I have taken a few in the Baltic, where, perhaps owing to the low percentage of salt, they run small, like the herrings. It is closely allied to the cod, from which it may be distinguished by the black marks on either side beneath the first dorsal fin, popularly regarded as the finger-mark of the apostle who took the tribute-money.]

[The *Hake*, another ally of the cod, is also a fish rarely taken by the amateur, though he may probably have an opportunity of seeing more than one should he spend a night aboard a pilchard-driver, as these powerful and voracious fish pursue the pilchards right into the net, where they occasion much damage.]

Already mentioned incidentally in connection with the worm with which it shares its stolen shell, the "soldier crab" is a familiar object in every rock pool, where the sight of a whelk-shell crawling over the ground occasions for the first time as much wonderment as the sight of the first caddis, which many take for an inanimate stick. This crustacean secretes so poor an armour that it is compelled to seek shelter in a whelk-shell, not, as many have asserted, ejecting the whelk, which would be an impossibility, but looking about for an empty shell. This dwelling it is compelled to change when it grows too bulky, usually after casting the small shell that keeps some of its soft parts within bounds, and then combats frequently ensue with other hermits in possession of the coveted quarters. In addition to the useful worm, one species of hermit at any rate has a mutual understanding with an anemone, which fastens on the shell, hiding the orifice from passing fishes, which probably take its pedestal for a stone, and getting in return free rides and possibly board as well. The larger hermits are usually found in the shells of whelk or winkle, but I have taken smaller examples from nearly a dozen kinds. *Hermit crab*

The herring is here mentioned as a bait, although numbers are occasionally taken by the amateur, especially in Scotch waters, and it is even said to rise freely to a fly. This fish, the type of what is probably our most important family of food fish, is silvery, soft-finned, and lacking the curved lateral line characteristic of the majority of fishes. It is gregarious, and the immense shoals perform seasonal migrations, formerly considered *Herring* of immense length, but nowadays regarded rather in the light of short journeys to and from the shallow to the deep water. The attractiveness of herring as a bait lies in two qualities,—the silver sheen of the skin, and the oily nature of the flesh.

Launce, see *Sand-eel.*

Limpet Less used than the mussel, the limpet is at times a good bait for the smaller fish, though by no means easy to remove from the rocks, to which it clings with a glutinous secretion evidently insoluble in water. To remove a limpet from the little pit in which it rests, a performance rendered still more difficult by the shape of the smooth shell, requires a force equivalent to about 60 lbs.! Though to all appearance a fixture, the limpet is able to move very slowly over the submerged rock. It is an extraordinary creature in many ways, for its "foot" is its stomach, and on its tongue are a couple of thousand teeth. Its mode of feeding on the weed over which it moves has been happily compared with browsing.

[The *Ling* is another of our fish that lie in the ordinary course without the scope of the amateur, though I recollect one case of a large but ill-conditioned example being caught off the Dover Admiralty Pier. It is "bearded" like most of the cod family, to which it belongs, its nearest ally being the burbot of some of our rivers.]

Lug-worm If asked to name the best all-round sea-bait, I should be sorely puzzled to choose between the mussel and the lugworm, though I think the mussel would take first place. Yet there are few fish that refuse lugworm, which makes it the greater pity that it is not more agreeable to handle, the fact being that there is no bait more disgusting. It is not necessary to be fastidious in order to recoil from this pulpy worm, with its inside of yellow seeds and the deep red blood that leaves a lasting stain on everything with which it comes in contact. The lug is a swift burrower, diving head-first in the wet sand between high and low water mark with amazing rapidity, so that some practice is requisite before one can dig it out with a fork, particularly as the water at once rushes into the gap and hides all that is going forward. Even when the disappearing yellow tail of the worm is in full view, great care must be exercised in seizing it gently but firmly, between the second and first finger of the right hand, and above the tail, which is full of sand, and easily breaks away. Both this and the ruptured body are useless as bait. Viewed anatomically, this shore worm, with its gill-tufts and the curious digging proboscis, is rather an interesting creature. Mr. R. B. Marston recently showed me some dried salted lugworms which he had received from a Yarmouth sea-angler, and they were agreeably tough and free from smell of any kind.[1]

One of the most sporting of fish for its size, one of the best for the table when grilled fresh, and one of the most deadly of baits for other fish, both large and small, this familiar species is as important as any with which we have to deal. The worst feature about it is the rapidity with which it loses its freshness, a fault of all the fast

Mackerel

[1] Watson and Hancock of Holborn sell jars of preserved lug. When fresh bait is unobtainable, these preserved worms take a few fish.

surface-swimmers, the larger relatives of the present species. Nothing, we are told, can be perfect on this earth, but I have always thought that the mackerel would take some beating. Its shape is elegant, its colouring (*not* judged from the fishmonger's slab) superb, and its action in the water as gallant as that of any fish, as it will sheer to right and left as long as it has breath. The fact of its life history that most concerns the angler is its periodic inshoring, when, from May until early in August, it is caught on whiffing-lines near the surface, and often within a stone's throw of the beach; later, or earlier, in the year, it must be sought further out on ground-lines. The so-called "mackerel-midge" are not, as some have stated, the young of mackerel, but the fry of the rocklings, our smallest gadoids; and they are named after the mackerel for much the same reason as that which rules the specific name (*piscatorum*) of the lugworm, to denote an affection that recalls that of the Sandwich islanders who love their European friends, especially when *roasted*. Bournemouth Bay is usually visited by hundreds of thousands of small and flabby mackerel late in June. They are caught by the leisurely seaners from Poole, and generally attract a number of thresher sharks into those quiet waters.

Mullet, Grey. There seems to be some doubt as to the precise number of species of grey mullet found on our coasts; indeed Mr. Cunningham hints in his latest work at the possibility of only one. I am of opinion, however, that there are at any rate two, the thick-lipped and thin-lipped, and I know them both well from the Mediterranean, where they are common. These fish have no teeth, but their digestion is assisted by a compensating arrangement in the stomach, which need not be particularised in this place. The importance of this fact to the angler however, is that baits for these mullet must be soft. Some anglers bait with macaroni. Further, the grey mullet is a very timid fish, taking alarm on the least disturbance. It also enters fresh-water, the Sussex Arun being one of its favourite south-coast rivers, the Kentish Stour another.

Cooked with the trail, the "woodcock of the sea" has, I suppose I may say without fear of contradiction, no rival among table fish. Nor has it anything in common with the last fish from which it is systematically separated by many families. It is a familiar enough fish in the shops, with its bright red colour, largely due to the trick of scaling it immediately on its removal from the water, and the two sensitive barbules beneath the lower jaw. There are two races, a large and a small, of this fish, both of which are taken for the market in a fixed net known as a trammel. But a few instances, perhaps a dozen in all, are on record of the capture of this fish with hook and line, but this would appear to be less rare than is commonly supposed. The last instance that came to my notice was at Bournemouth on July 22nd of the present year, when a large red mullet was caught on a line (mussel bait) on the "outfall" (see *Bournemouth*, Appendix). Mr. Wilcocks writes to me that, though he has only personally caught one, Mr. Maple of Shoreham took on one occasion no fewer than five, on lugworm. Mr. Maple himself tells me that the red mullet have of late been very scarce in the neighbourhood of Shoreham, but that, when

<small>Mullet, Red</small>

they are feeding, he finds no bait to come up to the lugworm. Mr. Wilcocks also says that one morning, an old bandsman took five on the north pier at St. Peter's Port, Guernsey. A gentleman signing himself "Oyster," recently wrote in the *Fishing Gazette*, in reply to a statement of my own concerning the rarity of the hooking of red mullet, that he had caught a number, one of them weighing a couple of pounds, on the French coast with leger-tackle; and Mr. Leonard Hare, who also noticed my statement, writes to me that he once took one when *whiffing* off the Cornish coast. One of the earliest records, says Mr. Wilcocks in his letter, of the capture of red mullet on the hook is to be found in *Salter's Guide* (1830) on p. 170.

Mussel — This is of all sea-baits perhaps the most reliable, especially in strange waters. It is too familiar a mollusc to need description, though mention must be made of the fibrous "beard," which it secretes, and with which it can on occasion pull itself from point to point, eventually making it fast to some post in company with others. The pearl-bearing mussels once common in the Conway and other rivers, have no "beard," and may therefore lead a roaming existence. The worst thing about the mussel is the enormous damage it does among the oyster beds. It is more difficult to open properly than any other bivalve, and a note will be found on the subject in a subsequent chapter. The white, yellow and red mussels are races only of a common species, the colour probably varying with the food in a manner that has not up to the present been satisfactorily explained. A red and a white mussel are

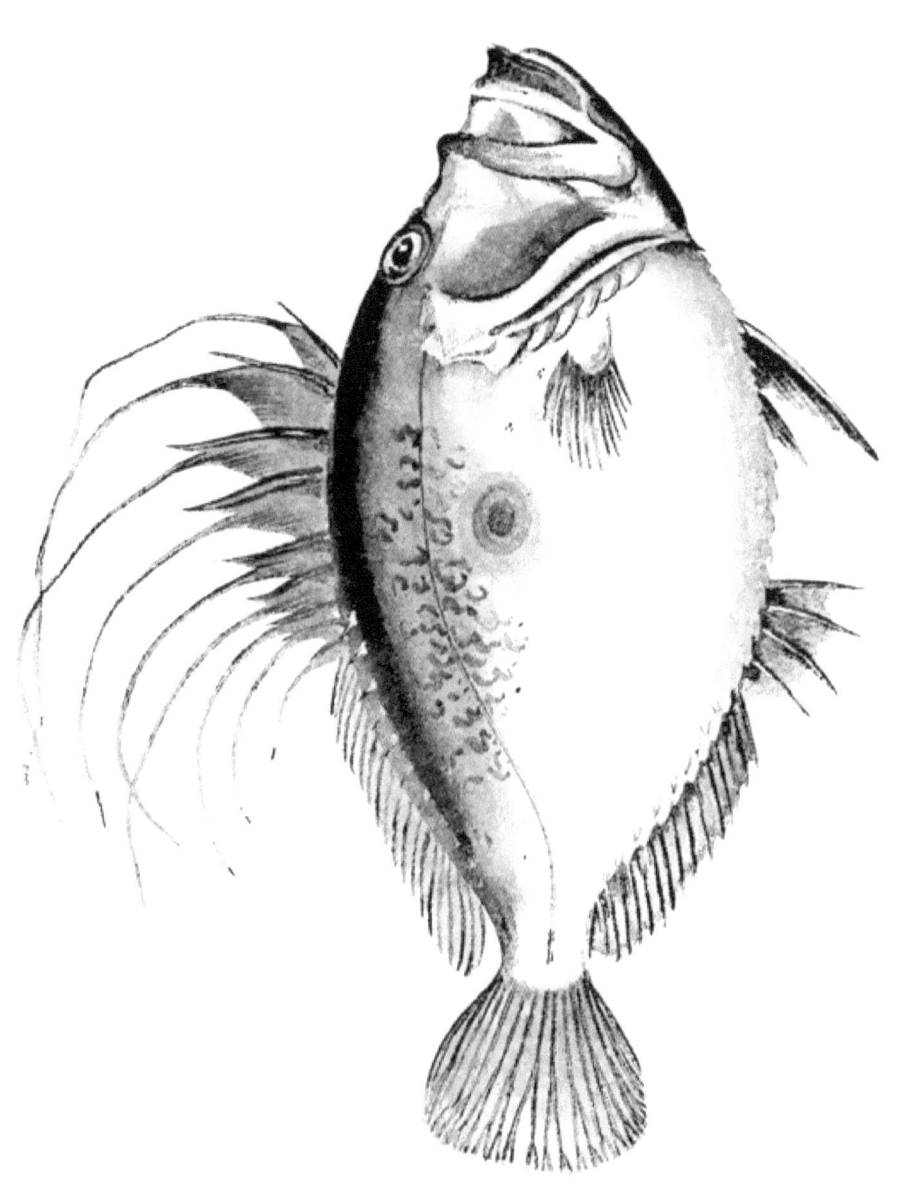

often a very killing combination for pollack or mackerel.

This is one of the commonest and most troublesome of our small sharks, but it is at any rate prized more than the rest by the fishermen, who eat it in many parts where they would not touch any of the rest. It is, judged without the prejudice that attaches to all its tribe, a handsome fish, growing to a length of 4 or 5 feet., and not unlike the smaller rowhound aforementioned, only its spots are larger, fewer and more blurred. This fish is particularly common in Bournemouth Bay, where I catch a number every summer; indeed, it is essentially a shallow-water fish. Nurse-hound

One of the commonest of our flat-fish, the plaice, gives good sport in the late summer and autumn, when it has attained to a weight of 3 or 4lbs., and will take the lug or mussel bait freely. Like the dab aforementioned, from which it may be distinguished by the red spots that cover the body and fins, as well as by the bony ridge on the head, this fish spends its life in the sand. The mouth is small and situate at the end of the snout, and the teeth will be found to be more strongly developed on the left, or blind, side. Plaice

One of the amateur's favourite fish, so far as sport is concerned, though of little or no use for the table and quick to lose its freshness, the pollack, may be distinguished from the rest of the cod family by the combined absence of barbule, projecting lower jaw and dark colouring. It is a handsome fish, being taken of a weight of over 20lbs., Pollack though the angler has come nowadays to regard a pollack of 10 lbs. as a good fish. It is found as a rule only among the rocks, the depth at which it feeds varying with the temperature, light and time of day. Cold and excess of sunlight drive it to the bottom, while it usually seeks its food, chiefly sand-eels and fry, close to the surface during the long early summer evenings, when it may be taken on surface-tackle from five in the afternoon until nine or even later. The pollack is a roving fish, a spell of cold weather sufficing to drive it into the outer water several miles from land, indeed it does not as a rule remain inshore for more than six months in the year. When feeling the hook, the pollack invariably heads straight for the ground, and this is the fact in its life-history that it most behoves the angler to bear in mind, for unless prepared to negotiate very warily, the finger being pressed on the rim of the reel to check the run, a smash will almost inevitably ensue. The rapidity with which the pollack decomposes has been alluded to; no fish is less fitted to bear transport inland, a fact to remember when sending presents of fish.

The iniquities of the blue shark and of more than one dog-fish have already been mentioned; and it remains to add a few words about the heaviest and most evil-smelling species of shark with which the amateur is likely to be troubled in English waters. A far deeper fish for its length than the more graceful blue shark, this specimen is netted in Cornish bays to a length of over 10 feet, the weight of which may be approximately estimated when it is considered

Porbeagle shark

that a porbeagle of little over 4 feet will turn the beam at 50 lbs. When hooked, this shark shows less fight than the blue, but I have always found it perform the usual shark tactics of swimming to the surface and slacking the line. In colour, it is between a green and grey along the back and sides, lighter on the belly.

This species, too well known to need either figure or description, *the* fish of pier- and boat-fishing alike, prefers the rocks, over which indeed it is imperative to bring up for really good pout-fishing, but is also taken from piers some distance from any reef. It has the beard of the cod family, to which it belongs, and its deep body is marked with vertical bands. Few of our fish take the hook at so early a stage, with the result that, although the pout grows to a length of a foot, and I have hooked many between the Foreland and the Land's End weighing close on 3 lbs., it is much more familiar at a length of 3 or 4 inches and a weight of as many ounces. The pout is particularly fond of frequenting the neighbourhood of wrecks, which furnish shelter to successive generations of the fish and sport to successive generations of those who catch them. It is known in Cornwall as "bib," and is almost invariably found there in the company of small "power-cods." *Pout or pouting*

In that favourite crustacean, the prawn, we have a sea-bait that has not up to the present attracted all the notice that it merits, which may in part be due to the somewhat high price of these animals. In the live prawn, however, there is, for those who do not mind the expense of buying *Prawn* or the trouble of netting it, a pollack-bait second only to the living sand-eel. Though not more delicate than other crustaceans, prawns do not thrive in the narrow confines of a bait-can, the courge (p. 119) being the only satisfactory receptacle for the purpose; and indeed the best way is, I have always found, to arrange with the owner of prawn-pots at so much a head for his catch (usually 2*d.* apiece), also hire himself and boat, let him row you out to the grounds where the pots are set (which are also the pollack-grounds), and remove each prawn from the pots as you place it on the hook. Of the anatomy of the prawn, on which something should be said in this place, it will suffice to mention the distinguishing toothed beak and the long and sensitive antennæ, the small pincers and the fan-shaped tail that enables the prawn to leap backwards a distance exceeding his own length, which is not more than 4 inches. The prawn is essentially carnivorous, and, by tacit understanding, no questions are asked as to the fattening of those excellent prawns of Indian and other Eastern rivers that make such unrivalled curries. Our own species feed on any flesh they can get hold of, and are even known to dispossess anemones of half-devoured meals.

Rag-worm. Two sea-worms of great value to the angler have been mentioned above, and a third, less useful yet killing at times for pollack, is dug from the black ooze of harbours and estuaries, known as the rag-worm, or, at Dover and some other places, as the mud-worm. In colour, it varies from pink to yellow, with the iridiscence characteristic of sea-worms, and the body is furnished with many feet with gill-tufts, the head bearing a pair of hooked nippers. The rag-worm is very fragile and perishable, in consequence of which great care is necessary, both when digging it and placing it on the hook, in order to avoid a breakage at one of the joints. It can only be kept in damp weed away from the light, and it is advisable to remove the dead worms (which assume a livid tint) as soon as possible.

Of rays and skates, depressed members of the shark sub-class, our seas have a number; nor will it be necessary to consider the characters of the homelyn, thornback, mavis and the rest. All that concerns the amateur is that moderately large specimens of these cartilagenous fishes are from time to time hooked close in shore, when care should be taken to avoid a blow from the tail, which in some species is armed with curved spines that inflict a most painful wound. These rays, which hover like birds of prey over the flat fish lurking in the sand, have the curved mouth, like the allied sharks, beneath the head, though they are not observed to turn on their side in the same manner when seizing prey. The more usual method for them is to dig up the sand with their shovel-like snout, and snap up the flat-fish and crustaceans as they are forced from cover. It is noticeable that, like the flat-fish, rays and skate are very deceptive in the matter of weight, and a comparatively small fish will, owing to the resistance of the water, put an immense strain on the rod. The liver of the rays is, especially when a trifle decayed, much valued as bait for bass.

Rays

As bait for conger, these small members of the
Rock- cod family are, as a rule, not to be beaten,
lings though I have alluded to one occasion on
which they failed to attract. There are three; one
species having three beards, while in the others the
number of these appendages is respectively four
and five. The fry, silvery and lacking spots, are
the "mackerel-midge," so greedily devoured by
surface-fish. Any of these rocklings, about seven
inches long, make first-rate conger-bait; and one
of the best ways of taking these slippery fish at
low water from the isolated rock-pools they in-
habit is to draw off the water with a small garden-
syringe. The cost of such a syringe is trifling, and
the saving of time and trouble incalculable, as
these fish are most difficult even to net. The
water should be drawn off quickly, as the rocklings will otherwise take the alarm and disappear
into various holes and crannies, from which it is
impossible to dislodge them.

After the lug-worm and mussel, the sand-eel, or
Sand-eel launce, must take precedence as an all-
round bait; indeed, for such fish (as bass
and pollack) as will take live bait, the launce
stands first. There are at least two species on our
sandy coasts—the larger, which grows to a length
of 12 in., being distinguished from the smaller
(maximum length, 7 in.) by the two horny teeth
in the upper jaw. They have much the same
habits, burrowing in the wet sand just above low-
water mark, or swimming at the surface, often in
the company of sand-smelts, fighting over all floating food, taking any small hook freely, and falling
a prey to the pollack beneath and the gulls over-

head. These fish are taken in the sean-net, or are raked out of the sand by moonlight with a peculiar weapon, not unlike a sickle.

Sand-Smelt, see *Smelt*.

When mackerel-railing, still more frequently when fishing for mackerel with the drift-line, the amateur may catch a fish that at first puzzles him, its general outline resembling that of the commoner fish. The colouring is more sober, a bluish-grey along the back and sides without any of the silvery bands, and there are also bony plates along the lateral line. This is a scad, or horse-mackerel. It is useless as food ; and is said, though I have not noticed it, to grunt on being removed from the water. This August, in Cornwall, my boatman caught one of over 3 lbs. Scad

Shark, see *Blue* and *Porbeagle*.

The shrimp is a smaller crustacean than the prawn ; indeed they cannot easily be confused, as the shrimp lacks the nippers and serrated beak of the other. In habits, too, it is different, and instead of springing backwards when disturbed, it prefers subsiding in the sand, throwing up a cloud with its long swimming-feet, and burrowing with incredible rapidity. The shrimp may be taken in the ordinary shove-net. It should, if possible, be used alive, but I have known pout, when in the humour, take the firmer inside of boiled shrimp in preference to any other bait. Shrimp

Skate, see *Rays*.

There is a small relative of the salmon, known in Scotland as the "sparling," and with us as the smelt, which is excellent eating, and which, on our east coast at any rate, affords some Smelt sport with a light rod and fine tackle. This fish is replaced, however, on our south coast by the so-called "sand-smelt," really the atherine, a small silvery fish lacking the adipose fin of the other. The atherine, which affects sandy bays, is caught in thousands every summer from Bournemouth pier. This summer (1897) the atherines came inshore early, so that the first were observed on the same day as the first swifts overhead; but for some reason or other, probably the cold, they disappeared again for nearly a month, after which the supply was inexhaustible throughout the summer.[1] Besides giving some sport for their size and being excellent on the table, these fish are among the best baits for turbot and other ground-fish.

The amateur is not likely, unless he do a deal of night-fishing, to catch many soles; but if minded to attempt their capture, he should bear in mind that they feed in the mud, and that the mouth is exceedingly small, the sole sucking in all manner of soft food. A lug-worm is as good a bait as any. The so-called "lemon sole" is more properly speaking a dab, in shape resembling the plaice group, to which it belongs. It is commonly caught, along with plaice and sand-dabs, from our south-coast piers in the autumn months.

Sole

This remarkable "shell-fish," pipe-shaped, as its name denotes, burrows in the wet sand just above low-water mark, and, although my opinion of it as bait is not high, it is so interesting on

Solen

---

[1] The sand-smelts do not as a rule enter the mouth of the Arum at Littlehampton before the end of August or beginning of September.

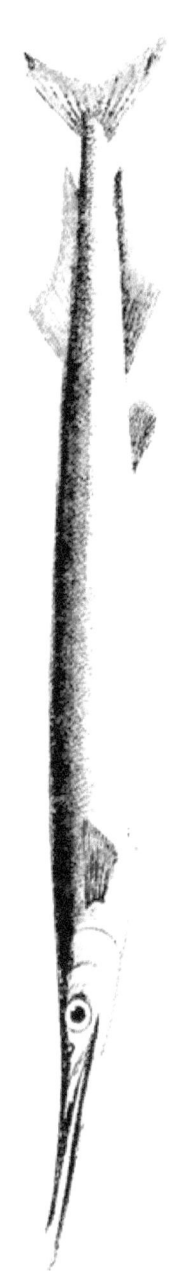

GARFISH.

other counts that brief mention must be made of
its chief peculiarities. The most curious feature
about this bivalve, which is also, from the sharp
edges of its shells, known as the razor-fish, is its
"foot," which it can use as a borer, anon inflating it
to form a bulb with which it obtains a foothold in
the wet sand, and draws itself up or down as the
case may be. One of the best ways of procuring a
solen is to put a little salt in the keyhole-shaped
aperture of its shaft, when up comes the tenant to
see what has irritated it. It must then be trans-
fixed promptly with a barbed spear—a conger hook
flattened out and lashed to a stick answers the
purpose—for if missed, it will vanish at lightning
speed, and all hope of getting that particular solen
goes with it. Its burrows are easily found, if the
observer has only the courage to walk backwards as
near as possible to the edge of the receding water
and keep a sharp look out for the two little jets of
water that spring from the orifice when pressed by
his foot.

Superior in flavour to all other flat-fish except the
sole, the turbot is as a rule only caught by the
amateur in its juvenile stage, the allied and Turbot
inferior brill being a still rarer catch. This
fish, which is taken weighing as much as 20 lbs.,
has tubercles covering the body in place of scales.
Its food consists chiefly of crustaceans, but it also
feeds on small fish, and, as already mentioned, a
sand-smelt is one of the best baits, and may, if not
more than four inches long, be used whole.

More often caught than desired, the fish of this
genus require careful handling in order to avoid

the sharp spines behind the gill-covers, as, in a lesser degree, those on the dorsal fin, on account of their poisonous properties. These fishes lie in the sand, the eyes only exposed, and readily take any bait that lingers in reach. They are unusually prevalent after a spell of easterly wind, and are commonly called "stingfish," a name which is, however, indiscriminately applied to the equally abundant sea-scorpion.

Weevers

This, one of the most familiar of the cod family, is generally known by the sobriquet of "silver whiting," to distinguish it, no doubt, from the pout and pollack, to both of which the name of whiting is locally attached. The distinguishing features of the whiting are the absence of the family beard, the black lateral line, the black spot on the pectoral fin, and the more elongated form than that of the majority of its congeners. The whiting is, unlike the pout and pollack, a sand-fish, though I have occasionally made good catches right on the rocks, more usually, however, on the hard sand at the edge of a reef. It feeds as a rule about a fathom from the ground in deep water, not more than a foot from the bottom if in a depth of less than ten fathoms. (This, of course, with the local exceptions permitted to every rule.) Whiting are taken weighing over 4 lbs., but a 3 lb. fish is a "specimen."

Whiting

In the wrasses, characterised by their thick mobile lips, and strong crushing teeth, most of them brightly coloured, we have a large group of fish practically useless for the table, but continually invading the hook, especi-

Wrasses

ally in the neighbourhood of rocks covered with long, waving green weed. These fishes can seize a bait of larger size than the apparent stretch of their jaws would lead one to suppose. In most, the scales are of large size, but in some they are imbedded, so that the fish are very smooth to the touch. Owing to the nature of the air-bladder, two of the species cannot regain their proper position when thrown back in the water, and consequently float, a prey to gulls and other fowl. A live wrasse (locally, "rock fish") is the favourite bait at Littlehampton for large bass, and is hooked through the tail.

DEATH OF THE BLUE SHARK.
[*From a Kodak snap by* HAROLD FREDERIC.]

CHAPTER II.

SEA-RODS, REELS, AND VARIOUS TACKLES.

SEA-FISHING with rod and line has in our seas come in fashion almost within the last ten years, while the float and groundbait have, for general use, arrived from inland waters at a date still more recent. By degrees, and almost imperceptibly, the term "sea-angler" has come to indicate one who uses the rod in salt water, though many still use it in the broader sense of any amateur sea-fisherman, whether he seek his sport with rod or hand-line. The suggestion made last winter by "Red Spinner," that the committee of the *British Sea Anglers' Society* should pass a law pledging members of the society to use the rod, has not, I believe, been acted upon, but has much to commend it, provided some loophole be left for the use of the more primitive hand-line whenever conditions render the rod less effective.

"Red Spinner's" suggestion

For it is certain, though in our new enthusiasm for the rod we are in danger of forgetting the fact, that there *are* conditions under which the hand-line is not only as good, but indeed better. The rod may, it is true, be

Case for the hand-line

preferable in nine cases out of ten, but there is a *tenth* case for the discarded hand-line. It was, I think, during my fishing experiences in Australia that the few but insuperable limitations of the rod were brought home to me in a way that admitted of no further doubt. The Pacific Ocean does not always act up to its name, and the ground swell is frequently appalling. In pursuit of that handsome red bream, the schnapper, a grand fish that should find a place in the arms of the colonies, we used to drift three or four knots an hour over the roughest of ground, a four or five pound lead on the line, and the gunwale of the little steam-tug dipping now and again to the very edge of the green water that hid huge sharks, ever ready to wrench a good fish from the hook. Amid such surroundings, the rod would have been no more than a farce. Insular prejudice is a hardy weed, and I took my rod out on the first occasion, but had not the folly to put it together, preferring to accustom myself to the use of the hand-line which I had unreservedly condemned in the old country. Sharks, however, and other southern eccentricities apart, there are cases even here on our own coasts in which a great depth of water, or a spell of extra and breezy weather—the necessity, in short, for using heavy leads of four or five pounds—may render the rod, if not a useless, at least a very tiring and unmanageable weapon. This was well expressed by "President," in the *Fishing Gazette* (April 10th, 1897).

<small>Sea-fishing in the Pacific</small>

Those who prefer adapting themselves to the requirements of the moment, instead of adhering blindly, like the most rabid among the dry-fly or wet-fly trout fishermen, to one principle under opposite conditions, will find a few particulars on the subject of modern hand-lining in the next chapter.

The first consideration is the rod itself. The main requirements of the sea-rod are strength and lightness; and the great difficulty that must present itself to the tyro about to purchase his rod is the matter of length. In this particular, sea-rods have undergone some strange changes. A very little travel on the coasts of continental countries shows us that the rod had its origin in sea-fishing on rocky coasts. Near Gibraltar and near Naples, you may see the natives using enormous bamboos, 20 ft. in one piece. The reason for this is obvious. Although the water is usually of a depth sufficient for purposes of fishing right up to the foot of the cliffs, just as it is round a large part of the 8,000 miles of Australian coast, there are generally small outlying rocks to clear; and it is with this object that the long rod is used. A case is found in the Channel in the Admiralty Pier at Dover, on the western parapet of which, owing to the position of the angler, it is impossible to fish with comfort with anything under 15 ft., 20 not being amiss. When the rod came into general use among amateurs in salt water, say about 1887, it was also the fashion, whether fishing from boat or pier, to use a long bamboo rod, often wholly out of proportion to the needs of the case. From that, opinion veered round, as it so often does, to the opposite extreme, and it became the correct thing to fish with those short rods of 6 or 7 ft., of which there are a variety of patterns still in vogue. For boat-fishing, especially where the company numbers three or more, and space is a consideration, there can be no doubt that these dwarfed rods are extremely convenient;

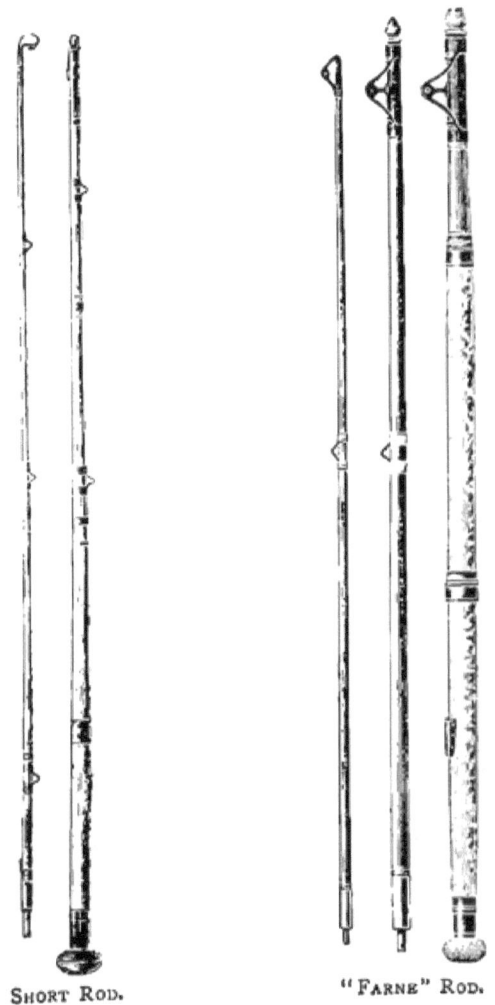

SHORT ROD.   "FARNE" ROD.

but there can also, I think, be no doubt that, being as stiff as golf-clubs, they give far less sport than something a trifle more springy. For general purposes, then, where it is not necessary to use leads of over a pound at the outside, the ideal rod lies in my opinion somewhere between the tarpon- and salmon-rod, and I have long found a three-joint rod of 10 ft., made for me by Little, a very sporting article. The butt and first joint, of bamboo, measure respectively 41 and 40 ins.; the top, of lancewood, measures an inch short of the last, and there is a spare top of only 25 ins., making an excellent stiff rod of 8 ft. 10 in. for pollack, or, when attainable, bass. If a little additional expense is not objected to, it is advisable to buy two rods at, say, a guinea apiece, one like the above—or the 10 ft. "Farne" rod sold by Hardy—for boat- and ordinary pier-fishing; the second, of 16 or even 18 ft. for exceptional cases. Do not pin your faith to what is known as a "general" rod. A jack-of-all-trades of this kind is an abomination, so far at least as sea-fishing goes, and I understand that it is equally objected to in fresh water; it is a makeshift under all conditions, and never exactly the right thing.

A compromise

Having decided on the length of the rod, one or two points remain which are of great importance in sea-angling. The simplest of these, which may be dismissed with a few words, is the additional comfort derived, especially when standing up in a boat, from the addition of a soft rubber knob to the extremity of the butt, which can be rested in the hollow of the thigh when playing a heavy fish, a practice that would not be comfortable with the usual wooden or metal extremity. If added when the rod is purchased, the cost of this improvement should at most be nominal; indeed, many sea-rods are supplied with it ready.

Rubber knob on the butt

SEA-RODS, REELS, AND VARIOUS TACKLES. 47

The winch-fittings are another important consideration in the sea-rod, for it is often found necessary, especially when a shark has run out and departed with thirty or forty yards of line, to substitute another winch of different size. It is therefore advisable to have the butt fitted with one of the new patent fittings that take any size of reel. More, as the support of the winch is very liable to a twist from a blow or other cause, I would strongly advise the angler never being without a few of those stout rubber rings, sold for umbrellas at a cost of one penny in the streets or at any rubber-warehouse. These are strong enough to keep even the largest winch in position, two being used before and two behind.

Winch-fittings

The most important items of the rod, however, are unquestionably the rings, the top ring above all. To keep the line from overrunning or fouling, and at the same time to allow of its passing freely through them, these rings should be large

Rings

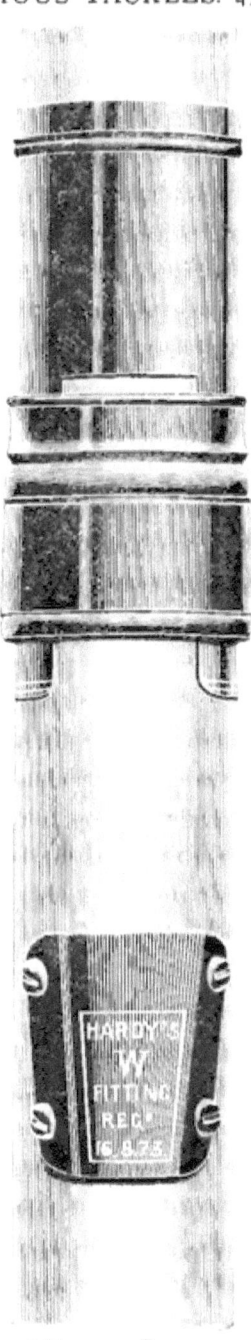

"WEEGER" FITTINGS.

and not too few, one to each foot of rod being a good average. The so-called "snake" pattern is unquestionably the best, for want at any rate of a better; it is in the form, not of a snake, but of the position adopted by caterpillars when moving over smooth surfaces, and half an inch is not too high for it. It cannot, however, be insisted that this ring is so infallible as was at first claimed for it. At the same time, if far from the ideal, it is the best on the market. The stouter the wire of which it is made, the less likelihood is there of the line catching round it, and the easier it will be found to shake the line in place should such a hitch occur.

SNAKE RING.

It is to the top ring, however, upon which fall the strain and friction, that the attention of practical anglers has been devoted, and some highly ingenious devices have been the result, pre-eminent among which stand Jones's pulley-block, of which I have unfortunately no drawing, and Bickerdyke's moving ring that adapts itself to any angle. Either of these contrivances must in reason minimise the wear and tear; and I have given them, and many more, a trial with the best results. At the same time, I think it honest to confess that I have for some years past used an ordinary top ring, such as might be found on any modern pike-rod, without having once suffered accident. This may, however, have been luck; and the modern recruit to the rank of salt-water fishermen will doubtless feel a strong preference for the very latest contrivances.

Top ring

SEA-RODS, REELS, AND VARIOUS TACKLES. 49

Two qualities are essential in this top ring; it must be large and smooth, half an inch in diameter and preferably of some material like bone or ivory. An inner ring, revolving loosely, so that it is possible

PULLEY END RING.

"BICKERDYKE" END RING.

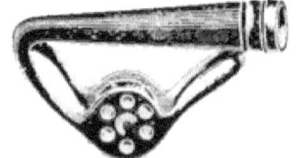

TOP RING.

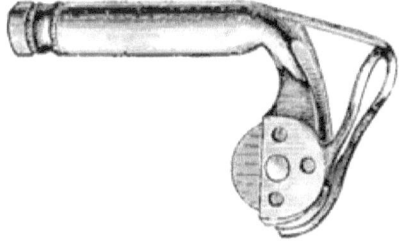

BRASS HEAD RING.

to present new surface to the friction of the line, is another excellent patent. Messrs. Hardy are shortly bringing out an improved top ring, which will sheer to right or left with the pull of tide or fish.

E

Next in importance, if not indeed first, comes the reel, or winch. Some one writing of tarpon-fishing, Mr. Harmsworth, I believe, tells us that the reel costs four or five times as much as the rod ; and, in a smaller ratio, the same holds good of sea-fishing. A sea-rod may be purchased for half-a-guinea ; but an efficient reel, able not only to hold a hundred yards of strong line, but also to reel it up in the shortest time and with the least possible number of revolutions, as well as to resist the rotting effects of sea-water, is not to be had much under twice that sum. I have used a variety of sea-reels, in ebonite, wood, aluminium, gun-metal and the rest, and ranging from ten shillings to forty ; and my favourite is the latest acquisition, a $5\frac{1}{2}$-inch combination of wood, bound with metal and aluminium, and furnished with the excellent " Bickerdyke " line guard. If I remember rightly, the price of this reel was eighteen shillings ; but it is easily recognised by the circular perforations in the barrel, which both lighten the whole and serve in a measure to dry the line by admitting the air. It is to all intents and purposes a star-backed " Nottingham " winch, free-running with optional check ; and the mechanism of the latter is simplicity itself, all the parts being of gun-metal. The barrel can be removed in a moment by a few turns of a screw, a preferable method to the spring catch by which this was accomplished in another reel of mine, a $4\frac{1}{2}$-inch vulcanite, furnished with a brake acted on by the forefinger, with which I did all my fishing for eight years, and with which, for the matter of that, I fish still whenever the other wants a rest. Yet another winch that I used with good results for a time was a composite metal affair that I purchased of Hardy, of Alnwick, but the sea-water played the mischief with it. The writer of the "Badminton" volume cautions us against these optional check winches with a steel spring inside ; but, wholly as I agree with him as to the desirability of excluding steel generally from the sea-fishing outfit, I cannot forget that the above-mentioned vulcanite reel, which saw service not only on our own coasts, but also in the Baltic, Mediterranean, Suez Canal, Red Sea and Indian and Pacific Oceans, a fair all round test with waters of various saltness, never to my knowledge admitted the water ; and a touch with emery paper, followed by a drop or two of oil, was all that was required at the close of each of its eight seasons to renew it for the next.

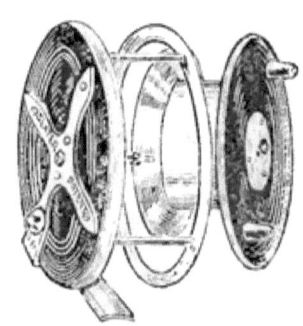

VULCANITE WINCH
(optional check).

We cannot, however, afford to lose sight of the deadly antipathy between steel and salt water ; and any and every contrivance for keeping them apart is welcome. I shall not include any account of the "Multiplying" winch ; for, in the first place, it is not a desirable weapon in the hands of the tyro ; and secondly, I am persuaded that an optional check Nottingham winch is, with certain slight modifications, all that is required. At the same time, I think it fair to mention, for the sake of those who are disposed to give that New World contrivance, the "Automatic" winch, a trial, that Alderman Newlyn, of Bournemouth, a sea-fisherman of long experience, has the greatest

"Automatic" winch

faith in it for mackerel-fishing from a boat; and he has often told me that, but for such a reel, he would have lost many a mackerel and pollack when, as often happens with those fish, they career wildly under the keel, and, making for the surface after the manner of sharks, get a slack on the line and shake the steel out. The "Automatic" reel, when it will condescend to work, allows of no such pranks, as it keeps the line taut. But, as I said above, these fancy reels are worse than useless in the hands of a man who does not understand their peculiarities.

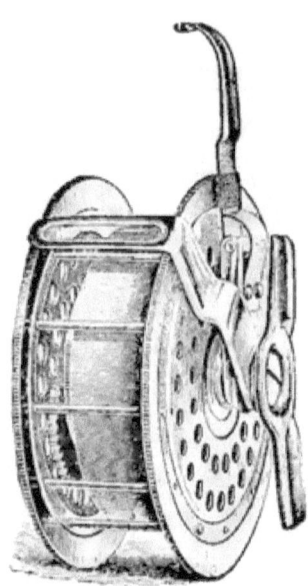

AUTOMATIC WINCH.

Line

Having disposed of the rod and reel, I come to the question of the line, one of those matters of opinion on which it seems sheer impossibility for any two writers to agree.

Let me say at the outset that I have no very pronounced opinion on the subject, and that the durability of a sea-line lies, so far as I can make out, in its treatment rather than in its material. The actual quality of line will always be a matter of individual taste and extravagance. Highly dressed pike-lines, costing from 1½d. to 3d. the yard, are very good for the work; but you can catch just as many fish on a fine tanned line at 8s. the hundred ; indeed, my Cornish boatman takes all his fish on a line costing 10d. the hundred ! One maxim I would insist on, and that is the more line you carry on your reel, provided, of course, that the free running of the latter be not impeded, the better. Accidents happen at least as frequently in sea-fishing as elsewhere ; and it is very annoying to lose a good fish for want of another ten yards of line, or, if a bad break occurs early in the day, in which perhaps 30 or 40 yards are carried away, to have to stop fishing, and weigh anchor from sheer inability to reach the bottom. Therefore, always carry a good 80 or 100 yards of line—a 4½-inch reel will take this with ease if properly wound—and it is a good principle to retain a "backing" of the better moiety of the last year's line followed by 40 or 50 of new. I hope this is clear. The half of the line nearest the barrel lasts far longer than the lower half, for the simple reason that it is less in the water ; and instead of fitting up entirely new lines throughout each season, it answers every purpose to renew the last half only, being careful of course to make the splicing very strong and of such a nature as to run freely through the rings. It is necessary to bear in mind that the effect of sea-water on most lines is little less deleterious than on steel, and that those who would rely on their line in the hour of need should not think it too much "fag" to soak it for an hour after each day's fishing in soft water, after which it should be dried, wound round and round a chair or towel-horse, the surplus water being first squeezed out by drawing the line through a towel held tightly between the thumb and forefinger. A line treated with this consideration will never

Treatment of sea-lines

break under a little additional strain, and should bear all that is likely to be put upon it for at least six months of continuous fishing; a line on which the sea-water is allowed to dry day after day may snap under a 10 lb. pollack within a fortnight of its first outing. It is quite useless to complain to the dealer from whom it was bought; for the mishap would be no fault of his. Some friction might, however, be saved if the dealers would only remember to warn their customers of the necessity of the daily washing and drying; indeed, the cost of printing a label with a few words to that effect would be so trifling that sea-lines might well be stamped with some such legend when sold. The materials recommended for sea-lines are excelled in number only by the dressings. I propose leaving both to the taste of the purchaser, the only essential conditions being that the line shall be strong, fine, and not given to kinking, that abomination of nine lines out of every ten. It is, of course, possible to use a much finer line with a rod than when hand-lining; for in the latter method, as practised at least in this country, a very fine line would cut the finger-joints. Moreover, unless an expert, the hand-liner is very likely to get too fine a line snapped by the sudden rush of a pollack or large mackerel, which is, to a great extent, counterbalanced by the elasticity of the top joint of the rod. The hooks figured on the opposite page are the average sizes in use for the chief fish.

Hooks

Having rigged up the rod, reel (the handles of which should face the angler's *left*, as the reel is to be used *beneath* the rod), and line, the next consideration is the particular fine tackle, or combination of gimp or gut, hooks and leads; and the remarks which follow may be applied with

Bottom-tackle

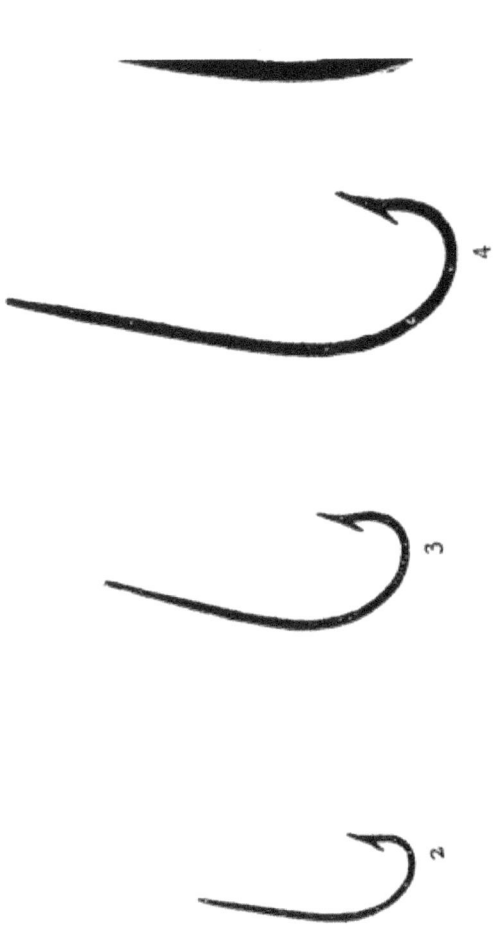

1. Smelt.   2. Flat Fish and Pout.   3. Whiting and Mackerel.   4. Pollack and Bream.   5. Bass and Conger.

FIVE GENERAL HOOKS (ACTUAL SIZE).

equal force to the hand-line, on the management of which some special hints are given in the next chapter.

There are three typical rigs of bottom-tackle, —the paternoster, leger, and chopstick. The multiplication of patterns and fads based on these three types is infinite; and if I explain the standard principle of each, the rest may very well be left to the angler's own ingenuity, for it is then merely a question of adapting one or the other to some unforeseen condition of things,—a swift current maybe, a dockhead, or an overhanging rock.

The history of these names, of the first more particularly, having been discussed by every foregoing writer and being of no practical interest, I will merely refer to the accompanying figures for

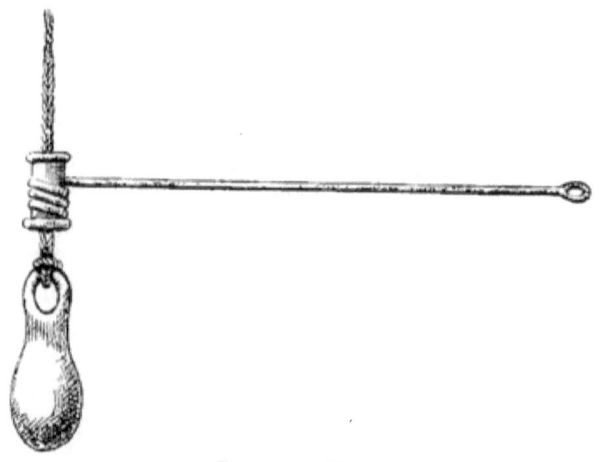

REVOLVING BOOM.

all the explanation necessary. It will at once be
Paternoster seen that the object of the paternoster is to search more than one depth; of the chopstick, to keep the hooks at the same depth, usually just clear of the ground; while the leger has to

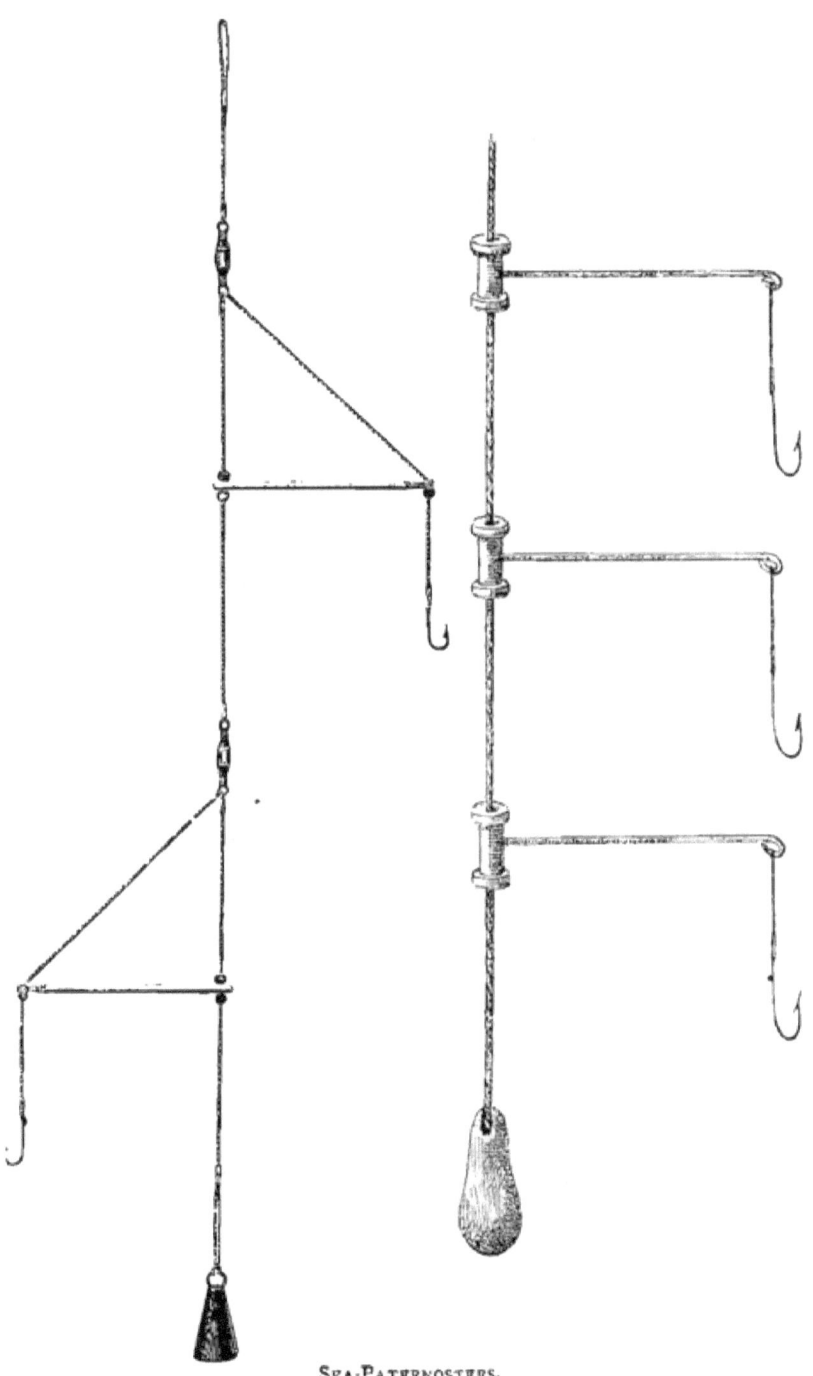

SEA-PATERNOSTERS.

fish on the ground, which bears the whole weight of the pierced lead, through which runs the line. As I said above, the variations on these simple models are infinite. The paternoster, the crude form of which was used by the monks of old to catch their pike and perch, has been invested in its new surroundings with arms of brass, cane, or even whalebone, all with the object of keeping the hooks clear of the mainline, as well as with patent swivels, interchangeable leads and a number of other dignities unknown in less pretentious days.

The leger (which in the vocabulary of the Thames barbel-fisher means little more than a split bullet,

Leger

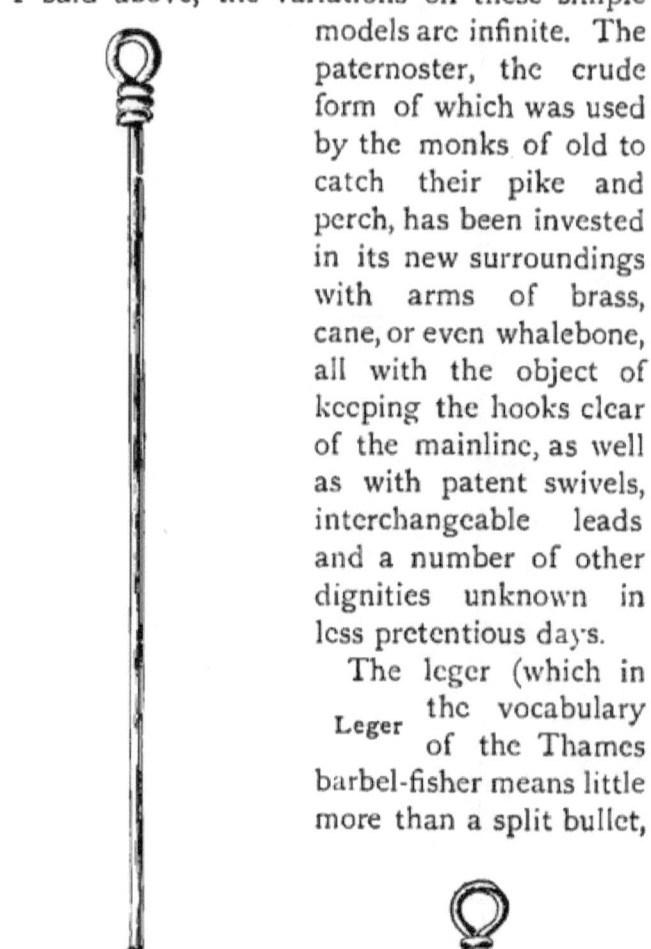
PATERNOSTER ATTACHMENTS.

or coffin-shaped lead, through which the line can pass freely *from* the angler, its progress in the opposite direction being checked by a large split shot nipped on just above the hook) has also been modified for use in salt water, a second hook being generally attached above the lead, in which form the tackle becomes, strictly speaking, a combined leger and paternoster. In boat-fishing, where the angler is directly over the lead, an ordinary plummet is found more sensitive than the regulation leger-lead.

The chop-stick, the favourite tackle of the professional hand-liners, has also been made up in a number of " rigs," not, however, for the modern amateur, but for the native fishermen of each county. These rigs differ chiefly in the length of the arms and in the position of the lead. For light inshore fishing, the pattern overleaf figured will be found most sensitive, but for deeper water something heavier will be preferred. {Chop-stick}

It has often troubled sea-anglers, when confronted with a strong tide, that each rod will not bear without undesirable strain more than a given amount of lead, and this difficulty has at last been got over by Mr. T. Y. Bramwell. My attention was first drawn to it in the *Fishing Gazette*, and it is so simple as to explain itself. The secret lies in the use of an independent hand-line for the lead, of the entire weight of which the rod is thus relieved, the rod line being merely caught in the clip, from which it is freed by the striking of a fish. Like the majority of excellent innovations, this device is so simple that the wonder is that it should not have been thought of sooner. Unfortunately, too, it is a tackle that does not present sufficient difficulties in construction to enable its inventor to patent it and reap the material benefit which he so fully deserves; but he will at any

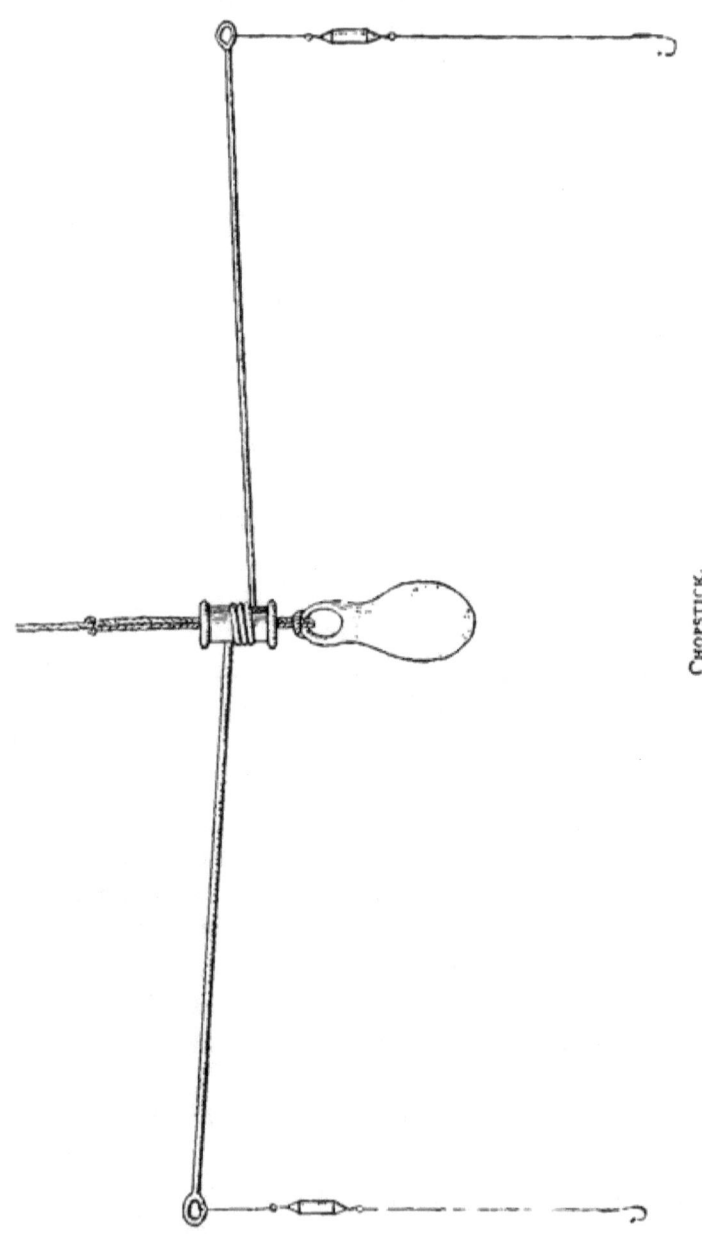

MACKEREL.

rate enjoy the thanks of all whose eyes he has opened. This "Spin-Brown" tackle, as it is called, can be applied to bottom-fishing or drift-lining, as well as to railing, for which its inventor originally designed it.

It will now be necessary to mention one or two other tackles in general use for certain methods of fishing; but the three foregoing, the paternoster, chopstick and leger, are the chief.

A style of fishing, the practical details of which will be more fully dealt with in the chapter on boat-fishing, *Railing* and known as *railing, whiffing* —in Cornwall as *plummetting*, not unlike the *plumb-lining* of the Windermere charr-fishers— or *reeling*, often requires a peculiarly leaded trace at the end of the main line. The material of which this trace is made depends largely on the size and strength of the fish in the neighbourhood, twisted or plaited, gut being a favourite, though I have managed good pollack and mackerel, the former up to 5 lbs., on single gut. For the beginner —and this is a general rule in the choice of gear—the stronger trace will be found safer, as the playing of anything over 2 lbs. on single gut is so much a matter of practice that it becomes a question no longer of the fish, but purely

"Spin-Brown" Tackle.

of the fisher. Having served a useful apprenticeship with gimp or treble gut, the angler will enjoy at a later stage landing fish of 5 lbs. or more on single tackle.

Railing is practised (see Chap. VI) with either the natural or the artificial bait, but in either case the trace is made to taper somewhat as it approaches the hook, which is generally fastened by a short snood of a single gut. In "plummeting" for mackerel, the Cornish method, the hook lies about a couple of fathoms (12 ft.) beyond the plummet,[1] and the 3-in. snood is of single gut, the line itself being very fine, save the upper few feet, where it is held in the

PLUMMETING LEAD.

hand. This last is thicker, and those whose hands are particularly sensitive can still further lessen the chance of a cut by the use of a wooden "toggle."

A good deal of ingenuity has from time to time been spent on the designing of leads for these railing-lines, the great aim being to make them as sensitive as possible, that is to say as little as possible in the way of the angler's hand at once feeling the slightest nibble at the hook that he is towing astern; and opinions differ much as to the best form. Personally, I do most of my railing, let me hasten to admit, without lead at all, this plan

---

[1] To be more precise, the hook on the light stern-line (lead, about 1 lb.) is 3½ fathoms from the lead; on the medium after-lines (lead, 2 lbs.) the distance between lead and hook is 2½ fathoms; while on the heavy for'ard-lines (lead, 3 lbs.) it is only 1½ fathoms.

SEA-RODS, REELS, AND VARIOUS TACKLES. 63

having the unquestionable advantage of enabling a lazy man to row at the slowest possible pace. For, obviously, with a heavy lead it is necessary to move at a speed of two or three knots an hour in order to keep the lead from sinking to the rocks; whereas with no lead at all, it is only needful to keep the craft just moving. I only fish in this way, I should add, just before and after sunset, when the pollack are playing close to the surface; but those who pursue this method earlier in the day, when the sun is high, will have to use some, often much, lead to sink the bait to the greater depth at which the fish then feed.

The choice then lies between some kind of pipe-lead, or the more usual boat-shaped arrangement,

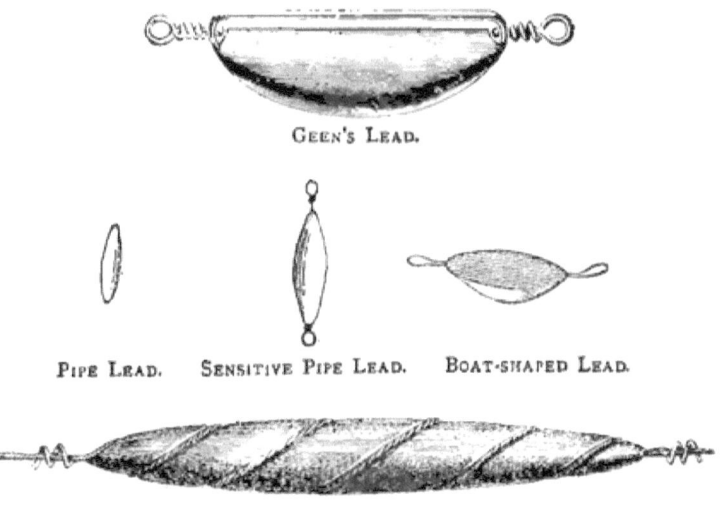

GEEN'S LEAD.

PIPE LEAD.   SENSITIVE PIPE LEAD.   BOAT-SHAPED LEAD.

JARDINE'S LEAD.

and I must say I prefer the former, and several at intervals, in preference to one of several ounces. The clip arrangement, alluded to above, would meet the difficulty admirably. Jardine's spirally-grooved lead is also very convenient for easy adjustment or removal.

The artificial baits, which rarely beat the sand-eel, and which will only occasionally kill at Bournemouth against the all-powerful local mussel, are legion, the chief being the rubber-eel, with or without a "baby spinner," and either white, red, or drab. Hearder, of Plymouth, supplies these baits in great variety, and they can also be found in most of the London shops. The "baby" can be used with or without a strip of mackerel, a sand-eel, mussel, or other natural bait. The caprice of the fish on any given day must be discovered; it cannot be guessed beforehand. Sometimes they prefer the spinner by itself; at others, it is necessary further to rouse their appetite by the addition of a fragment of fish or mussel. The rubber-eels and band baits sold by most makers are often found in practice to hang too far below the hook: if it is found that fish after fish seize the bait without being hooked, cut off, an inch at a time, the rubber beneath the hook, and results will usually improve now that the pollack can no longer nibble at the extremity with impunity. I confine myself, however, in the present chapter to the bare mention of such tackle as is referred to in the following pages; its manipulation will be dealt with in the chapters on pier and boat-fishing. The soleskin bait is, in combination with a "baby," very killing at times.

Many, "John Bickerdyke" among them, trail their sand-eel on some kind of spinning flight, the "Chapman" spinner being a favourite, as they might in fresh water. I have tried these arrangements in salt water times out of number, but have found nothing beat the far simpler device

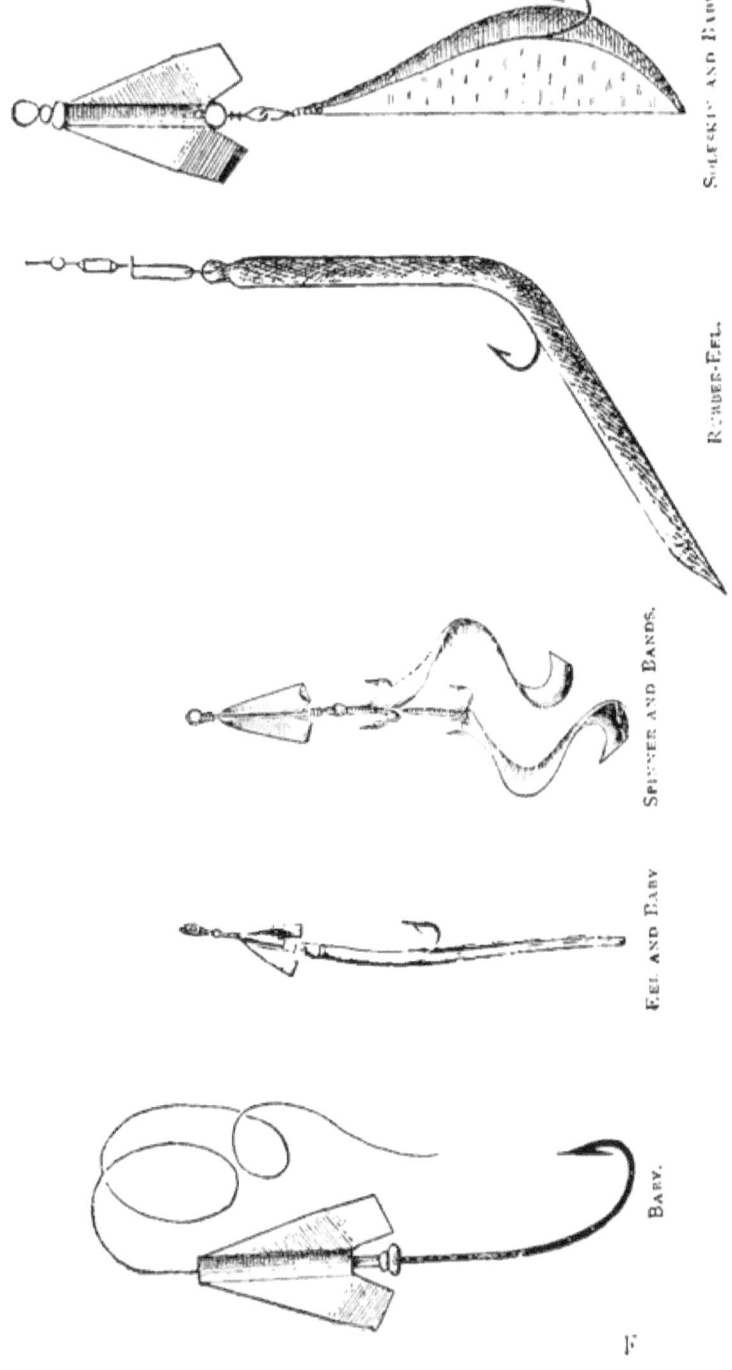

of merely passing the hook of a "baby" through the launce's upper lip. I have even taken very fair pollack on a dead launce hanging in this way at the end of an unleaded drift-line. Sea-fish are, at any rate up to the present, less discriminating than those of river and lake, and "deadly spins," attractive matter though they make for description, are in most cases superfluous.

Another killing method of using the rod, espe-*Float-fishing* cially off pier-heads, is in conjunction with a float, a stout adaptation of the tackle used in bottom-fishing in rivers. The sea-float, however, must be a portly article, capable of carrying several ounces of lead in the tideway, conspicuous too at a distance of forty or fifty yards. The best float I have yet come across was given to me by Mr. Jardine, the well-known pike-fisher, who has also a fondness for sea-fishing. It allows the line to pass freely from hook to rod, but, as in the leger aforementioned, its passage in the opposite direction is effectually checked by a small bristle or india-rubber band of such a size that, while passing through the top ring, it stops at the float. The advantage of this stop is obvious; the angler can fish a depth of twenty or thirty feet, and when he comes to reel in a fish, the float glides down the line to the hook, whereas with the usual fixed float it would be impossible to fish such a depth save with a rod of the same length! One of the best features in Mr. Jardine's float was a spare red top for use in flecked water where the ordinary white top, which cannot be beaten in still water, would so harmonise with the foam around as to escape notice, or at any rate severely try the eye. The spiral wire at either end of the float involves the

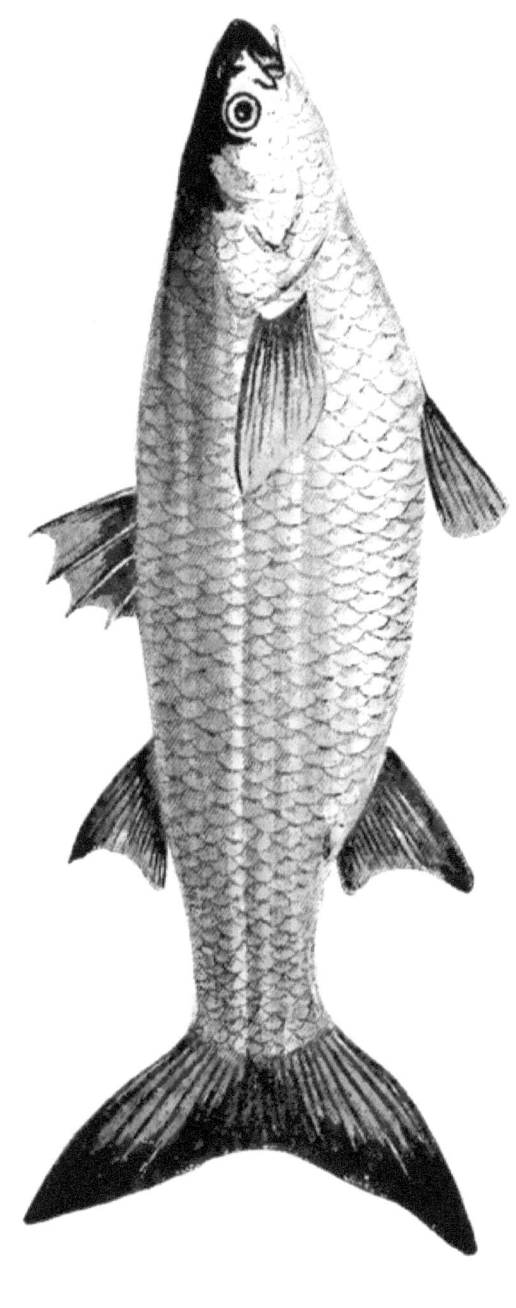

GREY MULLET.

same principle of easy adjustment as in the spiral lead aforementioned designed by the same angler.

The exact form of lead for use in float-fishing is largely a matter of taste. The split shot in vogue on the river are not of much use in the tideway, where something more solid is required. Small pierced bullets are as good as anything, though I usually have in my basket either a small coil of soft lead wire, or else of the thin sheeting which is sold in penny rolls, for plumbing the depth. Either of these can be added to the line, a fraction of an ounce at a time, until the float rides just as required, and each has the further advantage of taking up little room when bound round the gut being far less likely to disturb the fish than would a number of additional bullets of the same weight.

In the foregoing pages, mention has been made of all the typical tackles on which are based every combination which the angler is likely to devise. Thus, the drift-line is merely a float-line without either float or lead; the trot, or long line, is to all intents and purposes a number of paternosters tied together and used horizontally instead of vertically, between two weights that lie on the bottom, the floating trot being, as its name implies, the same, with buoys in conjunction with the leads.

There remain, however, a number of implements, which, coming under the convenient and accommodating head of sundries, need a few words before we quit the tackle department. On some of these, my advice will, I fear, appear revolutionary, conflicting not only with the verdict of other writers on the subject, but even with what I have said on previous occasions. On this I prefer being frank;

it is my object to give the best counsel at my disposal in the light of recent experiences, and I have no intention of sparing my own previous errors where I think it to the reader's benefit that I should recant.

First, the basket, or creel, a most useful and important receptacle. A deal has been written on this subject, much has been said for and against open or closed creels, still more in preference of a bag to any basket yet designed.

CREEL.

Now, the orthodox creel, of the pattern figured, is undoubtedly an excellent article; but to be of any use for holding one's lines and reels it must be of the largest size procurable—my own is over 2 ft. long, and I picked it up, as one picks up so many useful things at low prices, as a "misfit" that had been ordered but not paid for—and being as it is somewhat unwieldy, I cannot help thinking that its permanent place is at home or aboard a yacht. For ordinary everyday purposes of taking one's tackle, and bringing back the fish, I find a couple of the straw bags used by fishmongers and poulterers answer every purpose. These cost only a shilling the dozen, and can consequently be renewed once or twice in the week, more particularly the one used for the carriage of fish. There are, it is true, a number of bags and baskets with

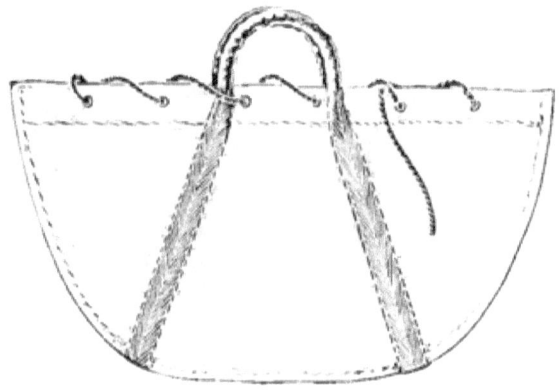

THE "GRESHAM" BAG.

separate compartments for the latter; but these do not answer the purpose, in my opinion, with sea fish, many of which, whiting, conger and mullet among them, impart an odour that is not to be got rid of by the usual method of scrubbing with soda and hot water. Perhaps the best bag sold for the purpose is that named after the "Gresham" Angling Society, to a member of which we owe the pattern. While on the subject of the carriage of fish, I may as well say a word, not knowing where I shall find better occasion, on the practice of sending presents of sea-fish to friends inland. As a matter of plain truth, it is, unless done with discrimination and common sense, a very silly custom indeed. Whiting, for instance, and pollack are often despatched in this way in the height of summer from watering-places a hundred miles or more from the metropolis; the recipients have perhaps to pay considerable carriage on them, even if they have been nominally freighted to the door, and they arrive in a condition that even offends the cat. In point of fact, it would have been difficult to select two fish less likely to bear the journey, though mackerel and sole would have been nearly as hopeless. If fish must be sent in this manner, let them at any rate be such as have a chance of reaching their destination in an eatable state—plaice, flounder, codling or dab. Let them be cleaned and rubbed with salt, and each fish done up in dry weed in a separate straw bag of the kind mentioned above; and, above all, let them be despatched with due regard for the time of arrival, so that they may not pass the night in the station. Flat fish are able to survive removal from the water by some hours if kept moist and cool; and it has been found possible to get them alive from Southend to Fenchurch Street by keeping them in wet seaweed, the hamper lying in the shade under the seat.

The next article that occurs to me is the gaff, which, as their function is identical, we may consider together with the landing-net. Here, again, the patterns are various, being indeed of less significance than the length of the handle, which should vary according to circumstances. For boat-fishing, for example, I prefer a handle of not more than 3 ft. in length, whereas for mackerel or mullet from piers and

Gaff and landing-net

jetties, a handle of 5 or 6 ft. will often be found indispensable. Of the variety of patterns that are designed for the trout stream or salmon river, and which are doubtless well enough in the right place, I would counsel distrust: they are not adapted to the rough wear and tear of sea-fishing; and even if the salt water does not tell sooner or later on the all too unprotected screws, the fragile parts are certain to come to grief, most often when beaching the boat, a very trying time when the seas run heavy for everything on board. The simplest thing is in sea-fishing, as in much beside, the best. My own gaff for boat work —I bought it in Australia for about a shilling—is a 3 ft. ash pole, into one end of which is wedged a hake-hook, the barb of which has been removed. The flattened end of the shank was obviously beaten back in a curve, driven into the hollow end of the ash handle, and kept in its place by a number of small wedges. I have brought a number of fish to the boat with it in both hemispheres, and never want a better. The gaff is, as a rule, used for large fish, the net for small, an indefinite division that leaves room for the exercise of individual eccentricity. As a matter of fact, it is a mistake to leave the beach

LANDING-NET.

without having both aboard; for it is always impossible to say what will be the size of the largest fish, and the net alone would come off badly with any of the spinous dog-fish that one hooks so often when fishing for mackerel or whiting. A great deal has been written in learned vein on the subject of gaffing. The tail is usually aimed at, as the specimen is less likely to be damaged; moreover, the strength of the fish lies in its tail, therefore that extremity should get the angler's best attention. There is also, I believe, some idea of its being possibly found desirable to return the fish, in

GAFF-HOOK (WITH SCREW CAP) FOR LASHING.

which case the gaff is less likely to injure it if inserted in the tail. These reflections are very charming on the edge of the salmon-pool; but at sea, I fear, we gaff bass, pollack, or dog-fish very much where we can, most often in the gill-covers. The confession is a humiliating one, but better made. Fish of less than a pound can usually be "hauled" without either net or gaff, though the hook-gut is not improved by the strain of these deadweights. My boatman in Cornwall rarely used either gaff or net, lifting pollack up to 10 lbs. weight into the boat with his left arm. Where, however, as in the case of the grey mullet and smelt, the lip of the fish is very delicate and likely to break, it is much safer to use a net for even quite small fish. If a second person is holding the net, let him keep it perfectly steady, with one

SEA-RODS, REELS, AND VARIOUS TACKLES. 73

edge dipping under the surface, leaving the angler to guide the fish into it. Any attempt on the part of the assistant to *scoop* up the fish will almost certainly end in disaster. In landing fish from a pier, a large net is preferable to a gaff, as the effective use of a long-handled gaff is exceedingly difficult, even for an expert.[1]

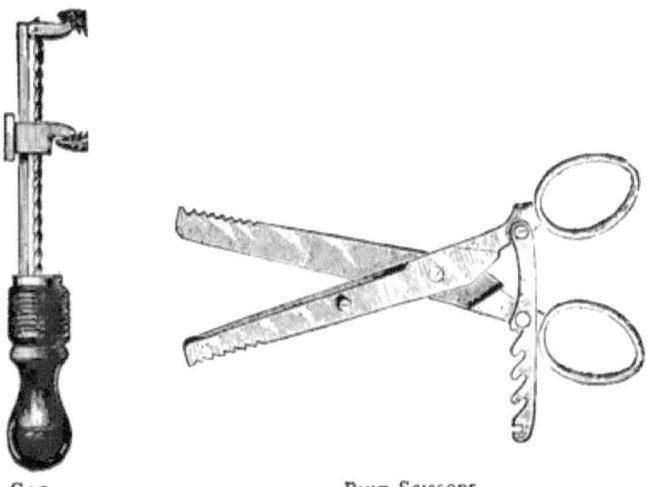

GAG.   PIKE SCISSORS.

But the fight is not quite over when a large fish is brought safely to the boat or landing-stage, for the hook has yet to be recovered from its often well-armed jaws; and, if the angler has no spare hook, time may be a great consideration. It is found necessary (a) to make the fish open its mouth, often no easy matter; (b) to keep the mouth open without bringing the fingers in contact with its teeth; (c) to push out the hook often from far down in the throat. To aid in these

Gag and disgorger

---

[1] The neatest manipulation of landing-net and rod I ever saw was at Littlehampton, where the mullet-fishers keep a stone or two in the net, the weight of which holds the latter in position.

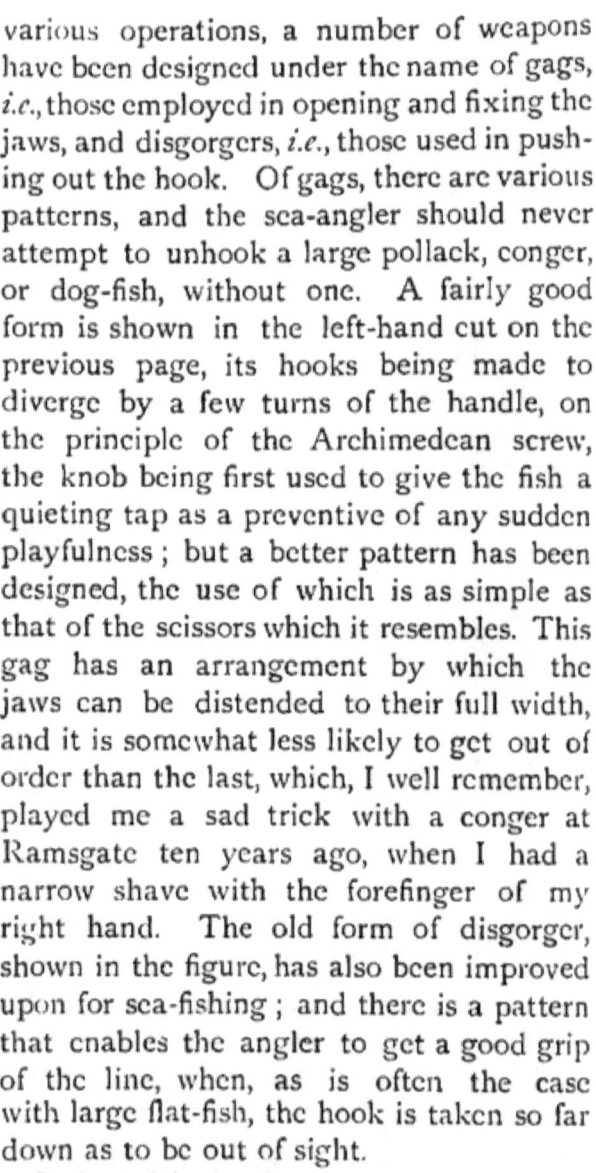

Disgorger.

various operations, a number of weapons have been designed under the name of gags, *i.e.*, those employed in opening and fixing the jaws, and disgorgers, *i.e.*, those used in pushing out the hook. Of gags, there are various patterns, and the sea-angler should never attempt to unhook a large pollack, conger, or dog-fish, without one. A fairly good form is shown in the left-hand cut on the previous page, its hooks being made to diverge by a few turns of the handle, on the principle of the Archimedean screw, the knob being first used to give the fish a quieting tap as a preventive of any sudden playfulness; but a better pattern has been designed, the use of which is as simple as that of the scissors which it resembles. This gag has an arrangement by which the jaws can be distended to their full width, and it is somewhat less likely to get out of order than the last, which, I well remember, played me a sad trick with a conger at Ramsgate ten years ago, when I had a narrow shave with the forefinger of my right hand. The old form of disgorger, shown in the figure, has also been improved upon for sea-fishing; and there is a pattern that enables the angler to get a good grip of the line, when, as is often the case with large flat-fish, the hook is taken so far down as to be out of sight.

In few of the implements of his craft does the fisherman's individual taste find expression in greater variety than in the form of knife which he produces when wanted, either for cutting up the

Knife

RED MULLET.

bait, killing the larger fish, or trimming the knots on his line. Yet nowhere perhaps is there less room for variety. In the first place, two out of the three operations just enumerated should not on any account be performed with a knife at all;

"Priest."

the fish should be killed with a blow from a belaying pin or the gaff handle, better still with a leaded hammer or "priest," of some pattern like that figured, which is made by Farlow; and the line should be trimmed with scissors, which enables one to clip the ends much closer without repeatedly scoring the gunwale or one's thumb, as so often happens when using a large knife for the purpose

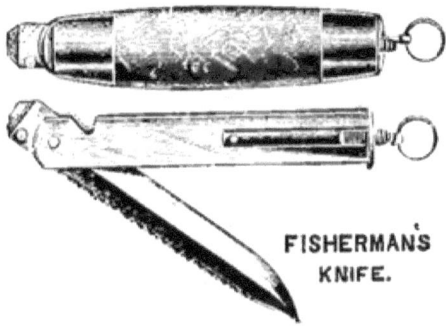

FISHERMAN'S KNIFE.

of trimming knots in a heavy sea. For the cutting of bait, two knives should be used; a small knife with rounded (*not* pointed) blade for opening mussels,[1] a larger weapon for cutting up mackerel, herring, or squid. On no account use a folding

[1] The blade should be inserted in the small orifice found on scraping off the "beard," and should then be worked completely round either shell to sever the mussel from its armour.

pocket-knife for either, or accidents will be frequent. Failing one of the excellent Norwegian pattern, which are far and away the best for most outdoor work, it is best to take an old table knife, in doing which be careful to select one with a stiff blade. Those in which, through long use, the blade has been worn thin, bending easily to left or right, slip into one's fingers at the least provocation, and are far better overboard.

This chapter may perhaps be brought to a close with a word more, in addition to what has been said above, as to the care of tackle,—a most important subject in all fishing, in sea-fishing more than the rest. The maxim of the French engineer, that no fortress is stronger than its weakest part, has been so often quoted in connection with tackle that I am afraid to take it as the text of the following remarks; but it should at any rate be borne in mind that every inch of the line, every strand of the gut, every part of the hook must be kept perfect, and that there is no co-operative principle whereby extra strength in one part atones at the critical pass for weakness in another. The great enemy, one ever at work against the owner of tackle, is damp. Paradox as this may seem in the case of tackle manufactured to endure long exposure to water, it is a fact that damp is almost as fatal to tackle as it is to guns and powder. It is customary to keep tackle in outhouses without regard to their dryness or temperature; but this is a most absurd practice. If there is a harness-room handy, as when putting up at an hotel, it is a good plan to earn—otherwise buy— the friendship of the ostler and secure a corner for your gear, for such places are usually kept at a dry and equable temperature. Otherwise, I generally keep my rods in the living-room, a habit that does not always meet with the enthusiastic approval which it undoubtedly deserves. It is important to remember, though the remark seems trite, that objects impregnated with so greedy an absorbent of moisture as salt can never be properly dry for long together. Yachting men know this well; but it might perhaps be news to others that a coat that has been dashed with salt spray in the summer will still be damp during the rainy days of November,

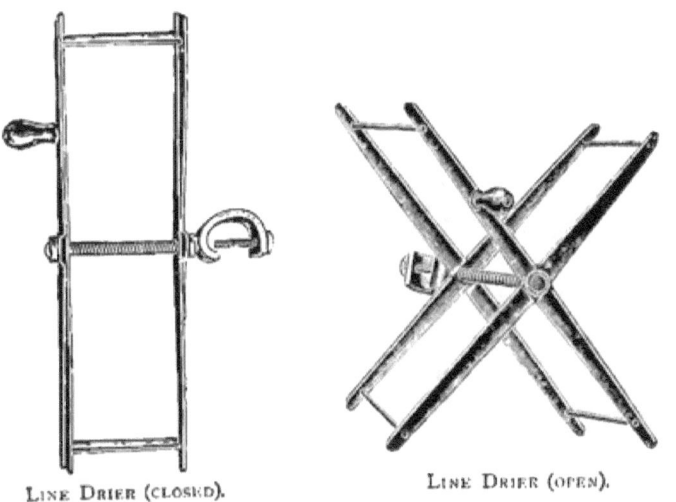

LINE DRIER (CLOSED). LINE DRIER (OPEN).

serving, in fact, as a rough barometer, or rather as an indication of the degree of moisture in the atmosphere. The object of which discourse is to bring home to the sea-fisher the great advantage, if not absolute necessity, of thoroughly soaking the lines each evening after the day's fishing to get rid of the salt, then allowing them to dry (over the back of a chair or towel-horse in the absence of a proper line-drier) before winding them back on the reels.

The rod should be kept as much as possible out

of water; but occasionally the sudden downward rush of a pollack will prove too much for the angler, and the top joint will dip, his best efforts notwithstanding. After an experience of this sort, it is as well to rub the top joint with a damp cloth on reaching home, drying it with another cloth.

In like manner the reels, the rod-ferrules, the joints of gaff and landing-net, anything, in fact, in the construction of which metal is employed, may with advantage be overhauled and touched with a drop of fine machine oil, at any rate once a week.

A little care for one's tackle, though many may vote it a bore, takes up but a few minutes each evening; and the trouble expended will be repaid a hundredfold, if only in the comfortable sensation when at sea that the gear may be trusted to hold its own against any fish likely to interfere with it. As may, indeed, all good gear properly cared for and handled. The rod and line, above all, need constant care, for it is on them that the strain falls hardest.

A word may here be said against the practice, prevalent at Littlehampton and some other ports, of not taking the rod to pieces after each day's fishing. Apart from the inconvenience of carrying the rod in this form, the habit is a bad one, tending to breakage, especially when again taking it to pieces after the season is over. An inexpensive mullet-rod, by which the owner sets no store, may perhaps be used thus, but it is not fair treatment for any good weapon that has to kill heavy fish.

CHAPTER III.

HAND-LINING.

IT has been said above that there are conditions under which, even in our seas, the fisherman of quite the most advanced views will do well to leave his rod at home and put his faith in the older hand-line. In the majority of cases, it is true, the rod not only answers every purpose, but, admitting as it does the use of lighter gear, beats the hand-line fishing alongside. I cannot, however, agree with the plea that the rod saves time in hauling ; for, unless in combination with a cumbersome reel of, say, a foot in diameter, its performance in this respect must obviously compare badly with that of the hand-liner hauling, hand over hand, a fathom at a time. Its advantage tells, however, in the fact that the elasticity of the top joint enables the rod-fisher to score on clear bright days with a three-yard trace of *single* gut for pollack and mackerel ; whereas with the hand-line he would, unless very skilled in its manipulation, be compelled to top his line with a shorter trace of *twisted* gut, a decided disadvantage with the water low and clear.

A very pleasant day or night may, however, be spent on the outer grounds, ten or more miles from the coast, where, as a change from the more delicate fishing inshore, the angler—the word is used in its broadest sense—may pit his strength against heavy skate and conger, fish reckoned in stone, not pounds. For work of this description, the rod is quite out of place. I do not assert that it would, with a few hours to spare, be impossible to kill a skate of 100 lbs. on a short stiff rod of the kind used for tarpon. It is injudicious in these days to pronounce any feat of skill an impossibility. But I may say, at any rate, that, so far as my own taste goes, it would be an intensely wearisome proceeding—a nuisance to every one in the boat and a strain of the severest kind on the tackle. With the hand-line, on the other hand, such prizes are brought to book in a few moments; and, apart from the novelty of tackling very powerful fish, they give, whether on rod or hand-line, the poorest of sport in the ordinary acceptation of the term, so that he who soonest gets his skate or conger into the boat may fairly be reckoned best man.

There are occasions, indeed, on which, out of regard for the probable arrival of sharks and their kind, it is not advisable to leave shore without at least one stout line aboard. A case in point occurred on the occasion of my first outing this spring, the 27th of April, and, so far as fishing went, the first fine day at Bournemouth since the previous September. We immediately struck a patch of small spring silver whiting, which bit greedily at mackerel-bait. Of a sudden, and after each of us had caught a number, there came a lull in the proceedings, and the fish had evidently gone off.

HAND-LINING.

The next development was for my light rod to bend in most uncomfortable fashion, the tug, tug, and heavy pull unmistakably denoting a dog-fish. For fully five minutes I managed to play the vermin, getting it in full view at the surface—it was a "nurse," about four feet in length—at the end of which space it got its teeth in action, and the single gut went. It was a matter for congratulation, indeed, that I did not lose the whole trace or damage the rod. Had there only been a conger-line in the boat, such as there had always been before and has always been since, half a mackerel would soon have settled the question; but having foolishly left the despised hand-lines ashore, we were powerless, and, after I had killed a smaller "nurse" of two or three pounds, we had to weigh anchor, as the old fish was still prowling round and keeping all else away. *[Case of a "nurse"]*

Other cases in which the hand-line is all but indispensable occur to memory. That of deep water has already been quoted; but for those who do not shirk the labour of reeling in ten fathoms on a four-inch reel every few moments, there are certainly modern rods and rod tops that enable them to disregard any depth likely to be encountered within ten miles of the coast.

Then there is mackerel-railing from sailing-boats, when you get over the water four or five knots to the hour, and draw the bait across a stiff tide, eight or ten (in clear water, even twelve) fathoms of line streaming out behind the boat. Where would the rod be then? The line used in this "plummeting" (the Cornish term, derived from the plummet-lead used) tapers somewhat from the thick cord held in the hand to *["Plummeting" for mackerel]* the fine brown snooding, a fathom in length, to which is attached the hook by its link of single gut. The plummet, the weight of which varies according to circumstances, from 1 lb. to 3 lbs., is furnished with two loops of stiffened cord, to one of which is fastened the mainline, to the other the fine hook-snood. The hook is then baited with a "last"—a name well merited by its powers of endurance, as one bait often suffices for a score of fish—cut neatly from the side of the mackerel's tail, and allowed to hang from the bend of the hook without any attempt at concealing the point, and the whole is cast astern. As the strain is very considerable in anything of a breeze, those with tender fingers will do well to ease the tension by the use of a toggle of wood, nothing more than a tapered plug fastened crosswise, which should be held between the first and second fingers of the closed hand. The lines are kept in motion with a give-and-take action of the arm; and the fish, as a rule, hook themselves. As the dip of the gunwale, especially off a broken coast, is often sudden, the amateur will find that he has quite enough to do in managing one such line and maintaining his balance; but the Cornishman will go out in a spanking breeze single-handed, manage three lines, and, pressing his bare feet into the service, handle his lugger with a skill that would take some beating. I have heard a good many complaints against the simple plummet-tackle described above, and have tried a number of "sensitive" leads and what not, designed to improve the fisherman's chances; but, truth to tell, these are not as a rule in need of betterment; and we only catch mackerel in this way down in Cornwall on our way out to the pollack- and whiting-grounds for bait, so little sport is there in it. Luck varies, of course, as in all fishing; a couple of hundred fish (the Cornish "hundred" of fish is equivalent to 126) may be recorded as a good two hours' catch for three lines.

I have also, more for the sake of experiment than in any doubt as to the result, been persuaded to try a number of patent and other baits against the local "last," or "snade," but the latter cannot be beaten.

It is, I think, plain that the strain on the rod would, in such fishing, entail a deal of extra work; and when, as not seldom happens, a clump of floating weed or a huge jelly-fish (locally known as "machiowler") drifts by and strikes the line full, doubling the already heavy strain, the top joint would almost certainly go.

It does not, however, follow that the use of the professional hand-line need involve the accompanying clumsiness of their lower gear. The bottom fathom near the hook should, on the contrary, be as fine as is compatible with safety, always having regard to the fact that the less skilled and patient the fisherman in playing his fish, the stronger need be the gear from hand to hook. It is more particularly in the two operations of casting out the lead and striking the fish that the expert with the hand-line is recognised. *Fine gear with hand-lines*

The most efficient all-round lead I know of is the boat-shaped lead of the Cornish fishermen, which can be attached to any part of the line by a hitch round its stiffened arms of cord, its usual distance above the hook being a couple of fathoms, or 12 ft. There are without doubt many ways of throwing out such a lead, but there is only *Casting the lead* one correct one that makes fouling next to an impossibility. The hooks, being baited, are put overboard first, the lead being retained in the right hand until the tide has carried out the fathom of

CORNISH SHEARING-LEAD.

slack snood below it. Then, and *not before*, the lead is pitched a good two fathoms against the tide, the line being allowed to run slowly out over the gunwale until the lead touches the bottom, when three fathoms are hauled and the whole made fast round a cleat. Thus, if the tide runs aft, the lead is thrown for'ard, and *vice versa*. Unless there is a mizen up to keep the boat head to wind, she will swing to the tide; where, however, the latter is streaming out broadside, the hooks are thrown out first as before, and the lead is dropped alongside as soon as the slack is all out. Above all, it is essential to let the line run out slowly while the lead is going down. Any attempt to gain time by letting it fly out unchecked, or, worse still, paying it out in coils, will only result in a foul; and the worst of it is that, although no fish of any consequence will take the bait with the line in a tangle, there is nothing to warn the fisherman that all is not right below, and he may fish on in a fool's paradise for some minutes before the absence of bites suggests something at fault. It is as well to bear in mind, when withdrawing the lead from the bottom, that a fathom may be roughly measured by the full stretch of both arms.

I trust I have made the matter quite clear, as, strange to say, the proper method of throwing out the boat-shaped sinker has not been described in any previous work on sea-fishing.

The other matter, striking, is simpler, but there is also a right way and a wrong. Striking with a hand-line in any considerable depth of water must be no finicking turn of the wrist, such as would doubtless serve in emptying a shallow pond of small roach; but what is needed to drive the steel well home is a good, smart hauling back of quite a yard of line over the gunwale, which, as subsequently in hauling the fish, should be made to bear the chief brunt. In short, the hands should be kept *inside* the boat from the moment of hooking the fish; and it is in this that the old hand is at once recognised. The exact amount of law to give each fish must depend much on its weight and, if known, its probable behaviour, as an instance of which may be cited the downward boring of the pollack as contrasted with the upward spring of the sharks. As a general rule, and always supposing the gear can be trusted, the main object is to get the fish into the boat, the finer cat-and-mouse play of the rod being unquestionably lost with the hand-line, though I have seen some skill exhibited in playing large fish. I recall the capture in 1894 of a 26 lbs. porbeagle shark on a hook on single gut by my Cornish boatman, George Marshall, of Mevagissey; but George is by nature a very clever fisherman, and a great advocate of the artistic playing of large fish over the gunwale.

Several contrivances have been devised, mostly, I think, by Hearder, of Plymouth, for use in connection with hand-lining, of which brief mention may here be made.

Winders In winders, there has not, it must be confessed, been any startling innovation; and the old pattern, nothing more than four pieces of wood joined in the form of a square, is still in general use. The only improvement has been the addition of a fixed handle on which the rest revolves, a convenience in reeling in. A still better arrangement, however, though also more expensive, is the pollack-reel, fitted with an upright piece of cane with a notch through which the line passes from the reel. The fish

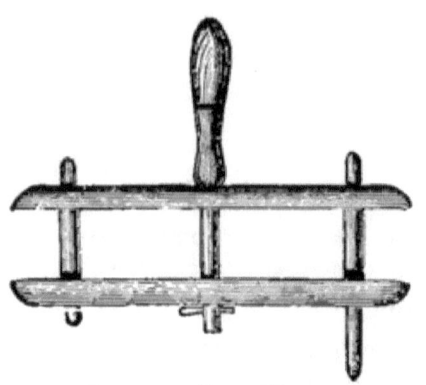

REVOLVING HAND WINDER.

striking the line causes the cane to bend and release the line, which is then handled in the ordinary way. The chief function of this reel is in cases where more than one line is in use. Sportsmen of the hypercritical school may object to the use of more than one line, as an approach to pot-hunting, but I am unable to agree with this view. The sea is a large stew, and there is nothing to object to in the use of as many lines as one fisherman can manage properly, for there is no fear of exhausting the supply. Two will as a matter of fact be found ample; but even then the second should, especially where there are large pollack about, be hitched round something springy, be it only an inch or two of cane stuck upright in the gunwale. This is the hand-liner's substitute for the top joint of the rod. Yet another of the Plymouth contrivances—and it should only be used where there are more than one line out—is the automatic striker. This sounds almost as bad as the winch from the further side of the Atlantic that strikes and reels up the fish, leaving the angler nothing to

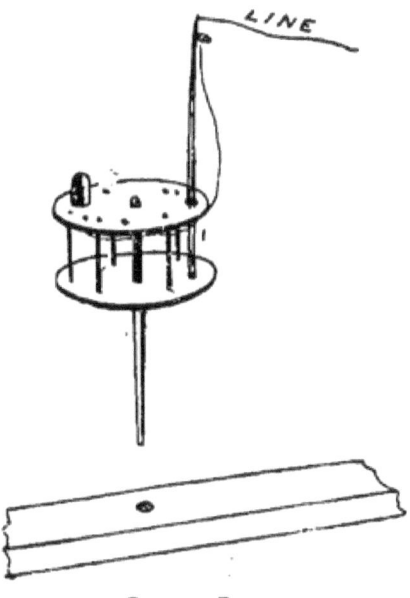

POLLACK REEL.

do; but it is not quite so offensive, though there is more than a smack of "poaching" about it. All it does is to hook two fish out of three, while the fisherman is busy with another line. Personally, I do not as a rule make use of more than one line at a time, but there are many who do, and for them there can be nothing objectionable in the use of this striker. Its action is sufficiently explained by the annexed cut, the bell acting in much the same way as the similar arrangement on the bamboo tackles rigged up for catching albicore and barracouta in mid-ocean.

Another matter to which some attention has been given during the past two or three years is some pattern of lead that will facilitate rapid

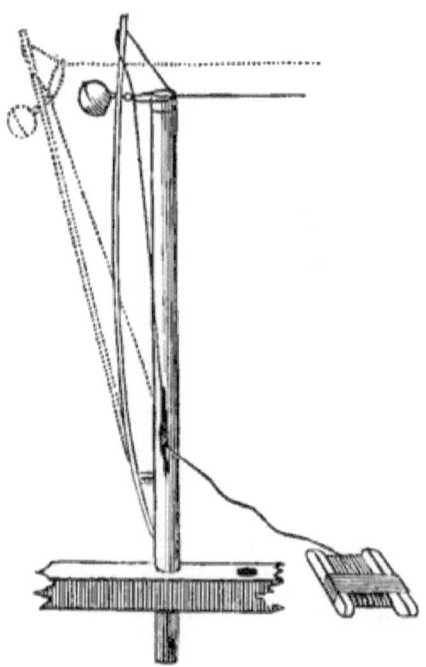

Automatic Striker.

changing, so desirable in the tideway, where the angler may start fishing with half an ounce at low water and require to add weight gradually until, when the tide is running very strong, 2 or 3 lbs. will, on the hand-line, be none too much. I have several of these new patent leads before me, two of which are figured here; while a third, the device, I believe, of Macpherson of Southampton, is shown

HAND-LINING. 89

on a later page. The conical figured pattern below explains itself, while the other, generally used in connection with the "Mahteb" sprool, is equally simple. This sprool, by the way, is excellent in deep, thick water; but I am unable to recommend it, portable though it be, for inshore fishing, as it is undoubtedly very conspicuous. The common fault

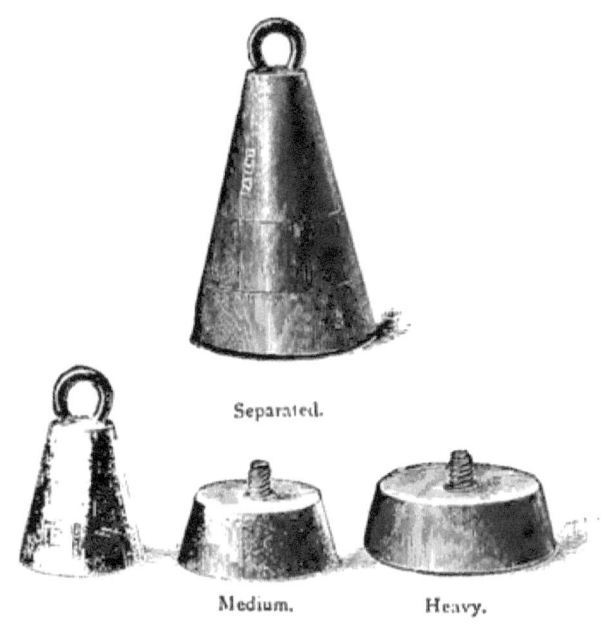

Separated.

Medium.   Heavy.
INTERCHANGEABLE LEADS.

of all these leads is that they do not admit of addition or diminution of weight in sufficiently small quantities. When fishing in the tideway it is often desirable, more particularly when the fish are biting shyly and at some distance from the boat, to alter the weight by perhaps ¼ oz. at a time. This may seem fastidious, but those who have not tried it can have no idea of the success attending very nice adjustment of the lead, which should be just enough to hold the bottom and not too much for the angler to feel the slightest nibble. It is not only in river-fishing that the largest fish give the most finicking bites. All the patent leads that I have yet come across necessitate altering the weight by 2 ozs. or more at a time, and the effect is bad. Some day, one is tempted to think, the difficulty will be got over by the use of small quantities of quicksilver, than which there is no better medium for the purpose. Meanwhile, I manage pretty well with a coil of pliant lead wire

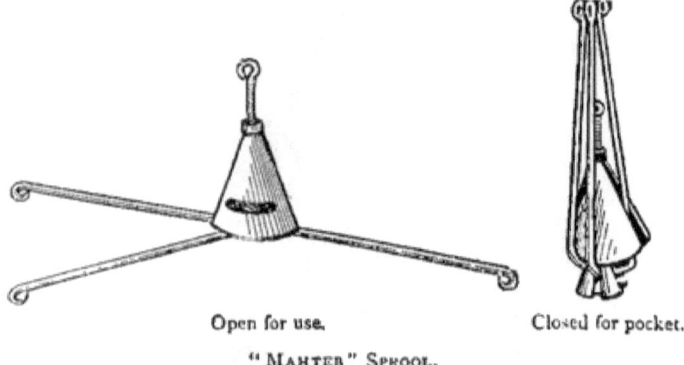

Open for use.   Closed for pocket.
"MAHTEB" SPROOL.

—the ordinary plummet-foil answers the purpose as well, but the wire is easier to fix on stout line— which enables me to add weight by the merest fraction of an ounce and in a shape not calculated to alarm the fish. All leads, by the way, should be attached to gut traces by an intervening loop of silk, as the metal—whether the lead be perforated or provided with a brass loop—frays the gut at once.

To the cases in which the hand-line is preferable to the more civilised rod may be added that of autumn beach-fishing from a sloping shore. Here,

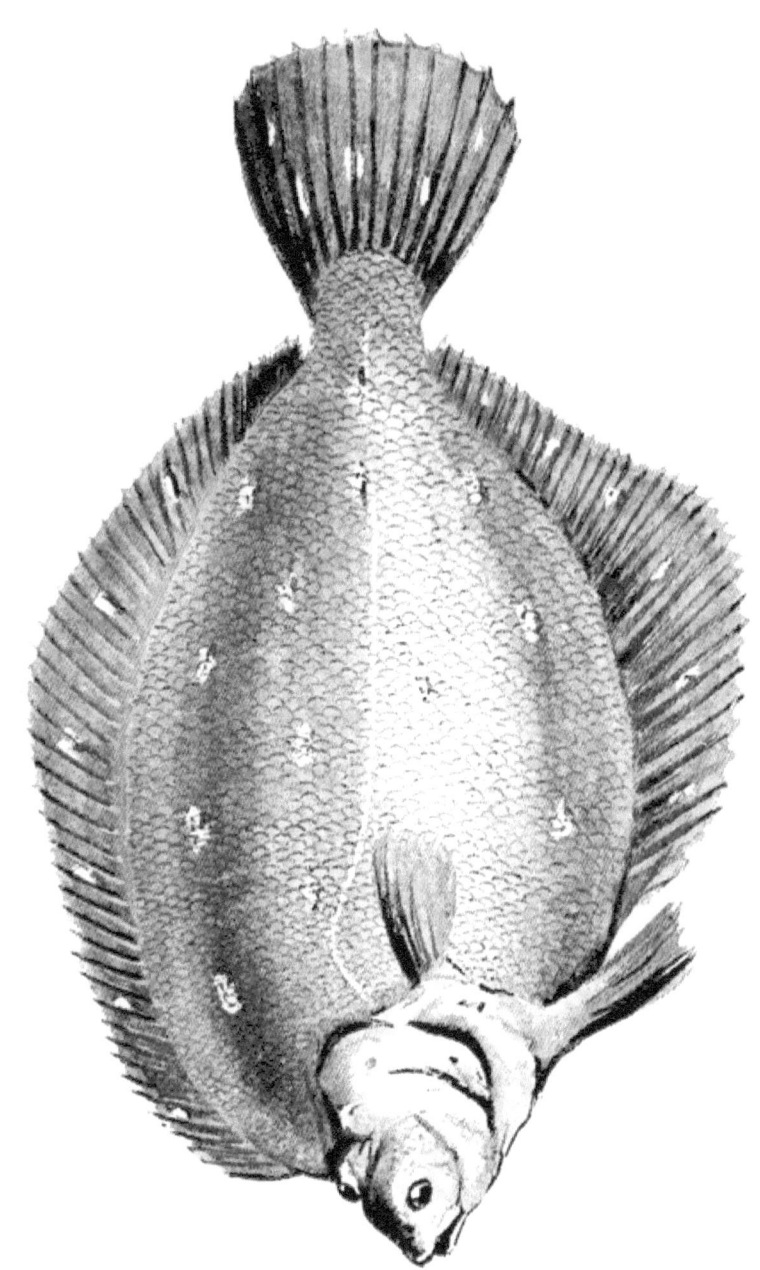

the rod may be a positive nuisance, the hand-line, on the other hand, being easy to manipulate at the edge of the surf and to lay down in the intervals of fishing. There are several methods of swinging the lead into position; one much in vogue among beach-fishers being the use of a forked stick, which takes firm hold of a button on the line close to the hooks. With heavy leads, however, and a little practice, it is not difficult to pitch the hooks to a considerable distance without any such aid, though some care is often necessary on pierheads to avoid accidents with others in the neighbourhood. I once saw an old lady's ear caught in this way by a hook that was hurtling through the air after a $\frac{1}{2}$-lb lead. She was obviously one of a large excursion, the members of which were that day gladdening the place with their laughter; yet in her few hours by the sea she managed to enjoy an experience such as falls to the lot of few. I remember with regret that, as the landing-stage was very crowded at the moment with youthful anglers, there was some slight difficulty in fixing upon the owner of that hook.

A plan that has much to commend it from such pierheads in the tideway as lend themselves to its use is to fasten a wine bottle, half filled with water to keep it upright, to the further end of the line, and let the ebbing tide carry it out, line and all. When the hooks have gone far enough, a smart jerk causes the bottle to fill and sink. The obvious objections to this plan are the time taken by the bottle in travelling out with its burden, and the impossibility of fishing when the water is coming in, the best time as a rule. On the other hand, it is possible in this manner to get the hooks much further than you could throw a lead. As the shape of the ordinary bottle is, however, peculiarly adapted to getting foul of the rocks, it is advisable—and this applies more or less to all fishing over rocks—to make it fast to the line with a weaker thread, as the hooks can then at any rate be recovered should the bottle, or lead, get hopelessly " hung up." Large conger—I have killed them up to 23 lbs.—are caught at night on the Cornish coast within stone's throw of the rocks. As there are, however, no ledges that even a chamois would care to essay in the dark, a boat is absolutely necessary. The handline also takes the place of the rod, and indeed, though I once killed a conger of over 20 lbs. on a stout rod, the confusion in the darkness was such that I shall not readily try it again.

A CONGER HOLE.

CHAPTER IV.

SHORE-FISHING.

As stated in the Preface, it is my intention to describe the different methods of sea-fishing for sport on topographical lines. This is, indeed, the most convenient standpoint from which to discuss the capture of the species under notice. In describing sport in a river, as Mr. Wheeley did in the preceding volume, there was no objection to taking the fish in order and repeating the styles peculiarly adapted to each. A bream is angled for with much the same tackle whether from punt or bank. In sea-fishing, it is different, and the pollack or bass will be sought in totally different fashion, according to whether the fisherman goes afloat after them or prefers the inexpensive security of the foreshore or pier.

Three kinds of sea-fishing may therefore be distinguished—from shore, pier or boat.

Shore-fishing is less practised in these islands perhaps than abroad. In Australia, more particularly (see Appendix), there are a great number of keen anglers from both sand and rock, the two categories under which this sport naturally falls. The rock-fishers face the most

In Australia

appalling climbs, scrambling to their favourite grounds over all but perpendicular faces of slippery rock, creeping along ledges a few inches broad, from which a single false step would plunge them among the sharks a hundred feet below. The baskets which they bring back from these perilous spots certainly include some magnificent fish, among them gropers of fifty pounds, schnappers of ten, and large traglin and leather-jackets.

In our own country the dangers are fortunately very much less, if only by the sharks, an appreciable item in the more southern waters.

At home

At the same time, rock-climbing always calls for a steady eye and foot, as well as some attention to local tides and vagaries in the way of currents; else many ridiculous situations, if nothing graver, are sure to result.

In fishing from sandy beaches, the whole procedure is of course very much simpler, the danger is practically absent, and the sport is, as a rule, inferior.

The localities on the British coasts that offer facilities for rock-fishing are somewhat limited, as, though many of our counties are more or less rock-bound, there are not everywhere positions easily reached and giving the angler command over water of sufficient depth to harbour desirable fish. The most advanced school of rock-fishers at home are the Aberdeen men, who have for many years been formed into an association; indeed, I am told there are at the present time as many as three such clubs of local anglers. Be this as it may, the Amateur Rock-Fishers' Association was, the subsequent birth and growth of the British Sea-Anglers' Society notwithstanding,

Localities

the first salt-water angling club in these parts, and as such is deserving of more attention than previous chroniclers have given it. I am indebted for the following particulars to Mr. George Mackay, a frequent contributor to the *Fishing Gazette*.

There are two associations, he says, at Aberdeen, the "Amateur Rock-Fishers" and the "Bon Accord Fishers," the former, and senior, club numbering about 150 members, while to the latter, only recently organised, belong about half that number. There is yet a third association at Stonehaven, with a membership of something over 30. All these clubs have distinctive badges and regular rendezvous; their subscriptions range from 2*d*. to 3*d*. per quarter, in addition to a light entrance fee. These associations have, one and all, done good work in regulating their competitions and collecting information; but their chief influence has been in the direction of elevating the *morale* of the rock-fisher and bringing any objectionable pot-hunter to his bearings. Aberdeen rock-fishers

Mr. Mackay further gives an account of the tackle and baits used in this rock-fishing in the north, and they serve admirably as an example of the right gear for rock-fishing generally. The best rock-rod, he says, is a bamboo in three or four joints, 18 or 20 feet in all, a formidable though inexpensive weapon. For bait-fishing in the deeper pools for large fish, such a rod cannot be beaten; but the comparatively few rock-fishers who angle with fly or other artificial bait use a lighter rod of about 12 feet in length. Silk lines, apart from their expense, are not found so good as those of barked or unbarked cord; and as for reel, although it adds to the angler's comfort when obliged to give law to Tackle used a heavy fish, many of the rock-fishers dispense with it altogether.

<small>Rod and hand-line</small> The rod is eminently suited for rock-fishing, just as hand-lining is the better style on a sandy beach. It stands to reason that the use of the rod enables the angler to keep his hooks clear of the side, while, on the other hand, it is often awkward to lay a rod down on a sloping beach, even with the supports used in bank-fishing inland. There is, however, no hard and fast rule; and I have seen the line used with success from the rocks, as I have used the rod myself from the beach.

The fish chiefly caught in this shore-fishing is the cod. On the east coast, beach-fishers also make fair hauls of whiting; and in Scotch waters, there is, as we have seen, the coal-fish, or saithe, as an uneatable [1] yet sport-giving alternative. The size of the hook depends of course on that of the fish expected, and rock-fishers usually keep several sizes by them. For the average run, 2 lbs. to 4 lbs., a 0 round bend with a long shank and whipped on to double gut is most in vogue. Two hooks are very commonly used, one above, the other beneath the lead, the latter being so arranged as to be capable of change with minimum loss of time, its usual weight ranging from 4 to 12 oz., according to the strength of tide for the time being.

<small>Baits</small> But the cod is the shore-fisher's first string, both north and south of the border, and there are few better baits for it than two or three medium-sized mussels whipped on the hook with a

---

[1] I am assured that the coal-fish is, when *properly cooked*, delicious. While in no way changing my own opinion of so insipid a mess, I gladly insert this piece of information for the encouragement of tourists fond of novel dishes.

turn of yellow wool or silk, wool for preference, as the silk (or, in a still greater degree, cotton) is apt to cut through the bait.

Soft crab, or rather the soft interior of the common shore-crab—curiously enough it is *the* bait for groper in Australian rock-fishing — is another favourite bait; and Mr. Mackay even tells of a rock-fisher, who was hard up for bait, making an excellent catch of coal-fish with a fish of that species cut in strips. They use the black crab for preference, as it has not the market value of the red. The latter, it is noticed, has to be sought in the rocky crevices, whereas the former may be found among the weed and in the pools left at low water. The inside only is used for bait, that of a large crab being sufficient for two baits at least. It is, like the mussel, tied on the hook, and is perhaps still more killing. Other baits, less in favour, are herring, lugworm and sand-eel.

There is then nothing peculiar in the tackle used in this fishing, a stout rod, with running line and twisted gut paternoster, answering every purpose. Some anglers, with plenty of time at their disposal and a weakness for trying experiments, catch their rock-fish with fly or spinner; but I cannot, save under very exceptionable circumstances, recommend either of these practices, sporting though they be, to those who want to make a good basket. Sportsmanlike methods should, it is unnecessary to say, be followed in salt as in fresh water, but there is no need to choose out of a number of legitimate ways of taking fish the one least likely to meet with success. Therefore, the majority of rock-fishers will elect to use natural bait. It is usually handy at low water, and the angler can then often get a supply so as to fish the whole of the flood.

Float-tackle is also first rate in those localities in which the ground is too rough for the lead to be dragged with safety. Unless, however, the rod is considerably longer than the depth fished, a condition that rarely obtains, the float must run freely and be stopped on the "slider" principle explained on a subsequent page. In the ordinary course, the best fishing from rocks is obtained in tolerably slack water; but occasionally sport is to be found close to a headland, round which the tide runs with some force, and in such spots the float may be allowed to travel, Nottingham style.

In Australia, the methods were rough and ready. A heavily leaded line, on which were strung two or three large hooks, mounted on twisted flax and baited with soft crab, was swung into the deep water, often under the very snout of a wobbegong shark, and in a few moments there was generally something substantial at the lower end, which was hauled up to the ledge without more ado. I have seen fish of ten pounds and more hauled in this way through a hundred feet in the calmest way possible. Excitable as he is in election time, the Sydney loafer is imperturbable when rock-fishing; and the daring with which he will spend his life leaning over the giddy "Gap," the last land touched by the ill-fated *Dunbar*, just outside the Heads of Port Jackson, and drawing up huge gropers and other fish, hanging on the while with his toes, is worthy of better objects. Sea-fishing is, I am ready to grant, an excellent and harmless pastime, but as a man's sole occupation in life it falls rather short of the mark.

SHORE-FISHING.

On sandy beaches, the procedure is, as will be readily imagined, far more tranquil, the fish being usually cod and whiting. The hooks, baited with mussel as before, are, with the aid of a heavy lead, and sometimes of a forked ash-pole, swung out behind the breakers, and the fish very often hook themselves, though the angler, as distinguished from him who fishes only for the pot, will usually prefer holding the line and striking at each bite.

I have long thought, though it must be admitted that I can quote no successes in support of the notion, that the true secret of successful bass-fishing will be solved from a sloping beach, so often have I seen large bass after an August gale feeding just behind the rollers in the surf, where it was impossible to get at them from either boat or pier. Unfortunately, at the very season when the bass come so close in shore, the beach is crowded with holiday folk, whose immediate neighbourhood the peaceful angler shuns at any cost, even that of an empty creel. I do not, however, despair of finding one of these days in the early morning, the right combination of bass feeding close in shore, and a beach with plenty of elbow-room. So far, it is a dream.

This fishing from sandy beaches is nowhere more practised than on our east coast during the autumn months; and I am indebted to Mr. C. H. Wheeley, who contributed the opening volume of this Library ("Coarse Fish"), for the following practical account of autumn beach-fishing for cod near Great Yarmouth.

A flat lead, pierced with a short wooden peg to prevent rolling or dragging, is attached to a stout line by a leather snood, and above it, a foot or more apart, are fastened two cod-hooks. The best bait is lugworm, which is not easy to procure at Yarmouth, but may be obtained from Winterton, or, by rail, from Heacham, where William Chapman supplies it, or did when I was there last. The next best bait is the mussel, which should be tied on the hook with a strand of Manila fibre, else it is apt to be thrown off in casting out. Anglers should bear in mind that the action of salt water on zinc is in a very short time fatal to lug and ragworms, both of which should be kept in *wooden* pails. Several lines are usually employed by each fisherman, each being made fast to a cane or stick driven into the sand, the pull on which shows when a cod is hooked.

<small>Cod fishing near Gt. Yarmouth</small>

Getting out the lines is the most important feature of this beach-fishing. Swinging the lead round the head is not to be recommended, as the impetus it imparts to a cod-hook enables the latter to inflict a serious wound. A stick or cane is therefore used, having a short spike in the top, a brass ring being attached to the line two feet, or a little more, from the lead. The ring is placed on the spike, and it is not difficult, with a little practice, to send the lead out with such force as to carry out all the line, which should lie coiled on the sand. Should the sea be too rough at Yarmouth, there is sport in the river; and, when the tide does not run too strong, there is good cod-fishing from the pier-head at Gorleston.

Some more hints on beach-fishing for cod, for which I am indebted to Mr. Gerald Geoghegan, will be found in the Appendix, under *Aldeburgh*.

In short, for those who cannot endure the motion of boats, this shore-fishing provides many attractions; while to the lazy, whose sole idea of comfort, rudely broken by the trouble of looking after a boat, is to fall asleep over a pipe, it comes, even if not the ideal of sport, at least very near the ideal of enjoyment.

It is, moreover, practicable in many excellent spots where neither pier nor boats are available, and in weather that would not permit of going afloat. So many anglers are precluded from sea-fishing by their fear of the sea itself, that I am persuaded that there is a great future for two as yet little favoured methods, the above-mentioned shore-fishing and the live-baiting for bass in rivers, to which allusion is made in the next chapter.

CHAPTER V.

FISHING FROM PIERS AND HARBOURS.

On the whole, it must be admitted that the majority of our piers offer so little in the way of sport as to make it scarce worth the trouble of putting a rod together; though in some few cases—that, for instance, of Deal pier in the fall of the year—really good sport may be obtained in this way, which is sure for the rest to commend itself to those who suffer in small boats, or who object to the constant expense of their hire. The poverty of pier-fishing lies less in the absence of fish than in the great number of pleasure steamers and boys that between them spoil the angler's chances. This is proved by the excellent bags made from a few Government piers, closed to pleasure craft and the outside public.

The best time for pier-fishing is, for those who have the energy, between dawn and breakfast-time. In former years—the fishing has gone off sadly of late—I had some good mornings on Bournemouth pier with the pollack and mackerel and dory, fishing from four in the morning, and with no other company than that of the guillemots, busy a few yards off filling their crops with sand-eels and smelts. The early bathers, arriving on the scene at half-past six, would put an end to the sport, but by that time I had generally caught sufficient. It was often tantalising, it is true, to leave just as the fish were feeding mightily. The pier-fishing at Leghorn was never disturbed in this way!

In the course of the following pages, allusion will be made to a number of our piers; but, although it would be easy to name a dozen better and half-a-dozen worse, it will be as well, as an example of the average, to say something in detail of that at Bournemouth. Having visited it on many occasions during the past seventeen years, I know something of the fishing to be obtained there. Ten years ago, it was still remarkably good, and we used to get turbot of several pounds in weight during the months of July and August, fishing up to nine o'clock in the evening. Now, things are sadly changed indeed; and, as the town has increased, so, as is usually the case, the fishing has gone from bad to worse. I have seen no turbot there this summer of a pound in weight; the only bass would have gone six or eight to the pound, and, beside these, the flat fish were dwarfs. Yet the variety remains considerable, and among the score or more of fish that I have seen taken from that pier are bass, pollack, whiting, codling, pout, grey and red mullet (very rare), conger, mackerel, scad, dory, plaice, sand-dab, "lemon-sole," sole, turbot, brill, gurnard, sand-eel, atherine, wrasse, and skate—no bad choice! There are reasons why, if it were not for the steam traffic in the summer months, the fishing from this pier should be excellent. It lies in a kind of back-

Bournemouth pier

water, such as the fish love to foregather in after coming inshore in spring. On the one side is the joint estuary of those grand salmon and pike waters, the Avon and Stour; on the other, lies Poole harbour, an excellent shelter for all manner of sea-fish in hard weather. There are several patches of rock in the immediate vicinity, and the town sewers attract great hordes of flat fish and whiting to within five hundred yards of the end.

Yet the fishing is, as I have said, ruined by the steamers that ply between this place and the Isle of Wight, Swanage, Lulworth Cove and elsewhere; and too many avail themselves of the cheap day-tickets to fish without pause throughout the spring and summer months, retaining every fish, even though it would not turn the beam at an ounce.

Mussels One great attraction of this pier is the inexhaustible supply of mussels that cover the piles. Ever since I have fished from it, when it was shorter than now by half its present length, it has been the custom to scrape bushels of mussels from the piles week in week out, daily bait for half a hundred anglers. Not only are these mussels drawn upon by those fishing from the pier itself, but they also furnish bait to all who fish in boats. I must myself have used quite 2,000 mussels this summer, counting, that is, all that were wasted. Yet there is no end to them, and there would be no difficulty in scraping enough for a hundred anglers any day of the week. Like other molluscs, the mussel reproduces its species very rapidly, a provision particularly interesting to the Bournemouth amateur, since these pier mussels are, as a rule, his one resource, the only alternative being an exceedingly wearisome journey to Poole

Harbour after lugworm (though, in these days of bicycles, lug finds its way to Bournemouth far more frequently than it did five or ten years ago), an occasional squid from the diver's net, or some half stale, and wholly exorbitant, mackerel from the fishmonger. The mussel, however, meets every requirement, as not only is it to be had for nothing, or at most a small payment to one of the pier attendants for scraping the piles with a rake, but, fortunately, the fish of that bay seem to prefer it to anything else, living or dead. When I say that I have more than once known local pollack to take it in preference to the living sand-eel, and that it will beat the lugworm on three days out of every four, the esteem in which it is held will no longer be doubted. It is remarkable, when one comes to think of it, that so many fish take mussel as if it were their natural food, although their teeth are not by any means adapted to breaking the shell. Possibly, the very novelty of the thing may appeal. I have mentioned a score of species that have, to my own knowledge, been taken from this pier, but it must not therefore be imagined that the half of them are to be found in its neighbourhood throughout the year. Indeed, the only resident kinds are the flat fish, plaice, and lemon-soles for the most part, and even these keep in the sand during the colder months, and refuse bait of any sort. The sand-smelts and sand-eels come along the coast in May and remain till October, their stay coinciding with that of our later migrant birds; the bass are only irregular August visitors, being far commoner some years than others; while the dory and pollack are attracted mainly by the smaller visitors, and time their stay accordingly. I know of no pier on our coasts where the curious lazy action of a dory gorging itself on sand-eels can be witnessed to greater perfection on a calm summer's day than at Bournemouth.

The silver launce are sporting merrily in their thousands, one getting hooked every now and then, but usually managing to wriggle its way off the hook ere the landing-net is under it (it is absolutely necessary to employ a landing-net when catching these slippery customers for bait); when of a sudden there is a commotion, a flat, solid looking fish comes slowly into view with a peculiar rolling, undulating motion, not so slow, however, but it is able to seize several of the launce in its mouth and crunch them in full view, after which it sinks, equally slowly, out of sight, doubtless to take up its position behind the brown fronds of weed until confidence is once more restored and another raid is possible. These dories are caught mostly by chance. Sometimes a week elapses without one taking the hook, sometimes half-a-dozen, averaging half a pound in weight, are taken during the morning. The pollack come out to feed too, but their manner is different; all dash from the first. I have never seen a pollack near the pier of over a pound in weight, though I have in former years caught many of five and even seven on the rough ground about two miles to the south-west.

John Dory

The bass are, as elsewhere, exceedingly capricious in their coming and going; the only time they are fished for is during a heavy gale from the south-west towards the end of August, just when summer visitors talk about the weather breaking up, forgetting that September is, nine years out of ten, the finest fishing month of the twelve. The place for bass-fishing on this pier is

Bass

as limited as the time, for it is only from the sloping ledge facing the East Cliff, enough to accommodate with any degree of comfort not more than four fishermen, that the Bournemouth bass are ever taken.

The mullet is a rare catch indeed, still rarer the red mullet, of which two only have to my knowledge ever been hooked on this pier. *Mullet* This is, however, quite up to the average in red mullet records, as not more than fifty have ever been *recorded* in this country as having taken the hook, the trammel being the sole means of supplying the demand for this most delicious of fish (see p. 29).

Conger of very small size are taken from time to time, though there are plenty to be had on *Conger* the Outer Durley rocks. The best pier I know for conger is at Hastings (the old pier), where any breezy day in August it is possible with a strip of fresh squid to catch a dozen, running to a weight of 7 or 8 lbs. down to 3 lbs. These small pier conger can, of course, be managed on a rod, the more so as, unlike pollack, they rarely strike for the piles, but move off in stately fashion for the open sea, which greatly facilitates matters. For congering, however, on a proper scale, stout hand-lines and a boat are necessary, and the best sport is to be had at night. Of which more will be said in another chapter.

One of the most important factors in deciding the kind of tackle to use from any pier is *Tide* the state of the tide. We will keep to Bournemouth as an example.[1] No practical fisher

---

[1] The remarkable phenomenon of "double tides" is, owing in all probability to the action of cross currents in Poole harbour and the Solent, felt at Bournemouth. There are, that is to say, both second ebb and flood after the low and high water marks have been apparently reached.

man should be without a tide-table; they are to be bought at any stationer's, the usual cost being a penny a month. Let us suppose that you consult such a table at breakfast one morning in August, and find that it was high tide at three, when you were still in bed. That means that it will not be high again until nearly half-past three in the afternoon, so that there will be fairly slack water from nine to twelve. Obviously, then, it is of no use taking down your float-tackle, as there will be no tide to carry it clear of the piles; and the object of this method in salt water is, as already shown, to cover more ground than the stationary line can be expected to do. The leger-tackle will therefore be the best; and as a very slight acquaintance with Bournemouth shows you that the flowing tide moves along-shore, as at every place on our south coast, from west to east, you will place yourself so as to get what little advantage you can out of the slowly rising water, at the south-east corner facing the Needles; that is, of course, if you find the corner unoccupied. If, on the other hand, you had found from the tide-table that it was high water at eight, take down your float-tackle by all means, and the long-handled landing-net, for never was there better chance of a mackerel or two, fishing from the very end of the pier, and allowing the falling tide to carry the float, which should be stopped (page 123) about twelve feet above the bait, out in the direction of Swanage. Smelt-fishing from this pier, as from any other where these little sham smelts abound, may be practised at any time, as can also that equally harmless sport with tiny flat fish and pout. These bite eagerly throughout the summer; and there were few days in August when I could not secure a hundred pout from Hastings pier, averaging six to the pound, with a few consolation half-pounders thrown in.

But in serious pier-fishing, the importance of tides must always be the paramount consideration, especially where the water is too shallow at low tide to admit of any fishing at all, which by no means indicates that the sport at high water may not be excellent. The one pier on which, I think, the state of the tide means little or nothing South-is that interminable structure at Southend, end pier where autumn anglers make large bags of whiting and flounders and dabs the whole day through. The worst of it is that the October day is so short, that, as the tram is no longer working, the double walk of a mile and a quarter each way makes a good deal of work for the short time available. Near town, however, and reached by two lines that believe in cheap fares, Southend is sure to enjoy a long reign with a certain number of sea-anglers residing in the metropolis. Otherwise, the further you get from "the great smoke" the better the sport. Cornwall, Scotland, and Ireland, the Channel Islands, the fjords of Norway, —these are some of the localities in which sea-fishing meets with wonderful success. For all that, if, as the gentleman who is reintroducing the long bow for sporting purposes thinks, difficulty is the cream of true sport, there should be some consolation in the reflection that it wants more skill to deceive a single bass or grey mullet in the disturbed, over-fished waters in the home counties than to bag a hundred lythe further north. I have caught in little over an hour forty large perch and bream, few weighing less than three-quarters of a pound, in a river running into the Baltic, and not a hundred yards above its juncture with that exceedingly brackish sea. To the Germans, with their coarse tackle and carelessly fixed baits, this was a wonderful feat; and I fear I entered no protest when they explained to me that I was a very skilful perch-fisher. Yet I knew well that in our own Thames at home I should not make such a bag in a week, and that any of the thousand and one bank anglers who spend the seventh day in those parts would beat me left-handed. I merely quote this, though apart from the subject, to show the small merit of making a good bag in teeming waters fished only in the most unsophisticated fashion.

Baltic fish

On our own coasts, however, matters are very different; and although the tyro will sometimes catch the fish of the week the first time he wets a hook—for luck rules here as in most other pursuits—it is the angler who shapes his actions, not so much perhaps by book instruction as by that common sense which grasps the special requirements of certain combinations of wind, weather, and tide, who will in the long run make the best bag.

For pier-fishing, rods should always be used by those who are strong enough to manage them, though very small boys will doubtless have to be content with hand-lines, if only on account of their low cost. But with rods, improbable as it may at first seem, just double the number of anglers can conduct their operations from a stage of limited accommodation, for the simple reason that the rod enables the angler to

Advantages of the rod

pitch his lead in any given place—a sheer impossibility, even in the most practised hands, with the swinging hand-line, the lead of which may when released pitch in the right spot, but may equally well land in the ironwork, if not indeed in the hat of some lady overhead. With the rod, too, it is far easier to direct the movements of a large fish, whether the object be to keep it clear of the piles or of the next man's gear. In the case of one angler hooking a really large bass or conger, etiquette and personal comfort alike suggest that those on either side shall reel in their lines and give him every chance. Where, however, greed rules in place of good fellowship, and the lines are allowed to hamper fair play, it not infrequently happens, more especially when the hook is fast in a conger with the strength and manners of a runaway cabhorse, that there is a general foul, in the midst of which the eel usually breathes once more the air of liberty, leaving the disappointed one to disentangle his hooks from those of his neighbours, whose notions of politeness were on a level with their judgment. The necessity of leaving the field for a few moments to the rod that has hooked a fish is stronger than ever in the case of float-fishing, where there is no lead of any weight to check the sidelong struggles of the desperate fish. Given, however, this common-sense give-and-take policy, there is no reason why float-fishing should not be carried on at very close quarters; all that is necessary being that no one shall fling his float and line wildly to right or left, but that the floats shall, one and all, be dropped quietly into the water immediately beneath the angler's feet, leaving it to the tide to carry them out. Thus will the lines keep parallel, and a foul be next to an impossibility.

It is possible with the rod to use chopstick-tackle from the pier; with hand-lines, this form of gear should be used only from boats. The reason for this should be obvious: the object of the chopstick is to hang just clear of the bottom, and not to lie on the ground like the leger. There is, however, so much hidden ironwork beneath most of our larger piers, that this up-and-down fishing is, save for very small fry, exceedingly risky; so that, without the rod to keep the line well clear of the piles, some form of throw-out tackle, either leger or paternoster, is wanted. Yet for the last fifteen summers, at least, I have seen boys and men alike throwing out chopstick-tackle, never stopping to think that it is not in the least adapted in such a position for that degree of sensitiveness which is essential if the angler is to fish artistically by touch, instead of merely leaving his line to fish for the pot, while he walks round the band-stand upstairs.

I must now enumerate one or two of the chief fish taken from our piers, with some methods particularly applicable to the several piers most in vogue.

Bass This excellent fish is a true perch, and, consequently, of high rank; but so rare is the capture of bass of any size that a very few pages will suffice on the subject, though many amateurs spend most of their time in its generally fruitless pursuit. Fly-fishing, a very artistic and very unprofitable method of approaching bass, is not, so far as I am aware, practicable from piers, the ironwork being in the way of a cast. Nor, save at Bognor and Littlehampton, have I ever seen bass taken from a pier by spinning, though, at the two places named, the ebbing tide runs so swiftly to the westward that sport may occasionally be had by allowing it to carry a spoon or Devon minnow for fifty or eighty yards, then reeling slowly in, the tide imparting a brilliant spin, and so on *da capo*, until a fish is struck, which is usually managed in the course of a fortnight. The best plan at Bognor is to coax it up to the sand, this being, at any rate when I was last there, one of the only piers on which, in the absence of projecting alcoves or lamps, such a course would be possible. At Littlehampton, where the only available position for such fishing is at the end of the high, narrow west pier, or on the Beacon opposite, the walk to shore, though possible in the former place, would be a long one indeed; and the only thing is to chance it, and haul the bass, when thoroughly tired of life, to the longest landing-net handy. Perhaps, on the whole, it is as well that catches of this description are very few and far between. Further up the opposite side of the swift Arun, however, close to the railway quay, I have seen some brave bass taken, and have even made some fair baskets myself; and a fish of good weight is occasionally taken at spring floods as far up as Arundel, the bait being a live roach. The only bass I saw caught on the west pier this year were about 3 ozs. in weight, and of these pigmies an angler caught over a score one afternoon. But this brings me to the subject of fishing for bass with natural baits, the most usual, and, save perhaps in certain remoter and less fished waters, the most likely to meet with success. The methods in vogue are three in

I

number, and are—drift-lining with live or dead bait; float-fishing; and what may by contrast be termed still-fishing, in which the position of the bait, whether on a paternoster or other throw-out tackle, is fixed by a heavy lead. The first and second of these methods are unquestionably the most pleasant, but can only be practised in smooth weather. The third, on the other hand, as I shall have occasion to show, is often most successful when there is half a gale blowing from the south-west.

In any case, I would recommend a rod. So sporting a fish as the bass deserves at least to meet his fate in sporting manner; besides which the enjoyment of killing one large bass on the rod is equivalent, in my opinion at least, to that of hauling in half-a-dozen on a stout hand-line. But the tackle, though fine, must be very strong throughout, for in the bass the angler has a fish which, without perhaps the first violence of the pollack, will often make a second and even third run when almost within reach of the net or gaff; and this holds more truly of the medium-sized bass of, say, six or eight pounds, than of the rare specimens that top twelve or fifteen, which I have occasionally seen show less fight than the smaller.

Except in the case of estuaries, as that of the Arun at Littlehampton, or that of the Exe at Exmouth, bass are rarely caught from piers, unless there is a good sea on, so that live-baiting and float-fishing are chiefly successful where either a river is running in from the sea, or, in the case of harbours, where there is a constant supply of offal and refuse to attract these foul feeders inshore. And further, I would counsel the float-tackle for the estuary and the drift-line for the harbour.

Let us, as an example of the former, take a morning's fishing at Littlehampton. We have brought a good supply of soft green crab, which we had to get by train from Macpherson of Southampton, knowing it to be the correct bait hereabouts; and our tackle consists of a short (9 ft.) rod, Nottingham reel carrying a hundred yards of fine, strong line, and a couple of traces of twisted gut, three yards each, a pike-float and some hooks, also on twisted gut, (for size, see p. 55). This, with the long-handled landing-net, so often alluded to in these pages, completes our equipment. We have timed our arrival just after low water, and we put our tackle together against the railway quay. There is no need for the float to slide in this case, for the bass are generally to be found feeding, if at all, not more than five or six feet from the top, so that it is possible to fix the float at the proper depth without interfering with the due netting of any bass that may get hooked. The hook—one is all sufficient—is next passed through the body of the crab, from shoulder to shoulder, the legs and claws being removed. It is kinder to the crab, as well as more attractive to the bass, to kill it first and slightly crush it with the foot. This float-fishing at Littlehampton railway quay involves some little exercise, for which reason it used to be in great favour with a quaint old gentleman of the neighbourhood, who was so good as to assure me on one occasion that he had only caught two bass that season, the season being then nearly over, but that he would not miss his daily walk all the summer on any account; for, in truth, you walk here while angling for these fish. The reason for this is obvious. The tide runs smartly up towards Arundel, so that, starting at the lower, or sea, end, your float moves along close in under the wooden piles, and you have no option but to follow it, for much slack line between it and the rod-top would certainly give the fish a very considerable chance of escape. When the other end of the stage is reached, all you have to do is to return to the starting point and go through the performance again. Remember, there is nothing to be gained, as at so many places, by getting your bait out into mid-stream, for the bass come along —I have seen them on clear days (N.B. No use fishing when the water is very clear)—routing among the weed-covered piles for shrimps and the like.

It is also of the greatest importance to put no drag on the float, as it causes the bait to bob in a manner that would suffice to rouse the suspicion of a less wary fish than the bass. This is of course avoided by always keeping two or three feet of slack line between the float and top ring, neither more nor less. If more, the line will get waterlogged and not respond the moment you strike; if less, there is the risk of the bait being disturbed in the way mentioned. As soon as a fish is hooked, keep a tight hold of it; there are no rocks or sharp piles in the Arun estuary against which it can cut your line; and altogether, I know of few spots where, with ordinary patience, there is less excuse for losing a fish that is once properly hooked.

Float-fishing for bass is also practised in a somewhat different manner from the east break-
Hastings water at Hastings. Eight or nine years ago we used to see some fine bass caught on that groyne, but I believe the sport has gone off sadly

of late years. The last time I fished at Hastings was in midwinter, only five days before I sailed for Australia; but I do not remember catching anything at all on that occasion, and it was so cold that we could hardly row home. Off the breakwater, however, it used to be the fashion to angle for bass in August on the rising tide, and preferably after a three days' spell of wind from the southwest, the rougher the better. For under the lea of this breakwater the water is always smooth enough for float-fishing, save during a south-east wind. The bait was placed about six feet below the float if within an hour after low water, three or four feet lower during the next hour, and gradually lower as the depth momentarily increased, until, towards high water, when the angler would be driven step by step to the higher end inshore, the bait would often do best at a depth of fifteen or eighteen feet. The pig's bristle arrangement (p. 123) was therefore necessary. The ground at that place is very rough, ledge on ledge of weedy rock, with deep gullies running between; and it is of the utmost importance to keep the hook clear of the ground, else a foul would inevitably ensue. I used to find the best way to land any fish from this none too secure place was to coax it over the lower end of the groyne, which is soon under water, when it could easily be dragged up on the shingle on the western side. I have not been near the place for nearly three years, so that the conditions which rendered this practicable may possibly have altered. An eighteen-foot rod did not come amiss on this breakwater, more especially in getting the fish over the end. The best bait was a good-sized strip of fresh herring, failing which a piece of mackerel, bloater, or squid would often account for something, even if it were only a five or six pound conger. Another class of sportsmen used to fish at the bottom with many small hooks baited with lobworms and catch good baskets of fresh-water eels that come working west along the coast from Rye Harbour, visiting the salt water to spawn and then die, after which their offspring make their way up the nearest river.

Drift-line fishing with either live or dead bait is fully discussed in the next chapter. As it is far more often practised for pollack from a boat, I have not thought fit to anticipate the subject in the present chapter. The difficulties, so far as pier- or harbour-fishing is concerned, are getting the current to take the hook and line clear of the ironwork or masonry, and striking quickly enough with some fifty yards of line out, for somehow or other this method rarely meets with any response until the bait has travelled some distance. No float is used, the single hook, at the end of a three-yard trace of salmon-gut, being allowed to drift with the current, unchecked but for a half-ounce pipe lead. Bass may be taken in this manner with the green crab used as above; but the bait of baits, if only pro-

Sand-eel bait curable, is the living sand-eel. I was always at a loss for this wonderful bait until the present year, which was the more annoying since millions of these fish are, as I have had occasion to mention on a previous page, to be seen and caught throughout the summer from Bournemouth pier, close to which I have spent the last two summers. Last year I tried a number of devices, not for hooking the slippery little launce, for that was always easy, but for keeping them among the living until such time, later in the day, as they should be required. At all times very delicate creatures, the ordeal of being hooked, played and unhooked was not calculated to act as a tonic; and I found to my chagrin that not one out of the dozens I sometimes caught in the course of a couple of hours could be kept alive for even an hour or so. I tried a bait can with wet sand. But nature refused to be reproduced on so mean a scale, and the eels were all dead within ten minutes of their capture. Next I tried a floating creel, but some escaped, the rest were soon floating belly upwards. Then, thinking to lessen the shock of hooking and unhooking, I reduced the barb of the roach-hooks on which these little fish are to be caught, the bait being a morsel of mussel, but even this availed not. I finally invested in a "courge," an invaluable basket cage, pointed at either end like a torpedo,

COURGE.

which enables it to move through the water swiftly

and smoothly when in tow, its chief function. This courge comes in exceedingly handy, not alone for keeping live bait, but also for keeping alive the fish one catches; nor, for all the wonderful tales I have read to the contrary, have I once found the one devour the other. It is also advisable to remove the dead from time to time, as, although a current of water is continually running through the courge, death seems in such form to be infectious. The living sand-eel, then, hooked through the tail, the lip, or the back of the neck, one being about as good as another, is the most killing bait for drift-line fishing, whether from harbour or boat, and for bass and pollack. The orthodox way of catching the sand-eel is of course with the sean, and I have even heard that it will take a fly, but I never saw this. The method I have described, however, will be found useful at places where, as at Bournemouth, there are plenty of launce and no sean; and if it is desired to make their capture as sporting as possible, without regard to keeping them alive, they may be caught on a very light trout-rod and single-gut cast, and the bait may be worked through the water like a submerged fly. And truly, few fish give more play for their size than a sand-eel about six inches in length.

What I have called still-fishing for bass from piers is a simpler affair, practised for the most part with hand-lines, and consists merely in getting the baited hook or hooks on the sand just behind the breaking rollers, for it is in the surf that bass are most likely to feed at the bottom. As it is only during lively weather that there is surf enough for this work, the right place can obviously be reached only in one of two ways,

Still-fishing

—from the beach in front of the waves, or from the pier behind them. Boats are at a discount on such days as one chooses for legering for bass. If practicable, the beach is in every way preferable, as the landing of a heavy fish can be accomplished by merely walking backwards until some one can get the gaff into its tail. At Bournemouth, how- Bourneever, it is the fashion, as already mentioned, mouth to fish from that portion of the landing-stage which faces the north-east.

Float-fishing, with a sufficiently heavy float,[1] would be very pretty work in the slack water behind the surf, but that the flowing tide runs all too strongly along shore to Boscombe, and it is not possible, save with a heavy lead, to get the bait right in the surf. One hook only is used as a rule, leger fashion, below the lead, though some few prefer the two- or three hook-paternoster. (What these wholesale gentlemen would say or do if by any chance they got two bass on together, it is not easy to imagine.) The best bait for this fishing is a strip of herring and another of mackerel, the hook being passed twice through each. It is absolutely necessary to keep all your attention on the rod or line, never leaving hold of it; for on the first moving away, generally, but not always, prefaced by a trial nibble, it is important to strike hard and then look out for squalls. The bass has not so decided a course of action as either the mackerel or pollack. He does not invariably sheer like the former, nor does he head for the ground like the latter; his chief object is to create as much disturbance as possible, and his great weight,

[1] A float can easily be made to carry more lead by the addition of a pierced cork, through which the float is stuck.

for somehow even a small bass seems heavy on a light line, and the power in his tail make him a formidable antagonist, especially where your movements are hampered by posts and girders all around, to say nothing of half-a-dozen others fishing at your elbow. It is impossible to lay down any rules for behaviour under such conditions; all one can say is, stick to your bass as long as possible; never, unless there is neither gaff nor net handy, attempt to lift him out on the hook, as the latter will in nine cases out of ten break away; and do not be in a hurry to land him, as every extra minute the fish is played on the hook tires him into a more suitable frame of mind for the final act in the tragedy. And when you do get your bass safe and sound on the grating, be not over anxious to grasp the prize, for the percoid dorsal fins are exceeding sharp, and make a nasty job of it with a careless hand.

Mackerel-fishing from piers is not a very general amusement, and I do not know of any book on sea-fishing in which it is mentioned. It is only during the last two years indeed that I have practised it myself, and I came upon the idea quite by chance. One evening on Bournemouth pier, I found an angler just arrived from Birmingham, and with proper enthusiasm trying his luck in the salt before he had had bit or sup. But, alas! it was the old story; he was using his old roach-tackle, lightest of rods, tight gut line, perhaps four yards of it, just enough shot to sink his little porcupine float, and a small hook embedded in a mussel. I soon got into conversation with him, in the free and easy manner permitted to the craft, and learnt, as I expected,

Mackerel

Bournemouth

that this was his first essay in the sea; and I was on the point of telling him that the result would probably be a smash with a small pollack, when away went the float, the rod-top bent under water, the line sheered wildly to right and left, there was a wicked gleam of silver,—and away went line, float, everything. That young man had lost his all, nor was he comforted by my thanks for his having taught me a new way to catch mackerel,— for of the identity of the lost one there could be no shadow of doubt—hitherto rarely hooked on that pier.

Mackerel, then, were to be had within a few feet of the top at the end of the pier. I had caught several fine mackerel that very week in my boat; but the prospect of catching them on a light rod and from the pier was a pleasant one, for not a little of the delightful play of a good rod is lost when one is so near the water as in a boat. The next thing was to set about improving on the Birmingham man's gear, which was evidently not equal to the occasion; and this I did by fitting up an old trout-rod with small check bronze winch, fine line, pike float, three yards of single gut, $\frac{1}{2}$ oz. pipe-lead, and a 6 Limerick hook.

It only remained to arrange the lead so that, while keeping the bait at a depth of from ten to fifteen feet, it would permit of reeling in line until the hook was in my hand, and as my rod was not more than nine or ten feet, it was obvious that the float must not be fixed. The principle of the Nottingham "Slider" float is no new one, and the difficulty was got over in this case by binding half a pig's bristle, of the kind used by cobblers, to the line, the requisite distance above the bait, in such manner that it would pass freely through the rod-rings and not through the float. The rest was easy, and very good sport I have since had with this tackle. All that is necessary, so far at least as Bournemouth pier is concerned, is to fish any August day just after high water, and to go right to the end of the pier, facing due south. The tackle is put together, a good large mussel, *red* for preference, is fixed on the hook, cotton or wool being unnecessary, as the bait is out of reach of the small flat fish at the bottom, and when the mackerel takes it he takes hook and all. Never put the rod down, for striking is absolutely essential, and should be simultaneous with the disappearance of the float. In nine cases out of ten, you will have hooked your mackerel; but the battle is by no means lost or won yet; for the mackerel, than which no fish in the sea has more dash for its size, has a good deal in its favour,—the chance of fraying the gut against the sharp mussels below, or the still greater chance of getting a slack on the line and shaking the hook out. Your business is to tire the fish, keeping the line taut, but guarding against any sudden rush by holding a foot or so of slack in reserve in the left hand. The way in which a two-pound mackerel will sheer from right to left, wildly entangling every other line within reach, as if for all the world it knew that these are so many more chances of escape, is exceedingly embarrassing; and I know of no fish of so small a size that calls for more coolness and judgment, especially when, as is usually the case, some one on the upper deck gives the alarm, and a dozen or more people come tumbling down the hatchways, or staircase, to see the fun, and hamper the angler all they know, hemming him in until free movement is out of the question. It is of no use being disagreeable on such occasions; for the British tourist is, at home as abroad, endowed with a skin that the elephant might envy when his country is invaded by the tsetse.

The only thing is to keep cool, concentrate your attention on the fish, and gradually coax it within reach of the long-handled landing-net which some one will always be ready to hold for you. Then follows a short and fervent prayer that your henchman for the time being may not indulge any of his originality in the direction of *scooping up* the fish, but may be content to follow instructions and hold the net, the handle of which should be not less than five feet in length, perfectly steady at the surface of the water, one edge slightly immersed, and leave you to guide the fish into its meshes. Although the shoals break up at the end of July on that part of the coast, and are for the matter of that not to be found at any time close to the pier, the mackerel is rarely, if ever, a solitary fish, but several feed in company. It is advisable therefore to waste no precious time in admiring your first catch, but rather to bait up again as quickly as possible, as the conditions may not remain favourable for more than a few minutes, at most half an hour, and there will be plenty of time to weigh and measure your fish after the rest have gone off the feed. The secret of success with these pier mackerel lies in the discovery of the exact depth at which they are feeding for the time being. For although they rove far in pursuit of sand-eels and the like, they are generally found feeding at some particular depth,

Use of landing-net

Depth

and it is futile to dangle the bait six feet above them, or, worse still, to send it careering beneath their tails. There is nothing for it, then, but to continue varying the depth, increasing it from, say, eight to fifteen feet until the float goes under. If no luck is had somewhere between these two levels it may generally, though not always, be assumed that there are no mackerel in the neighbourhood.

Pollack This is another fish that is taken more from boats than piers, and, as in the case of the mackerel, most works on the subject, while giving instructions for pollack-fishing with the whiffing or drift lines, are singularly reticent on the subject of pollack taken on our piers. In point of fact, they do not as a rule run to any great weight, but I have known them taken to a weight of six pounds, which, with a fish of such dash, is not to be despised. It is fair to add, however, that one pound is above the average weight of pier pollack. These fish will often be attracted by a moving bait in preference to one which is at rest; and it is for this reason that success often crowns the efforts of those anglers who, on the Deal or Eastbourne piers, work a parchment bait, an article that bears about as much resemblance as the average salmon-fly to anything living or dead, with rod and line, up-and-down fashion, just before sunset. The best bait for these pier fish, however, is unquestionably the rock-worm; when that is not obtainable the rag-worm is a good substitute, but on no account to be reckoned the equal of the other. The very best **Dover rock-worms** rock-worms I have ever used come from the chalk-beds at Dover, or rather a mile or two west, just beyond Shakespeare Cliff. Never very cheap, the average price that rules even on the spot is scarcely ever less than fourpence a score, and the normal supply is as a rule disposed of by previous arrangement to regular customers. The best way for the stranger will be to seek out a loafer in the narrow old streets near the Lord Warden, where loafers are as thick as thieves, and offer sixpence a score, making it quite plain at the outset (and whether it be strictly true or not) that he knows the smaller rag-worm perfectly well (N.B., it is called *mudworm* at Dover) and will have none of it. The real rock-worm is a splendid pink animal, very muscular looking for all its want of backbone, and provided with retractile nippers, with which, more especially if applied to the tender flesh between your fingers, it can give a very good account of itself. The hermit-crab worm, alluded to in the next chapter, is also admirable. One large worm (or two or three small) should be hooked through the head, just above the said nippers, and the hook—a single hook is sufficient—should be either kept about three feet from the bottom, somewhat higher towards evening, when the pollack feed nearer the top of the water, with the pike-float and bristle as described for mackerel, or, better still, allowed to drift out with the tide, a lead of not more than two or three ounces being attached to the line a foot above it. A third method is to use a paternoster with two hooks and a heavy pear-shaped lead to keep it in position. But on whatever tackle your pollack is hooked, the method of bringing him safely to bag is always the same. This will not come instinctively, but only with a knowledge, often gained by rough experiences and loss of valuable gear, of the pollack's strange tactics when trying his best to regain his liberty. For we have here a fish that is at any rate consistent in its behaviour; and of the thousands of pollack that I have caught I never yet knew one behave differently. Instead of sheering wildly like the mackerel, dashing anon to the surface in the endeavour to slack the line and shake out the hook, tactics identical with those of sharks, the pollack invariably heads straight for the bottom. Down he goes; and not all your strength, even if you know your tackle to be equal to any strain, will quite check the first rush of a large fish. Your great object must be to keep the fish as far from the rocks as possible, and, indeed, unless the water is very shallow, he ought not to be allowed to reach them even for a moment. The first rush over, the rest is plain sailing. Gallant as is his first and only bid for freedom, he makes but a poor show when that does not avail, and few fish of such strength show the white feather sooner. Perhaps an honourable exception may be named in the blue groper of Australian seas, which shows about as much sport as would a wreck. Another good bait for pollack that feed round piers is the live prawn, or even shrimp, hooked through the tail; and it is a good plan to work it with a short, light rod in such little bays or eddies as are often observed round steps, for it is there that the best pollack often lie in wait. Hand-lining for pollack from a pier is a very precarious affair, as in the first place it is next to impossible to keep a fish of any size clear of the piles, nor is there as a rule any "give" in the handline to enable gut tackle to withstand the downward rush. Occasionally, however, small pollack are caught on hand-lines. The

[margin: Behaviour of pollack]

best pollack-fishing is of course that obtained in boats, whether moving or at anchor; in other words, with the whiffing gear or on the drift-line. Some remarks will be found under both heads in the next chapter.

The flat fish caught from our piers are mostly small plaice, dabs, and "lemon soles," more rarely flounders and small turbot. They are all small-mouthed, so the hook must be small; and they all feed on the ground, so it must lie on the bottom. It is therefore found best to fish for them with throw-out tackle, leger fashion; and beginners lose a vast deal of gear through insufficient knowledge of the local obstruction in the shape of sunken chains or piles, such as are always to be found in the immediate neighbourhood of piers. To obviate such vexatious breakages, it is a good plan when throwing out tackle for the first time in unknown waters, to try the ground first with a stone made fast to the extremity of the line by a strand of weak string. Throw this out as if it were the leger, and as soon as the stone has reached the bottom, drag it *slowly* over the ground to the pier; if there are any obstructions, the stone will catch in them and the line may be released from the weaker string with a sharp pull. I always test any new water in this way, and thereby make the acquaintance of sunken rocks and other snares at a less price than the sacrifice of good gear.

A few hints on the subject of throwing out from piers may not be out of place. In throwing leads from the beach, where there is no one else within a dozen yards, style goes for little so long as the lead is swung a sufficient distance; but it is a very different matter on a crowded pier, with others throwing all around. Here, there is a *right* way, as well as a wrong. With a rod, the performance presents no difficulty; the lead is reeled up as close as possible to the top ring, and, if fishing with a Nottingham free-running winch, the angler has the choice of throwing direct from the reel, easily done with a little practice (Do not practise on the pier, but in a field or away up the beach) or from the coil, pulling a dozen fathoms (24 yards) of line off the reel and coiling it at his feet. When a sufficient impetus has been imparted to the lead, the finger which has previously restrained the line by pressing it against the butt just above the reel, is removed, and the lead flies out, carrying the hooks to the right spot. It is without the rod, however, that an accurate throw demands some little skill. Five and twenty yards may in this case be taken off the winder and allowed to fall in natural coils on the ground, or stage; the winder is next made secure to the chain or post; and, seeing that every one is standing clear, you grasp the line firmly in the right hand, and about a foot above the lead or top hook (if the hooks are above the lead), and swing it with your whole force in the desired direction. It is not necessary to swing it pendulum-fashion for some moments before letting go; nor, above all, can I recommend the dangerous fashion, particularly dear to small boys who have no control over the gymnastics of a pound of lead, of swinging it round the head horizontally, as if it were a bola, to be hurled at some luckless vicuna. I have often seen this done, and, the lead being released at the *wrong* moment, painful blows inflicted on those near at hand.

There are many forms of tackle suitable for throwing out from pier-heads; but the chopstick (figured on p. 60) is *not* of their number, though commonly used in this way. The simplest, and perhaps the best, is an ordinary leger (p. 57), with one hook above and another below the lead. Watson and Hancock sell a very fair pattern, which they call their "Pier Wonder," a somewhat modest title indeed. Its shape is seen in the adjoining cut, and I have nothing to say against it except that it would be a great deal more sensitive if the wire on which the lead runs were about twice its present length. These flat fish bite at times so shyly that it is of the utmost importance to have very sensitive tackle, the more so as the fish is often lost unless struck immediately.

"Pier Wonder."

The hook should be small, of the size figured (p. 55), and long in the shank, as these fish all have an awkward habit of gorging the hook in an incredibly short time, and the gut is easily frayed by their small, pointed teeth, to say nothing of the time wasted in getting each fish off the hook, a process easily accomplished with a long-shanked hook by a peculiar turn of the wrist, easily learnt, but, without such a hook, impossible of accomplishment without the aid of a penknife or disgorger. A very useful form of trace for flat fish is sold, under the name of "bay-set," by Laing, of Aberdeen. It consists of three small hooks on a 2½ ft. trace, and costs but 3*d*., I believe.

As already mentioned, it is of importance to strike promptly, on which account the rod, or line, should be held the whole time, with the line as taut as possible, and without shifting the position of the lead. Should you strike and miss, it is as well to be ready for an immediate repetition of the bite, as these fish have, like whiting-pout, the habit of following up a receding bait.

There are several excellent baits for this pier fishing for flat fish, and few of them will beat a strip of fresh sand-smelt, especially for turbot. Lugworm, if fresh, is also a first-rate bait; and mussel even better, the chances of making a bag with the last-named being much increased by taking a few turns of yellow cotton over the bait and bend of the hook, taking care, however, that the cotton does not form any impediment to the proper action of the point and barb of the hook.

Shrimp, either "live" or boiled, is another bait that meets with great success on some piers; and, where the fish run to a good size, small pieces of fresh herring prove hard to resist. In the Baltic, indeed, where I have made very large catches of plaice, 30 or 40 in an hour and few under three-quarters of a pound, we used nothing but the small Baltic herrings, which we bought direct from the netsmen at the rate of about six for a penny.

Flat fish are capable of surviving removal from what is commonly described as their "native element" for many hours, so long as their gills are kept moist, and it is a good plan, one that I learnt in Mecklenburg, to transfer each as soon as caught to a small net tethered in the water, in which they keep quite lively until the day's fishing is done. Anglers who visit Southend for a day's sea-fishing could probably keep the flat fish, the majority of their catch in the Thames estuary, alive until their return to town, if they would only stow them away in an old carpet bag in some wet weed.

A word must be said at the conclusion of these hints on the subject of the immature flat fish that invariably, more particularly in summer, form the bulk of a pier catch. It is far more sportsmanlike, even though it be not yet insisted on by legislation, to return these tiny fish, many of them no bigger than laurel leaves, to the water to grow for another occasion. The fool, who is usually selfish, argues that some one else will catch the fish; but if every action were based on such logic, the greatest good of the greatest number would assuredly be in a worse way even than it is at present.

If any one has a mind to try for these, the wariest fish in the sea, he must lay in a long, light gut line with small pear-shaped plummet, a few ragworms, a little macaroni, soft bread, paste made with pilchard, or other soft bait adapted to the tastes of fish that feed by suction, and last, but not least, an inexhaustible supply of patience. With these, as well as a short rod and Nottingham reel carrying at least 50 yards of fine line, he may possibly catch a grey mullet, if not one summer, why, the next.[1] It is above all necessary to remember that no sea-fish takes the alarm more

Grey mullet

---

[1] I have been more than once accused of exaggerating the difficulties of catching this fish. Chance, however, apart, it is essentially the fish for residents with many opportunities. Thus, there are anglers living at Littlehampton who catch between two and three hundred in each season.

easily, and that you can only fish at neap tides and in the early morning. After that, the fish go off the feed. At Leghorn, we used to catch mullet on long horsehair lines, a single gut hook at the end imbedded in a ball of paste, made of arrowroot biscuit and pounded sardines, and no lead. The weight of the paste was sufficient to give an impetus to so light a line, and when it had been flung 30 or 40 yards, the cork on which the line was wound was fixed on two stones in such manner that when a fish seized the hook, one stone fell off the other, and the attention of the fisherman, who was managing perhaps six lines, was at once called to the one that needed his immediate attention. This use of many lines may seem to savour of fishing for the pot, but there is some reason for supposing that a modification of this tackle used with a rod might answer from some of our piers, as those at Dover, Littlehampton, Cowes, and others where these fish are at times seen feeding.

Leghorn

A time-honoured practice may be witnessed throughout the summer months on the western parapet of the Admiralty Pier at Dover, where a number of veteran mullet-fishers hang out enormous rods, fixed in a clamp. I have watched these patient men off and on for ten years and more, but I never yet saw a fish caught. They bait with rag-worms.

Dover

Mr. Kirby, one of the latest exponents of mullet-fishing, gave an account in the *Field* some time since of how he caught large mullet in the Fleet, a backwater between Portland and Weymouth, the hook-and ground-bait consisting of boiled macaroni. A powerful rod was used, but was not brought into requisition until the mullet was hooked, the tackle being first used as a hand-line. On hooking the fish, however, Mr. Kirby found the only plan was to get it to the net as quickly as possible. The best time for this fishing was at slack tide. Groundbait, if it can be so called, is essential in mullet-fishing in still waters, and I borrowed from the Italians a very ingenious method of presenting it to the mullet of the private shipyard canal in which I had special leave to fish. The bait was in this case soft Parmesan cheese, and a lump was sent out on the water on a cork just before I put my rod together, the fragments that crumbled from the cork and fell into the water proving wonderfully attractive.

As I have already said, conger-fishing is essentially a night sport carried on from boats, and some remarks on the subject are offered in the next chapter. The smaller congers only feed by day, fish rarely exceeding a weight of ten pounds, though I once heard of one caught off Bournemouth of over sixteen about three in the afternoon. Although, however, that is by no means heavy for a conger, a fish of even that weight is not as a rule hooked until the sun has sunk in the west and the lights are creeping out one by one on the hillside. Those who desire to catch a small conger or two without the trouble of spending half the night in an open boat, can gratify their tastes almost any day in August from any pier, like those at Eastbourne and Hastings, in the neighbourhood of rocks, the best bait being a strip of squid, obtainable as a rule from the local trawlers, or half a fresh herring. The hook for these day conger need not be very large, the size used for bass serving the purpose admirably, though in night-fishing for the heavy eels a very substantial hook is generally

Conger

used. The hook is passed twice through the bait and the heavy lead is swung well out. I have heard a great deal about the necessity for striking a conger as soon as it bites, but much of this is imaginary. While I am fishing over rocks for large pout or what not, I usually leave out a couple of conger lines baited with herring or squid, and on these lines the fish hook themselves, all I have to do being to haul and unhook a small conger every few minutes, and rebait. When after heavy conger at night, special line, or "snood," is necessary for attaching the hook to the main line, and a certain number of swivels are very desirable for reducing the friction; but the conger caught from piers in the broad light of day are not likely to give much trouble (6 lbs. 9 ozs. is the largest I ever took in this way; it was on Hastings pier, August 1889), and these details are given more appropriately in the remarks on boat-fishing. In all cases, however, it is well to bear in mind that these sea-eels prefer baits being both *soft* and *fresh*, and all bones should be removed where any exist; squid may also be pounded with a stone or stick, and should be scraped clean of the ink-like fluid that invariably covers it, and which is indeed one of the chief means of defence of a creature blessed with many enemies. This fluid rots the fisherman's nets sadly.

Whiting-pout, or Pouting
These are so easy to catch, have such a knack indeed of impaling themselves on hooks intended for better fish, that any hints which I give on the subject must be addressed to those juvenile fishers who muster strong on most of our piers. For although pout-fishing may be excellent fun in a boat over the

rocks a mile or so from shore, where the fish average a pound, the undersized specimens that furnish the greater part of the catch from piers are hardly such as should entice the more practised angler. Those who wish to secure a large bag of pout should use a light rod, gut paternoster with four hooks, mussel or peeled shrimp, either raw or boiled, for bait, and a ground bait of crushed mussels, shells and all, the latter being lowered in a net, which may be tethered close to the fisherman. A light lead, just sufficient to keep the bottom (2 oz. should suffice, but it depends on the tide running at the time), is used, and should be allowed to rest on the bottom, the rod top being very slightly lowered so as to slack the line. If there are pout about, and particularly if the tide is rising—an hour after low water is about the best time to start fishing—bites should soon come, the whole secret of success lying in striking quickly enough. You should stand with the rod in your left hand, the fingers of the right hand grasping the handle of the winch, and your attention so concentrated on the motion of the rod-top, the twitching of which plainly indicates what is going on below, as to strike instinctively during the moment of time, literally a second, during which the fish is endeavouring to worry the bait off the hook. Now and again, this pout-fishing is no bad sport, especially as few fish make a better dish when properly fried in egg and breadcrumb; and I once took thirty-nine in half an hour, quite half of which time must have been occupied in unhooking and baiting. When your boat gets over a "splat" of pout on the rocks, it is no uncommon feat for every one to pull them up three at a time until the supply is apparently exhausted. So local is their distribution, however, that it frequently happens that one line catches all the fish, while others in the same boat lie idle.

The true smelt, whose adipose dorsal fin proclaims him own kinsman of the salmon, is caught by anglers chiefly on the east coast, a light rod and float tackle, small hook baited with shrimp or mussel, answering every purpose. On the south coast, however, there swarms a fish known locally as the smelt, generally as the sand-smelt, more scientifically as the atherine, a name that saves the confusion which suits the pocket of the fishmonger. All round the Isle of Wight and the Solent generally, off Bournemouth and Exmouth and Plymouth, these little sand-smelts abound, to the delight of all the small boys of the neighbourhood. It is surprising, however, what different methods are employed within a few miles for catching the same fish. Thus, at Southampton I have seen urchins taking numbers of these fish from the docks on paternosters armed with many hooks, the same method being successful, if I remember rightly, at Weymouth. At Bournemouth, however, were it only for the large number of gurnard and pout that snap up every bait that approaches the bottom, to say nothing of hordes of undergrown flat fish that take every hook that lies a moment on the sand, this would be impracticable. A special method of catching these fish, as well as the aforementioned sand-eels that foregather with them, has been in vogue at Bournemouth as long as local anglers can remember; and this is nothing more than the use of a light gut line with a single very small pipe lead, or a few shot, and No. 10 hook baited with mussel. The lead is allowed just to touch the bottom, whence it is slowly withdrawn, the smelts following the bait through the clear water, and one or more of them making a determined rush at it just before it reaches the surface, when the angler, having regard for its tender mouth, brings each one hooked to bag as quickly as possible. In this way, when the water is sufficiently clear, it is no difficult matter to catch a hundred or so before breakfast, and a very first-rate dish they make for that meal. Moreover, the sand-smelt is a bait second to none for turbot and dory.

This large and important fish is caught from Deal pier between October and Christmas, when, unless the water is too thick, anglers are to be seen almost any fine day either at the end or half way along, their rods projecting from the upper deck. The favourite tackle is the paternoster, some local fishermen being in favour of a light lead only, which drags on the sand. I believe this is a method much used by Mr. Sachs, the veteran of Deal pier. Lug-worm or mussel are always good baits, but sprat or fresh herring will answer as well, indeed few fish are more catholic in their tastes. Cod show but little fight. There is a stately assertion of strength in any fish over 5 lbs., but after this first move, the cod soon turns up the game, coming to the gaff like a lost anchor.

Cod

Deal

Codling and silver whiting are also caught on the same tackle and baits and at the same season, but the hooks may be a size smaller.

* * * * * *

I have dwelt on pier-fishing at some length because it seems to me to offer, if not the best of sport, at any rate some very substantial advantages. First, there is its cheapness. The continual hire of boats at 2s. the hour is an impossibility for many and an extravagance for more. From the pier, on the other hand, many a good day's fishing may with a little attention to detail be had for a few pence. On a few piers indeed, as at Deal and Eastbourne, a trifling charge is made for each rod or line, but it is so small as to cause no one inconvenience and yet keep the pothunter away. Again, even where expense is no object, there is the very grave question of sea-sickness which debars so many from enjoying themselves in small boats save on the very calmest of days, and even then the roll from a passing steamer is sufficient to cause distress. The pier gives sport of a kind to the most squeamish.

It is not to be denied, however, that, considered in all its aspects, pier-fishing has not a few serious drawbacks. In the first place there is the superabundance of humanity, which nothing will get rid of short of an east wind, and then unfortunately the fish go too. Then, too, people subject to colds will find the landings of piers unequalled for draughts. The wind seems to blow from every quarter of the compass, as well as from overhead and underfoot. Another very objectionable feature about these stages is the facility offered for losing various articles of value—watches, money, walking-sticks, tackle, and the like, through the gratings.[1] For this reason, solid piers of stone or wood are

---

[1] The remedy for this is to tie everything securely to your person. Never care about looks; but tie your watch, penknife, hat, everything of the kind to your buttonholes. Money is better left at home altogether.

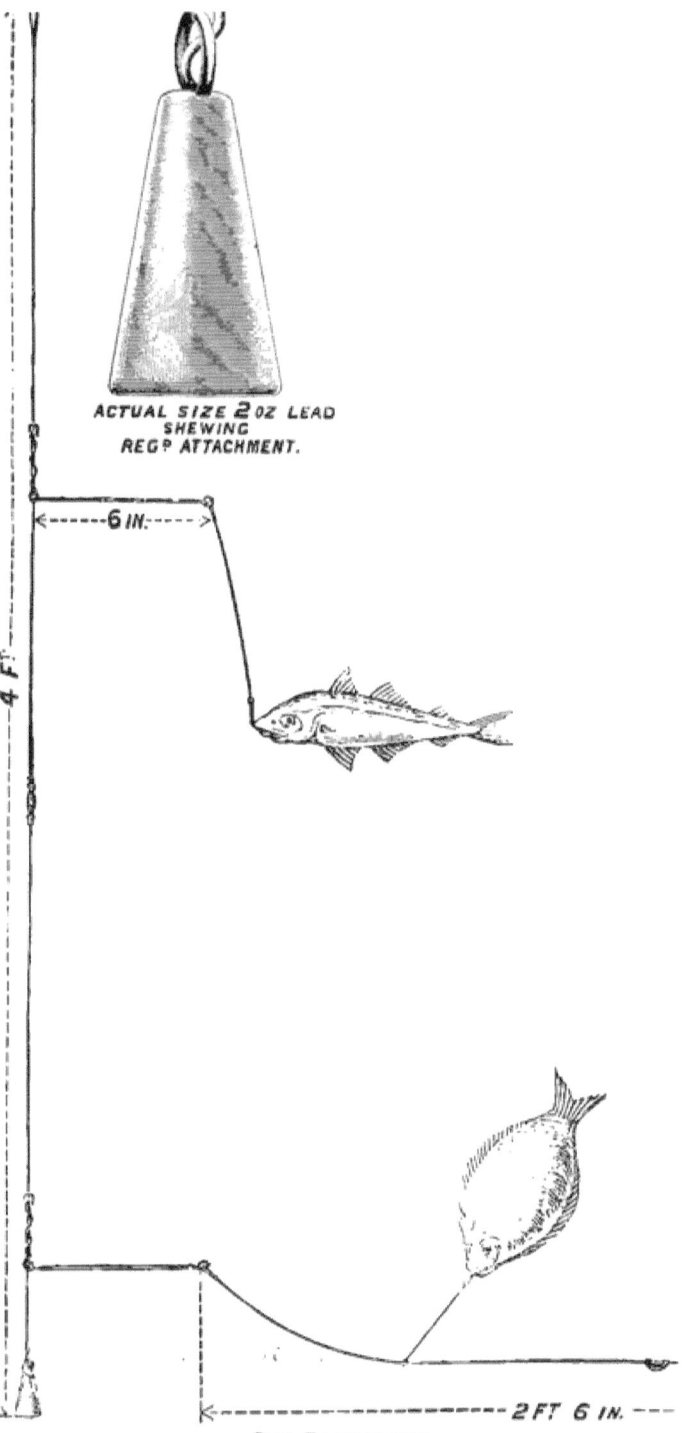

PIER PATERNOSTER.

to be preferred to those of iron, the more so as they attract to themselves in a very short time that coating of limpets and seaweeds that prove so alluring to fish, as cover both for themselves and for the smaller creatures on which they prey.

One of the most constant annoyances of pier-fishing is the fouling of the hooks and lead in the piles, sometimes through carelessness on the part of the angler, more often through the

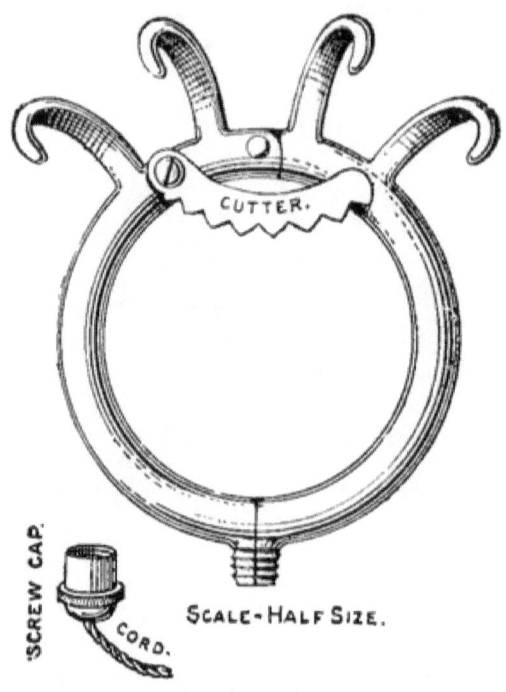

Clearing ring

CLEARING RING.

unexpected rush of a pollack, or the wash of a passing steamer. In any case the difficulty of freeing the hook is aggravated by the presence of dense bunches of mussels, from which it cannot possibly be recovered, as the gut will not stand the strain. I have for years used when in a dilemma of this kind a very effective clearing ring, or "messenger," patented by Watson and Hancock of Holborn, the claws of which can with a little practice be made to hold the mussels and drag away the whole bunch. This serviceable ring will screw on the long handle of your landing-net, or can be used from a boat with a cord. The former is, however, preferable when the distance is not too great.

A BASS-POOL ON THE ARUN.
(*From a photograph by J. White, Littlehampton.*)

CHAPTER VI.

BOAT-FISHING.

<small>Management of boats</small> OF the management of large and small boats it is not proposed to treat in this place. Some useful hints were given in Wilcocks's *Sea Fisherman,* and so serious a subject would need far greater space than I have at my disposal. The two most difficult operations in breezy weather are launching and beaching, the former being the most trying. One rule may be given, which is, I think, without exception, and that is, when launching a small boat in broken water put all the weight in the stern and of course head her seawards. If there are two fishermen going out, one should be seated in the stern, quickly getting amidships with the oars as soon as there is water enough to float her, the other jumping in as lightly as possible when she is in about two feet, but never on the top of a wave. In smooth weather, more than half these precautions can be neglected, and both may get away dry-footed.

In beaching a boat, it is safer, unless the sea is calm, to back in stern first on the top of each wave, backing water into each sea as it comes by the bow, which should be kept head on to the waves. It is always best to signal for assistance if available, lying off in the slack water for the purpose, as a ready hand to guide the boat out of danger will save at any rate a wetting. After a correct knowledge of the actual handling of boats, perhaps the most important qualification for comfort is to refrain from standing up too suddenly or jumping about. The man who jumps about in a small boat is best over the side, and there he will in all probability soon be.

What no one should be without is a knowledge of swimming; not merely how to swim for a short spell in a swimming-bath, where there is as a rule a premium on all manner of fancy strokes, but how to reserve one's strength, keep one's wind, and ward off cramp. No one who fishes in small boats in any kind of weather should neglect to practise *long* swimming, speed being no object, on every possible opportunity. He may never have to use it—I never have in some fifteen years of boating in all weathers—but the consciousness of being able to swim two or three miles if necessary is a wonderful factor in one's pleasure, especially when a squall comes up suddenly. Mercifully, those who cannot swim, including a large percentage of the able-bodied sailors in our merchant-service, if not indeed in the navy, rarely, I am assured, feel any fear of drowning. I have been out with Cornish fishermen who could not swim a stroke; and only once, when we were within a fraction of an inch of an upset in a boiling sea, did I see one quail. And on that occasion, it was not my boatman who was the more anxious of the two, for I realised how very small a chance

Importance of swimming

L

there would have been for me to have brought the two of us out alive. The spill never came, as it happened; but it was a tight squeeze, and made me vow at the time never again to go out with a non-swimmer—an undertaking I have since forgotten.

I have already mentioned the objectionable practice of standing up suddenly in a small boat. It is highly desirable to acquire, if it be not inborn, that presence of mind which shall never fail in an emergency, such as the sudden appearance in a fog of a steamer coming hull on—an experience that befell me in the present summer about a mile south of Bournemouth pier. These pleasure-steamers have now and again odd ideas about the propriety of answering the helm, and when we first sighted each other there was certainly not much more than 200 yards distance between us. My small mouth-syren was soon going vigorously. It is always advisable to have one of these aboard—they can be purchased at several shops near Charing Cross—for sudden fogs, though, as I afterwards learnt, it did not matter in this case, as the captain saw me at once. There was no question of reversing his engines, for a boat of that size and build would have passed over me long before she stopped; so that all he could do was to get his wheel over sharp, and the result was that he passed on my right by less than twenty yards, his wash swamping everything. Now, had there been a lady on board, she would inevitably have stood up and screamed. Next, both she and myself would have been in the water; and even had nothing worse happened, we should have looked ridiculous in the eyes of those on the steamer. If there had been another man in the boat, I should have got him to stand by with a knife and cut the anchor-rope, while I handled the oars and got out of the way of the steamer. But I was aft at the time and alone, and before I could have cut the rope and got back to the oars, it would have been too late. The very best thing, therefore, under the circumstances was to leave the responsibility entirely with the steamer, sit tight, and be ready to jump overboard in case of accidents. I do not quote this as a very thrilling adventure, but rather as a sample of the almost everyday annoyance to which one may be put wherever there is a combination of fogs and steamers.

The mention of fogs, to which the Channel is probably more subject than any other sea in the same latitude, reminds me of another very necessary adjunct to comfort, if not indeed, safety, in boat-fishing, and that is a reliable pocket-compass. When, as often happens even in summer, a dense fog springs up in the course of a few minutes, before the fisherman, intent on his sport, has any suspicion of its approach, not only may the beach, though not a quarter of a mile off, be entirely shut out from view, but the effect on the atmosphere is so remarkable, that the direction of sounds is perverted, and without a compass aboard the very best thing to be done is to remain where you are until the fog lifts. Should you have no compass and no food, the situation may become serious in an hour or two, and then you must endeavour—no easy matter, I admit, even for the old hand—to steer by the current. By this I mean that you must bethink yourself of the state of the tide;

Fogs

then, knowing that, on the south coast, the rising tide flows eastward, the falling tide ebbing westward, you must constantly pause in your rowing to see that you are going straight for the shore, which is accomplished by getting the boat quite steady and seeing which way a line streams out. If there is not any tide whatever, better wait till it starts. In any case, steering in a fog without a compass is such difficult and fearsome work, that the compass should rank first among one's baggage, far more important than lunch. Yet, I would wager, not one sea-angler in a score ever dreams of keeping one in his basket: well, experience, we are told, keeps a dear school, but fools will learn in no other.

Let your basket, then, include a compass, a mouth-syren, failing which a strong whistle will do, and a tide-table; the lunch and bait will be every one's care. Have presence of mind, above all; it can be acquired by practice, as I have often observed. Remember that you have two hands and two feet and a brain to direct them; and such a combination should be enough to get you out of any scrape; but they must act together and with as much deliberation as the urgency of the moment will permit. No hasty cutting of ropes or leaping overboard; but a cool summing up of the chances for and against, and then swift action.

The methods of fishing from boats are many. Besides the use of the paternoster, leger, and chopstick, as described in the chapter on rod-fishing, there are two methods confined to boats, whiffing (otherwise railing or plummeting) and drift-lining. One principle pervades these methods in common, and that is the

Methods of fishing from boats

BOAT-FISHING.

covering of as much ground as possible, the only difference being that in whiffing, the boat is rowed or sailed over the ground, while in fishing with the drift-line, she is moored or anchored, the line being paid out with the tide. A tide is therefore more or less essential for the proper working of the drift-line, though I have occasionally had sport in quite slack water.

It is unnecessary to go very deeply into the various tackles employed in railing or whif- Railing fing. Already, in the remarks on hand- or lining, I had occasion to give some account whiffing of the practice of "plummeting" for mackerel, as followed in Cornwall and elsewhere; and all railing is carried on in similar manner, save that, from rowing boats, at any rate, the rod may profitably be substituted for the hand-line. A short, stiff rod is the best; and the reel should hold not less than 100 yards of line, as not only is it often necessary on bright days to let out quite 50 yards before the fish will look at a bait, but it sometimes happens that the hook catches in the rope of a lobster-pot, low down by the hoop, in which case, unless there are a good 100 yards on the reel, a smash may be confidently expected. Unfortunately, too, where there are the most pollack, there also are the most pots.

At the end of the main-line there is usually a 3-yard trace of either stout single, or, as I would venture to recommend for the beginner of indifferent skill, of treble twisted, gut. The bait, or baited hook, is kept at the proper depth—it is well to bear in mind that railing is not necessarily surface-fishing, and that pollack may feed anywhere within a couple of feet of the bottom during the brighter hours of the day, cruising at the top only on the approach of dusk—by lead in some form or other on the main-line, preferably in pipe form; several small leads of $\frac{1}{4}$ oz. each being better than one of some ounces, as the smaller leads can be threaded at intervals, and keep the line sunk more uniformly. It is a good plan to have in your basket, in that compartment which should always be reserved for "sundries," a penny coil of fine sheet lead, such as is sold for plummets, as an inch of this bound on the line not far above the hook is inconspicuous, and may just make the required difference, when the depth has to be adjusted with great accuracy, as is the case when the fish are biting shyly on very sunny days.

The bait may be a plano-convex minnow, a "fly," or a rubber eel, the last-named alone or in combination with a tinned spinner—it is largely a matter of fancy—or a natural bait; best of all, a live sand-eel, next best, a couple of rag-worms. Large mussels are also used with success; in fact it may safely be said that, once you have ascertained the hour and depth at which the pollack are feeding, any, or almost any, bait drawn not too rapidly across their line of vision will in all probability provoke a rise.

Such are the broad principles of railing, whiffing, or whatever it may be called, and individual taste or experience will suggest a number of modifications to suit special conditions, the employment of a shorter or longer trace, of swivels between the trace and main-line to lessen friction, and of fancy patterns of lead, boat-shaped, coffin-shaped or pear-shaped.

A good deal has been written for and against

POLLACK.

each and all of these, and I fancy that I shall do best in leaving such unimportant details to the reader, cautioning him only against the use of more than one hook, with the rod at any rate, on each line.

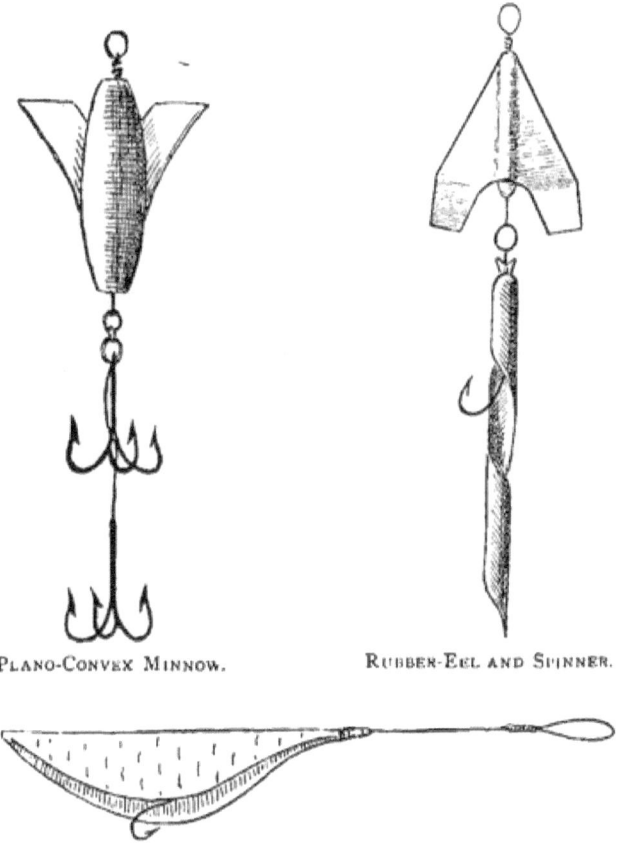

PLANO-CONVEX MINNOW.   RUBBER-EEL AND SPINNER.

POLLACK FLY.

I will rather offer a few hints on the general method of finding and catching the fish when the tackle is rigged up to your satisfaction. The very best time for this fishing is from about four or five on a summer's afternoon until eight or nine in the evening. Whiffing for pollack in the cooler months, or in the bright light of summer days, is very chance amusement. By sinking the bait to within a foot of the rocks, thereby endangering both line and rod in frequent smashes in the long weed, and letting out a great deal of line, putting in consequence a tremendous strain on all gear, it is often possible—I have done it scores of times—to make a good basket of pollack on the brightest of August days between eleven and two. But I cannot think this either so pleasurable or so artistic as the capture of larger fish when the sun is sinking in the west, and when pollack of 6 and 8 lbs. are as often happens, to be seen leaping at the surface like trout in a pool. At such times you may get within a dozen yards before interrupting the frolic, and it is possible to row backwards and forwards over the spot for a couple of hours or more, picking up a good fish at every turn. It is noticeable, as every pollack-fisher of experience knows, that the best fish are usually hooked as the boat is turning at either end of the reef, and if one's senses should ever be allowed to wander for a moment from the work in hand, this turning-point is the very worst moment to choose. The boat should be rowed (or sailed under a mere rag of a mizen) slowly over the rocks, a zig-zag course being preferred as covering more ground, though there may be cases in which the formation of the reef renders a straight course to and fro better than that known to seamen as "dogs' legs." A knowledge of the topography of the hidden bed of the sea is among the most important qualifications of the sea-fisherman, even if it be limited to the details that figure in the charts of the Admiralty

BOAT-FISHING. 153

survey. A good deal indeed that does not find a place in that work is of great use to the amateur, but can only be acquired in the course of residence at each particular place, and even then only by the most careful plumbing and entering up of notebooks. The best way is to try whether the fish are feeding about mid-water, increasing the lead by day, decreasing it towards evening. It is not, of course, easy to hit off mid-water at once, but, if there is no strong tide running, 30 yards of line with 2 ozs. of lead should, if the boat is only just kept under way, keep the bait somewhere about 30 feet deep.

There are three ways of increasing the depth at which the bait moves: by adding lead, by letting out more line, and by decreasing the speed of the boat. Conversely, there are three ways of bringing the bait nearer to the surface, by establishing the reverse of these conditions. *Adjusting the depth* The tide makes, of course, a considerable difference one way or the other, and it is therefore usual to minimise this by rowing across, instead of with or against it. This has the additional advantage of spinning the bait across the fish, which feed with their head to the tide. Here, then, is the best way of whiffing in strange waters: start with thirty yards of line out, two ounces of lead, and the pace of a snail; then add lead, $\frac{1}{4}$ oz. at a time, let five or ten yards more out, and continue adding lead and letting out line until the hook occasionally catches the weed. As soon as this is experienced, tie a fragment of white cotton firmly round the line, just above the reel, which will serve as a warning when the hook is going too deep. Should no fish be caught between mid-water and the bottom, reverse the proceedings, diminish the lead and take in line until the bait can occasionally be seen astern. Should both these extremes be reached without any recognition from the fish, run ashore and stay there, for the fish are evidently in no biting humour. Should the change of depth, however, prove beneficial, and a bite be felt, strike firmly, not by catching hold of the line and pulling it back through the rings—a man who knows how to use his rod and winch need rarely, if ever, touch the line—but by a decided backward lift of the rod-top. If the fish happen to be a small one, it may be reeled up to the net without more ado. Should it, however, be of some size, there are two courses to pursue, between which there is, I think, little to choose. You may either let your boatman stop rowing, and coax the fish to the side for him to gaff, or he may back water and bring you alongside the fish, you reeling in the while as hard as you dare. At all costs, keep the fish from the rocks, especially if there are lobster-pots in the neighbourhood. The cunning with which a pollack of large size will wind your line round the ropes and break away may be discredited by critics of animal instinct, but the fisherman's belief is not to be shaken. The grand principle on which to fight this fish is the refusal to yield one inch of ground. Should you have reason to suspect a faulty knot in your gut-cast, you had far better chance it and bluff the fish by mastery from the first, for the pollack is no brook-fish to tire lightly at the end of a slack line. In mid-water, he is nowhere; but let him once get sight of his native pools, his effort is supreme, and

Striking

Playing the fish

Pollack

more often wins the day than not. Provided you are able to keep the fish from the ground, you can play him, cat-and-mouse fashion, to your fancy; but, if he once get his head down and tail up, the odds are against the fisherman. With a bass it is different, and for this reason, if not indeed for his more salmon-like appearance, the great sea-perch will better please the recruit from inland waters. He may be played like any sporting fish; run after run he will give if in the humour; at other times, be it admitted, he will come to the gaff like any porbeagle. In railing with a hand-line, the heavy fish should be hauled gently over the gunwale, inch by inch, the hands kept *inside* the boat, as described in the remarks on hand-lining above. It is also customary to impart to the line, or lines (the fisherman in the stern sheets uses one in either hand), a swinging motion, backwards and forwards, by drawing the hand towards the body and alternately extending it the full length of the arm. Some anglers practise a like movement with the rod, alternately lowering and raising the tip to prevent the often uneven rowing jerking the bait and rousing the suspicion of the fish; but I have found that the springiness of the rod does all that is necessary.

 Some men go out railing alone, but the practice is not one to be recommended, as the solitary angler necessarily pricks about three fish for every one caught; and the effect on the neighbourhood may, even in sea-fishing, be demoralising. On a stream, it might mean the ruin of the fishing. For those, however, who from choice or necessity go out railing alone, I would counsel the hand-line in preference to the rod, as it is more easily picked up and got under control at a moment's notice. Also, strange as it may appear, I would advise the use of two hand-lines rather than one. Should the angler have the ill luck to hook two good fish simultaneously, the very best plan is to give two or three furious strokes, by which the boat spurts ahead, and the additional resistance may, though the odds are against it, keep the second fish on the hook while the first is being hauled. In any case, however, the second bait trailing astern will keep the pollack or mackerel in pursuit while one line is aboard. Two items of importance must not be lost sight of in this railing solo: the oars must be tied to the rowlock, and the lines must be made fast in such manner as, while checking the first run of the fish, they shall indicate its presence to the fisherman. Unless the first precaution, that of making fast the sculls, be observed, there is considerable risk, under the excitement of hooking a large fish, of letting go the sculls all too suddenly and losing one or both, when it would have been far cheaper to lose the fish. Where the boat has considerable way on, it is of course safe to let the sculls swing to the side, the resistance of the water keeping them in place; but when she is merely creeping through the water, as is often necessary in this work, they easily slip into the water, as any who doubt may try for themselves. Therefore, it behoves the careful man to tie them with a hitch of waxed cord. In Italy, where I have at one time or other done a good deal of boat-fishing, the oars are never fixed in any other way. As regards the making fast of the line, there are several ways of attaining the desired combination, one of the most convenient devices being Hearder's cane spreader,

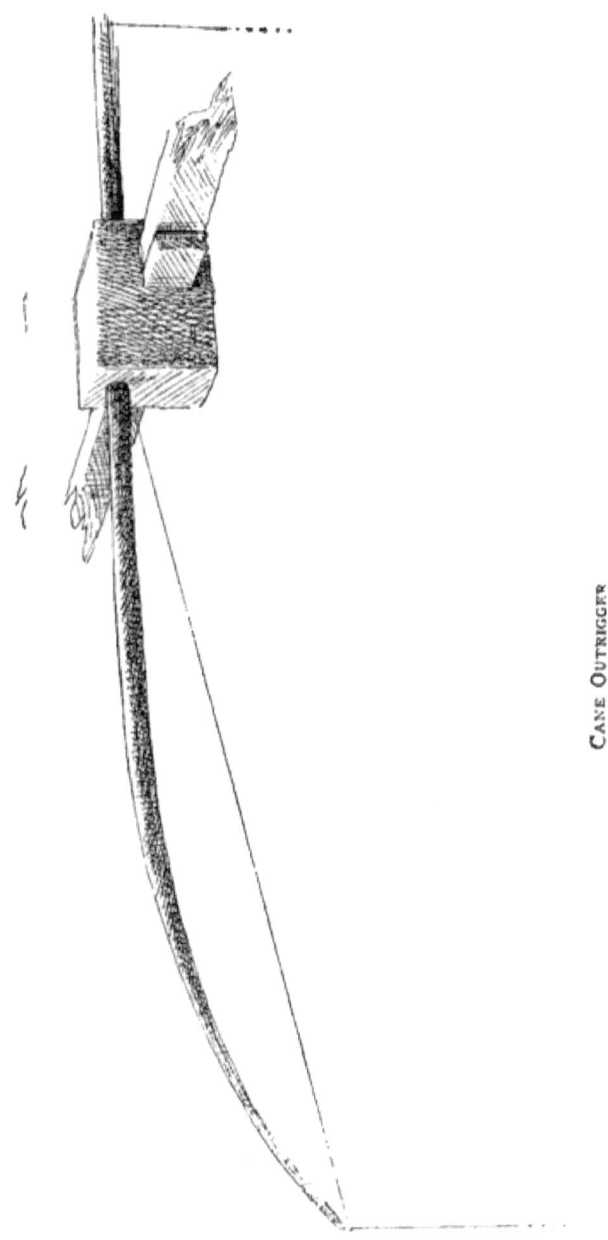

CANE OUTRIGGER

or outrigger, which is simply wedged on the gunwale, the line being passed round the outer end. Some fasten a little bell on this outrigger, similar to the arrangement used on the bamboo rod for catching albicore and barracouta at sea; but this appears to me quite superfluous in this case, as it is easy to keep an eye on the bending of the cane.

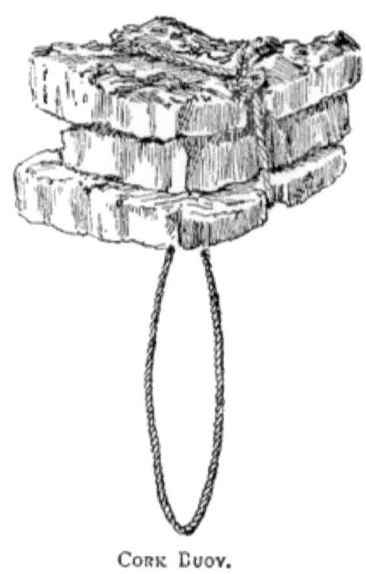

CORK BUOY.

In the absence of some such device, I have found it a good plan to hitch the line round a cork buoy, or even round the foot-rest, wedging the latter lightly under the thwart, so that, while retaining its place as the boat moves through the water, the hooking of a fish is sufficient to pull it overboard, and its buoyancy is just enough to play the pollack until it is hauled back in the boat.

The size of the hook and bait is always a puzzling choice to the beginner, if not often indeed to those of experience. One rule may, however, in railing as in other fishing, be kept in mind, and that is the advisability of using as large a hook as the fish will take, for the smaller the hook, the more time it takes to get it out of the fish. When the fish are shy, a small bait will often carry the day, and it is not a bad plan in that case to have a detachable swivel above each hook, so that the latter can be rapidly detached and left with the fish, a new hook being substituted without much loss of time. This plan, which is more commonly used with the long line, or boulter, should, it is unnecessary to say, be employed only with the more troublesome fish, and will for instance be found a great save-time in legering for large flat fish and whiting, which have an awkward habit of gorging the bait.

One last hint with regard to railing, and I have done. It has been remarked above that a fish is often hooked as the boat turns. Should this be found to be the case, it is often a killing plan to change her course every 20 yards or so, and if a fish is often missed at the turn, matters are sometimes improved by letting out a couple of yards of slack line just as she leaves the old course, striking sharply as the line tightens again. In this way I have brought to bag many a good pollack that, I fancy, would otherwise not have been mine.

A few words should, without anticipating the Appendix, be added on the topography of railing on our coasts. It is an unfortunate fact that much of the best railing-ground is also the best lobster-ground, in consequence of which, as at Mevagissey and Bognor, for instance, this method is practicable only on Saturday, when, as there is no market next day, the pots are brought ashore. On the other days, any attempt at railing would involve much loss of gear, time, and temper, as the surface of the sea is a perfect forest of corks, each with its slack line ready to catch the passing hook.

In certain years, Bournemouth Bay is as good a place as any I know near London for this method of taking pollack, for there is but one man with pots, and these he sets in fixed

Bournemouth

spots on the Durley and pier rocks. There remain a number of reefs, in all of which lurk pollack, though, oddly enough, they are not to be taken every year by railing. In 1894, I took a number of good fish in this way in the month of May. Two years later, I tried in vain with every possible bait, living and dead, morning and evening, and on every likely spot, but never a fish I took all May and June. Yet the pollack were there, for as soon as I brought up and put out the drift-lines I took them, though not of great size. So, too, in Cornwall no method is more killing for the pollack in some years, while in others you may row to and fro in the shadow of the Deadman by the week and never pick up a fish worth having. Railing is essentially an inshore method; five or ten miles from land, the drift-line will invariably give better results. That, at least, has been my experience. Thus, at Dover, there are occasionally, though decreasingly as the years go by, some heavy bags made in the long, light summer evenings within a few yards of the beach, every boat in the place, seaworthy or otherwise, being hastily called into requisition, and the pollack greedily seizing anything, living or dead, that is trailed along-shore. Lulworth, in Dorset, is one of the places where I have observed the fishermen rail in preference to any other method; and I have picked up a good pollack or two just without the beautiful little cove, though I was less lucky there than some. The local bait (and an excellent one it is) was the crab-worm, the pots, which are Lulworth's staple industry, usually providing a sufficiency of hermit-crabs. Otherwise, bait there was none, there being no shop in the place, and one had recourse to the artificial bait, the rubber-eel, and the rest, of which, truth to tell, Lulworth pollack have, or had, no great opinion. But for this continual lack of bait, as well as the absence of any other than boat-fishing, I should place Lulworth, with its hilly, unlighted streets, its simple lobster-catchers, and its solitary idle policeman, high among the desirable spots for a fisherman's holiday. As it is, many a good day is spoilt by insufficiency of bait and the uncertainty of the somewhat costly supplies from Weymouth.

It is undoubtedly, however, on the coasts of Scotland and Ireland—possibly due, as "John Bickerdyke" says, to the fact that pollack and coal-fish are not in much demand for the market—that railing is certain to give the best sport; and the catches, more particularly of the latter fish, the sillock or saithe of northern waters, are sometimes phenomenal. *Scotch and Irish coasts*

For mackerel-whiffing, the choice is somewhat wider, but results are a little uncertain east of the Wight. From the Needles to the Land's End, on the other hand, there are so many bays where this sport may be followed with the success that soon palls, that I hesitate to make any selection.

Weymouth Bay is perhaps as good as any, though I have taken hundreds of mackerel in this way off Exmouth, Dawlish, and in Torbay; while west of Plymouth, this "plummeting," which I have already had occasion to describe, is regarded as a means of picking up fresh bait on the way out to the fishing-grounds, rather than in the nature of sport. In railing for mackerel, it is well to remember rocks are not essential as in pollack-fishing, and a sandy bay will produce just *Weymouth, &c.*

M

as many mackerel of a bright summer's day as the most rocky coast. I have just mentioned once again the Cornish fishing. Let me take this opportunity of reminding the reader that Sunday fishing is still looked askance at in those parts. I am not presuming for one moment to consider the question in its moral aspect, my business in this place being to talk fish and fishing; but I do recommend respect of this primitive observance of the day of rest; and if the more advanced thinker from town wants to lay consolation to his soul for this barbarous superstition, let him regard this Sunday abstinence as a wholesome weekly close time, enforced by the chapels, instead of, as in the salmon-fishing, by the conservators. I do not say that it is not possible to bribe the younger generation into piloting you to the fishing-grounds on Sundays; nor is it to be denied that the spectacle of a calm Sunday may be, to the man of limited leisure, tantalising. I merely deprecate interference with a local prejudice, the effects of which are wholly good.

Sunday fishing in Cornwall

Another very characteristic method of fishing from boats is the use of the drift-line. As I have already mentioned, its principle, that of covering as much ground as possible, is not far removed from that of railing, only instead of the boat covering the ground and dragging the bait after it, the anchor is dropped in the present instance, and the tide does the work of carrying out the line.

Drift-lining

This drift-lining is in my opinion, whether practised with or without the rod, one of the most killing, and at the same time most enjoyable, of all methods, and I have employed it to catch not only the orthodox bass, mackerel and pollack, but also large flat fish and cod. Unless indeed the tide or current is so strong as to render it impossible, or, as less often happens, there is not even the little tide or current necessary to take the line out, I prefer this method to bottom-fishing under almost any conceivable conditions. In addition to the extent of ground searched, it has always seemed to me the most natural way of presenting the bait to the fish. The ease with which they are often deluded by three large baits depending motionless from a paternoster or float does not say much for their sagacity, but no blame attaches to their being taken in by a morsel of bait floating naturally on the current. As they invariably feed head to the tide, the bait approaches them with the line behind, and therefore not suspected until the hook is where it should be. There is, moreover, no lead worth speaking of on the line; and altogether, considering how inconspicuous is the tackle and how natural the presentment of the bait, it is not surprising that three good fish should be taken by this method, when practised scientifically, to one taken by any other.

In the first place, all the tackle should be as fine as is safe, a single gut trace being enough above the hook where the fish do not run heavier than 5 lbs. I am addressing the beginner; when he has graduated, he may find little difficulty in bringing to net on a single trace fish of twice that weight. When something stronger than single gut is fancied, plaited gut will be found less conspicuous in the water than the commoner twisted, and better still is a wire trace, though its career, as that of gimp, in salt water is likely to be brief. I

Gut

am told that more than one gimp impervious to the attacks of sea-water has already been put on the market, but it is my misfortune never to have come across so priceless an invention, so that, save for a day's work and then to limbo, my faith in gimp for sea-fishing remains shaken. The patent "Hercules" gimp is not a bad material for short service in the sea, and I have recently had traces of a still softer and equally powerful twisted wire from Little, of the Haymarket.

Gimp

Swivels on drift-lines are a matter of taste; personally, I never use them, having a notion that they are more likely to interfere with the natural movement of the line than anything else. In railing, they are of course indispensable, but for the drift line I think them superfluous, if no worse. As to lead, the amount used, if any, should be very slight. The exact depth at which, not alone the fish are feeding but the bait is working, must, as in railing, be ascertained by actual experiment on the spot. The best form in which to add lead in case of need is, I have always found, the foil or wire already mentioned, as it is inconspicuous and interferes little with the straightness of the line, which should cant away from the boat to the hook as rigid as a wire. It will easily be understood that this condition is impossible of attainment if a single heavy pipe-lead or bullet be used, as the lighter gut below the lead will inevitably sheer away at an angle with the main line above; but with three or four fragments of foil bound at intervals along the line, the whole is taken to the necessary depth without any abrupt change of direction along its course. A single hook only should be used in connection with each

Swivels

Lead

BOAT-FISHING.

line, as more would certainly mar the natural appearance of the whole, besides leading to complications should two good pollack get hooked together and differ as to the most promising course to pursue, while their agreement might be just as disastrous. The reason for the line lying straight between the fisherman and the hook is that success in this method often, more often than not indeed, depends on striking at the exact second, and any curve or angle in the line naturally impedes the communication of any movement from fish to fisherman and *vice versa*. As for baits, there are a number, all excellent, but the living sand-eel is probably best, although there are times and places where I have known it come off second to the mussel.

Mr. Wilcocks gives in his world-famed *Sea Fisherman* three methods of baiting with the living sand-eel; in the tide-way, he passes the hook in at the mouth and out at the gills; and in slack water, he fixes the hook either in the throat, beneath the pectoral fin, or in the nape above it. Now *{Mr. Wilcocks's methods of baiting with sand-eel}* the author of the above-mentioned work was my first philosopher and guide in the sport of which we are both so fond, and it is therefore not without hesitation that I advocate any method opposed to his practice; but I am bound to say that I have for years found the simpler plan of hooking the launce through either upper or lower lip equally effective and far easier to perform without injury to these exceedingly fragile creatures. As the bait obviously turns tail on the approach of pollack, this method places the line out of sight just as thoroughly as those advocated by Mr. Wilcocks. The courge, the only satisfactory receptacle for this delicate bait, has been figured on a previous page.

The bait may be kept alive in the courge for two or three days at any moorings; or, if moorings are not to be had, the courge can be sunk near the fishing grounds with a buoy to mark its whereabouts, and it is a good plan to cut or paint the owner's initials or name on the buoy in order to prevent errors. It is wonderful what a difference this makes; such are the morals of the foreshore, that the difference between mine and thine does not demand close attention in the case of nameless owners. It is also to be remarked that the luxury of scruples is indulged in to a far greater extent west of Plymouth, possibly, cynics say, because the communities are so limited and it is so hard to get away, the " iron road " being often miles from the sea.

Where sand-eels are unattainable, there are plenty of other baits suitable for the drift-line.

Mussel

Two mussels, one red, the other white or yellow, make a very deadly combination, and, as I have already said, will at times kill against the more popular eel. The hook should be completely buried in them, as both pollack and mackerel take the whole bait, and there is no need for the point of the hook to project.

Then the prawn, or even the shrimp, is a first-rate livebait, and should be hooked through the tail, the reason for this being that, when

Prawn

threatened, these crustaceans retreat face to the foe, and if the gut line were seen projecting from the face it is unlikely that any pollack would be taken in for a moment. Also, be careful to insert the hook well above the first ring or joint; for the backward leap of the prawn at any rate is effected, as already mentioned in Chapter I, by the fan-shaped tail, and it is of the utmost importance that the hook should not interfere with this operation, on the perfectly natural performance of which so much depends. A rock-worm of large size, or a bunch of the small harbour ragworms, hooked through the head, will also be found a good bait, though, personally, I prefer mussel.

<small>Worms</small>

Down in Cornwall again, where drift-lining for pollack gives great sport, and where, off the Tom Ash ground outside Fowey, I have taken a dozen pollack within the hour, none of which weighed under 8 lbs., the best of all baits is a slab of pilchard, which is cut in the following manner: the knife is inserted at the shoulder of the fish, the edge of the blade pointing to the tail, and the entire side of the pilchard is cut away from the backbone till just before reaching the tail, when the blade is turned downwards and the spine severed. Next, the tail-fin is neatly cut away, and we have left a long slab of pilchard thicker at the end next the tail. The hook is then passed through the thick end, the gut being drawn after it, and then passed once again through the middle. For bass, this is slightly varied: an incision is made on either side of the neck, and the head is drawn out with the trail attached, part of the latter being left with the trunk. The hook is then passed twice through the body, and a double hitch of the gut is taken round the narrow part above the tail-fin. Finally, the latter is removed, and the bait hangs neck downwards. A more killing bait than this, large, silvery and leaving a trail of oil, could scarcely be

<small>Pilchard</small>

imagined, and the head is usually thrown out in advance as ground-bait, or "guffin."

So much for the baits used with the drift-line. The method of using this sensitive tackle is not difficult, beyond the fact that it calls for the whole attention ; and though it is customary to put out a line of this kind to fish "for the pot," or to keep dog-fish and sharks employed, while bottom-fishing, it is quite impossible to fish with the drift-line scientifically unless holding it all the time. And truly, this is half the enjoyment, for the fisherman soon comes to recognise that a very insignificant picking at the line may mean a very good fish. Mackerel may be taken in this way indeed within a couple of fathoms of the surface, and I well recollect on one occasion seeing the blue fish shearing down in the clear water, while we brought nearly a hundred of them, all of good size, to the boat in less than an hour. Yet, so important is it to strike at the right moment, when the bait just disappears in the mackerel's mouth, or on feeling the first decided pull, that we saw many shear away merely pricked and, nothing daunted, follow the bare hook to the top. Pollack are, however, taken at a much greater depth, which, as the line cants away at an angle of from 30° to 60° with the gunwale, means a distance of thirty or forty yards from the fisherman, and it is for this reason that no slack line must be allowed to intervene, as it would seriously impede the due striking of large fish. It is in this drift-lining that you are most likely to hook a blue or porbeagle shark ; and care must be taken in dealing with these fish, owing to their aforementioned trick of slacking the line and swimming to the surface as soon as they feel the steel. Whether fishing with rod or line, it is essential to have a fathom or two of slack in the boat to guard against sudden squalls, and the shark should be played gingerly up to the gaff, gaffed in the head, stunned by a blow on the snout, and slung in a bight of line over the bow. On no account let the brute within the precincts of the boat if you can avoid it; and be still less inclined to quiet its struggles with a knife, for the odour of a shark's blood, above all that of a porbeagle, is not lightly forgotten, and will cling to the boat during the rest of the month. The pollack must be handled with due regard to its fancy for diving to the rocks, mentioned in connection with railing; and I have always preferred a large net to the gaff, because the pollack is by no means an easy fish to gaff. Its gill-covers, however, stand out boldly from the head, and the Cornish fishermen are very skilful in inserting the fingers beneath them and dragging the astonished fish safe over the gunwale. With the bass, it is not customary to take such liberties, as its gill-covers develop in the direction of sharp spines. The bass is therefore, on the comparatively rare occasions on which it nowadays comes to the hook, lifted aboard tenderly with a short gaff, or "gogger."

<small>Sharks</small>

<small>Landing-net</small>

Enough space has now been devoted to the subject of drift-lining, which is one of the best of all methods of summer fishing and usually feasible. For some reason or other, this method has been particularly associated with harbours; but, although these are perhaps the only places where it can be practised without the use of boats, I have invariably found it answer admirably anywhere within ten miles of the coast. Far from land, I have generally found both this and railing give inferior results to heavy leaded lines, probably because the strong currents render the drift-line nugatory, while, as for railing, the fish do not, as a rule, pursue the fry so close to the surface as they do inshore.

There remains bottom-fishing with paternoster, chopstick or leger; and the three chief considerations about this fishing at anchor are: (1) the anchor, or killick; (2) taking "marks"; and (3) ground-baiting.

Of these three very important matters I proceed to offer some particulars. In order to keep the boat on the right grounds, which are found, as presently described, by taking "marks" or bearings, it is necessary to use some kind of anchor or stone—the latter being known as a "killick"—with rope attached. The general rule is to use the anchor, or grapnel, on the sand, the stone among the rocks. There are cases in which, with soft sand and slack tide, the stone suffices to hold the boat up on the sand; but there are fewer cases in which the grapnel may be used without danger of breakage on the rocks.

Anchor or killick

There are many patterns of small anchor suitable for rowing and small sailing boats, the best form being, in my opinion, the new patent anchor sold by the Liquid Fuel Engineering Company, of Cowes. It is easier to release from the mud, and can be bought in several sizes, from 4½ lbs. weight upwards. The anchor is bent on to a sufficiently

PATENT ANCHOR.

stout rope by a bowline or other safe knot. If the bottom is foul, it is advisable to bend a buoy-line to one of the flukes, so that, if it gets hung up, an extra strain on the latter will release it. The patent anchor does not need any such device, as it rarely gets foul, though I certainly recollect one instance in which we had to abandon one.

There is a right way of throwing out an anchor as there is also a wrong. The first precaution necessary is to see that the rope is fast at either end and all clear. It is best at the bow, so that the boat may ride smoothly head to tide or wind, whichever prevails. If you are alone in a boat, the best plan (with the rope astern) is to get her well under way, then ship the oars, pitch the anchor well out astern, and make fast over the bow when the boat is over the desired spot (see below), provided of course the anchor is snug on the bottom. If, as is better, the anchor rope is fast to the ring in the bows, the solitary rower may for the moment sit with his back to the stern, get the boat in motion stern first, and proceed as before, throwing out in this case well ahead of the boat. With a second in the boat, the proceeding is yet easier. While one keeps the boat gently under way, the other, taking up his position at the bow (assuming that the anchor is made fast there), throws it ahead, the rower backs water until the rope is taut, when all is made fast. In calm water, it is unnecessary to let much rope out; when there is any breeze or swell, however, it is found more comfortable to let out all the rope available, when the craft rides much more smoothly.

The stone, or killick, is easier to manipulate, as it may be dropped gently alongside, there being no need, as with the anchor, to pitch it ahead. It must be borne in mind, however, that, even among the rocks, the holding power of a stone is far less than that of an anchor, and that for craft of any size a very heavy stone may be necessary, especially in any but the calmest of water; indeed, on the sands it is rarely efficient. The rope may be bent on with a clove hitch; but there are some forms of stone, those for example that taper abruptly towards one or both ends, in which this knot is not the best. The great aim of any knot used for this purpose should be that it is only pulled the tighter by every additional strain.

There is rarely room enough in a small boat for a spare anchor or stone, and in the majority of cases the loss of the only one aboard is the beginning of the end, there being nothing for it but to go ashore. Two alternatives, however, sometimes remain; it is often possible to bring up on some lobster-pots, mooring the boat to the largest bundle of corks, taking care of course to disarrange the pot-line as little as possible; or, on the other hand, it is occasionally possible to make a very good bag drifting over the different grounds. Indeed, there are cases in which, where the tide runs so strongly that the lead will not hold the bottom, something is gained by hauling in the stone and letting the boat drift with the tide, which removes a great part of the drift from the line, and enables the angler to fish on the bottom. Compared, however, with the accurate taking of bearings as described in the following paragraph, this drifting is at the best but chance work, and any success that may attend it should be regarded in the light of the exception rather than the rule.

How to take "marks," or bearings, is one of the first articles in the sea-fisherman's creed, and it is a very simple matter, accuracy being the only essential. Even the river-fisher has his favourite "swims," or "pitches," his bays for pike, his deeps for roach, the overhanging patch of willows for chub, and all the other backwaters, eddies, holes and the rest. But the vast sea is so very different from any river. Here, unless you know the exact whereabouts of particular patches of rock, or banks of sand, you have only the merest chance of catching more than a stray fish or two.[1] Not all the ground-bait will as a rule tempt the pout or bream a quarter of a mile—a short distance indeed as distances go at sea—from the rocks among which they have for the time being taken up their abode. The angler in fresh water takes up his position on the bank, or moors his punt, throws in his ground-bait and awaits the coming of the fish. I speak of course of bottom-fishing, analogous to the methods now under consideration, and not of the fly-fisher who selects a rising fish over which to throw his hook.

The sea-angler does nothing of the kind, for he would have to wait in all probability several days and nights before catching fish enough for a meal. On the contrary, he goes to the fish, or to some spot where they are likely to be found. This may be a patch of sand, a reef of rock, a bed of weed, or a stretch of shingle, and it is found again by its "bearings," in other words by making it the

Taking "marks"

[1] The importance of "marks" varies, of course; thus, "John Bickerdyke" tells me that off Cowes there are none of importance, the boats being anchored a few hundred yards out, and constantly shifted according to the tide.

meeting-point of two imaginary lines from different parts of the neighbouring shore, as near as possible at right angles, and noting objects that lie along each line. It must be clearly understood from the first that these "marks" are for re-discovering old grounds, not for finding new ones. The bearings for the Outer Durley rocks off Bournemouth may be quoted as a practical example of the method adopted: the flagstaff on the end of the pier being got in line with the middle of the patch of trees beyond the square red-tiled house just above the Bath Hotel on the East Cliff, while a conspicuous red house in Alum Chine (the third from the pier) is brought "dead on" the sloping roadway beneath it. These "marks" have served the purpose for some time, though I fished the reef long before there were either red houses or roads in the Chine, and we then had two tall pines, one of which seems to have disappeared before the invasion of bricks and mortar, to guide us. Moreover, on very calm days, it is generally easy to pick up Jack Bridle's corks, he being the only man who sets pots on both this and the Inner Durley rocks. With a breeze on the water, however, or worse still a strong tide to drag them under, the corks often baffle you until you are right over them. Old Harry Rock, outside Swanage, will also be found to cover the extreme point of St. Alban's, the headland beyond.

There is one great fault about many of these bearings in that they are of a not sufficiently permanent nature. As it is, the pine that served the purpose so admirably in the old days, is no more; and, in the case of houses, there is the additional danger of more of the same pattern springing up, to make the confusion worse than ever. On this account, it is desirable to select natural marks, the work of nature being as a rule more lasting than that of man. Nature's improvements, now that she has got the earth into working order, are very slow; and we are safe in choosing for our marks hills and headlands, uncovered rocks, and the like. Among the buildings least likely to alter their appearance or position for a reasonable period, are lighthouses, coastguard-stations, churches and windmills. A better second string for the Durley, though available only on clear days, is Branksea Island, about a yard of which is opened.[1] At night, it is of course necessary to have an accurate knowledge of certain green and red lights that assist in fixing the bearings. Enough has been said, I think, on the very important subject of taking proper bearings. As it is often necessary to take up the exact "marks" with fastidious accuracy, attention must be paid to the direction in which the tide is running, and allowance made for the length of rope let out. This is of such great moment that I offer no apology, even at the risk of some repetition, for endeavouring to make it perfectly clear. Two typical cases obtain,—that in which the tide is with, and that in which it is against, the boat. In the first, the best plan for the man at the oars is to paddle gently up to the mark, stern first. A few yards before the exact spot is reached, his companion pitches the anchor over the bow (now, in the wake of the boat, as she is going stern first), and the rope is brought up sharp and made fast as soon as the boat is exactly

---

[1] By a yard is meant, of course, so much *as appears* at that distance to measure a yard—in reality, perhaps a hundred!

in position. In the other case, where the boat is approaching the mark against the tide, the oarsman should sit round facing the bow, and overshoot the mark by a few yards. The anchor is then pitched ahead, and the boat allowed to drop back over the mark, the rope being brought up sharp and made fast, as before, when over the ground. Those of my readers who know all about the matter under notice will perhaps think that I have unduly prolonged these instructions; but it is very difficult to make the correct procedure quite clear to the beginner without saying much that to the old hand is trite.

The hardest grounds to pick up by shore marks are those which lie five or ten miles out at sea; and yet it is surprising, as those know who have fished off the Cornish coast, how easily the local professionals pick up such grounds. In such cases, some group of rocks standing off in the water, as, for example, the picturesque Gwingeas, that, like a lion *couchant*, guard the western approach to the harbour of Mevagissey, is generally requisitioned; and indeed it is always better for the "marks" on one line to be not too close together. A good deal more on the subject of "marks" will be found in the Appendix.

I have now, I think, made it fairly clear how to find out known grounds, and, having found them, how to keep your boat in the right spot.

It remains to get the fish. On really good grounds, particularly at some little distance from the coast, where they are not overworked, there will as a rule be plenty of fish. It may, however, be found necessary to bring the fish to the spot, or at any rate to keep them there. River-fishers will at once understand that I am about to speak of the process of ground-baiting, a principle woefully neglected in salt water. It is, of course, **Ground** influenced by a number of conditions in **bait** the sea that do not in the ordinary course bear on its use in fresh water, as, for instance, the tides, great depth, and distance from which it is often necessary to attract the fish. Nor is it so simple a matter as in some quiet inland water, free from disturbance of any kind, where the bait remains within a foot of where it was dropped until discovered by the fish. Apart from the tides and currents that interfere with its position, the bed of the sea teems with crabs, which, scavengers that they are, soon seize upon any edible matter that they come across. It is therefore necessary to enclose the ground-bait in some kind of receptacle, and, for want of a better, a cage or wicker, or for that matter a square of string net, may be lowered by a cord, which is occasionally jerked to free a little of the mixture. The ground-bait should be so placed that the tide sets from it past the hooks. The object of this is that the fish, following up the track of oily particles and fragments of bait to its source, shall be compelled to pass close to the hooks. A similar principle is, I believe, involved in the use of the brainy water when baiting for chub with pith. A useful arrangement, not unlike a miniature diving-bell, is supplied by Messrs.

DIVING BELL FOR GROUND BAIT.

Peek, and this is very suitable for sea-fishing. Care must be taken, however, not to let it touch the bottom, else the catch is released, and the bait comes out *en bloc*.

As regards the composition of ground-baits used in salt water, I may say that it is not nearly as complicated as that of the wondrous compounds of clay, bran, bread, worms, and all the rest that are employed for the mustering of bream and roach. A couple of dozen common shore crabs, a quart of large mussels, and a handful or two of the "innerds," obtainable at the fishmonger's; these pounded together make an admirable "guffin," as they call it in Cornwall. In Australia the correct name is "berley"; and indeed the colonial compound is particularly offensive, among its choicest ingredients being condemned tinned salmon, sour herrings, and cheese. Some of the most cunningly compounded of ground-baits for sea-fishing which I ever came across were those in use among the Livornese, with whom I fished for three or four months some years ago. The simplest of these consisted of a couple of fresh anchovies. The whole proceeding of getting it near the hooks was so inelegant that I hesitate to enlarge on it; but, to put the matter tersely, the native anglers used to chew the fish and *impel* it, without using their hands, with wonderful accuracy right against the line. There being little or no inshore tide in the Mediterranean, the principle aforementioned did not operate, yet this primitive ground-baiting conduced unmistakably to a full bag. Two other ground-baits I learnt from my Italian acquaintances; the one a stiff mixture of anchovies, sand, and shells, which was thrown out in pellets; the other, very useful in angling for grey mullet, a lump of Parmesan cheese tied to a small cork bung, the latter being set afloat just before fishing, when the particles of cheese would crumble into the water and attract the grey mullet from all quarters.

It will thus be seen that, without all the mysterious selection and baiting of "pitches" over night, or the adjustment to the material of the hook-bait, the principle of attracting fish to the neighbourhood of the hooks, and, what is almost more important, keeping them there (almost all sea-fish being of a more or less roving disposition), may be introduced with excellent results into angling in the sea. One more hint, which I have not yet given. Allusion has been made to those vagrant robbers, the crabs, which are so unremitting in their attentions to the bottom hook. A good plan for keeping them at reasonable distance is to tie half-a-dozen fish-heads —your fishmonger will supply these daily, gratis— to large stones, which are then pitched in the water at some little distance from the boat. To these the crabs of the vicinity will quickly attach themselves; and such is the fighting instinct beneath their corselets, any that chance to shuffle that way will soon join in the *mêlée*, leaving the ground-hook to the flat fish. I mention this under the heading of ground-bait, because it is more than likely that the fish-heads may also attract fish in your direction.

In taking leave of this important subject, the claims of which are not as yet fully recognised by the sea-fisherman, I may say that ground-bait is less necessary among rocks than on the sand, there being enough weed and animal life to attract fish of all kinds, while there is often the additional attraction of baited crab-pots. The extent to which these latter are appreciated by all manner of fish may be gathered from the fact that large bass and conger are often taken in them, so coiled as to be unable to escape.

There remains the consideration of a few fish which are commonly taken in boats on the bottom tackles already mentioned, or on others closely resembling them; and of these, the chief are the bass, bream, cod, conger, various flat fish, gurnard, mackerel, pouting, and whiting.

Bass One of our most successful bass-fishers is Mr. J. C. Wilcocks, now in his seventy-first year, if I mistake not; and he recently sent me some hints for catching these fish at the heads of Poole Harbour (I wasted some of the best years of my life formerly over those same Poole bass!), which are of general application to bass-fishing from boats. I therefore give the gist of them here, and as Mr. Wilcocks killed 150 of these fish at Shoreham in the course of four seasons, his methods are sure to command ready attention. Speaking of fishing generally at the mouth of a harbour, he says that the living sand-eel is the only reliable bait, and the wicker courge the only satisfactory receptacle in which to tow it to the grounds. The bass wait in the low water between the haven points for such sand-eels and shrimps as may come that way, and Mr. Wilcocks anchors his boat in the tideway and lets the line drift over the fish. The essential condition is that the sand-eels shall be lively; and in support of his vote for the courge, he quotes a case in which a Shoreham gentleman took his eels to sea in a pail, the result being that they had lost

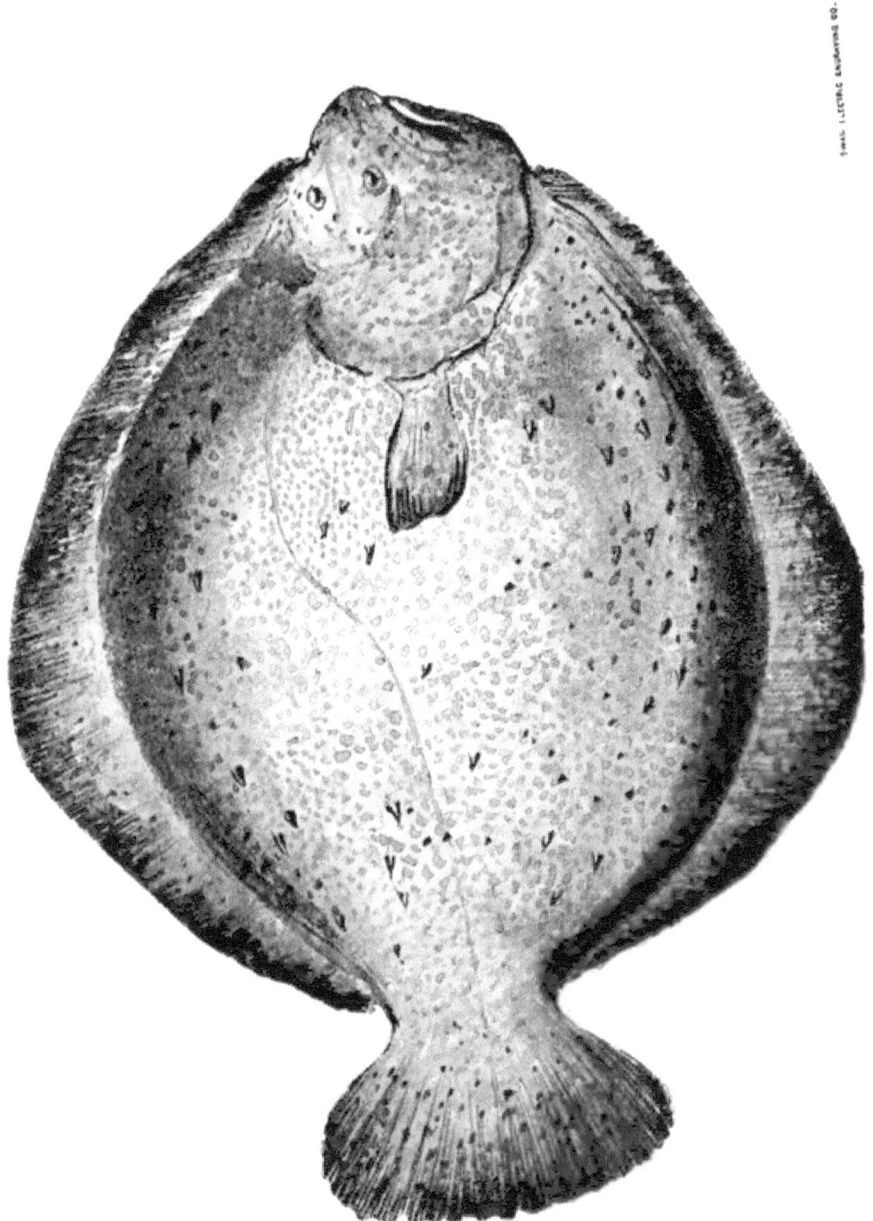

all vitality by the time the fishing-ground was reached, and he got no sport whatever. For fishing such a harbour-mouth from shore, Mr. Wilcocks recommends a rod and gut leger, or float-tackle, baited with soft crab.

Bream-fishing, when the fish run large and numerous, is about the most exciting sport, while it lasts, that the British seas can offer. We have no bream, it is true, to equal the glorious red schnapper of Australian waters, nor is our black bream sought on such delicate tackle as in the colonies; but there are scores of reefs on the south and south-west coasts, where you may with luck catch a hundredweight of the common red sea-bream in an afternoon's fishing, few of the fish under a pound and a half in weight, and some of twice the size. They are not particular, these bream; and once the boat is brought right over their particular patch of rocks, usually a couple of miles at least from the shore, a strip of fresh mackerel or herring, put on the hook without any particular regard for covering the point, will catch them. Nor, where the fish are biting greedily (usually towards sunset), is there any precise mode of striking, as they hook themselves. The best tackle for them is the hand-line, the time taken in hauling a large bream on the rod through perhaps twenty fathoms (120 feet) of water, being a serious loss. I hope that my verdict for the hand-line may not be misconstrued into a plea for pot-hunting. Were our bream large enough to give really good play, I would unhesitatingly advocate the rod, even at the sacrifice of two-thirds of the numbers caught; but in the pursuit of shoal fish in deep water, the aim of the angler is, as I understand it, to make the biggest bag he can by fair means, and the rod is certainly but ill adapted to the conditions that usually obtain in bream-fishing. In conjunction with the hand-line, there is no better bottom tackle than the Cornish boat-shaped lead with cord loops, figured on p. 84. The proper manipulation of this lead and line has already been given; it remains to add that the hook, of the size figured (p. 55) may be a fathom below the lead. Bream may be hauled direct into the boat, or guided to a landing-net; being very spinous fish, not unlike perch, they should not be handled carelessly.

Cod. The cod, caught in some numbers on Deal and other piers, does not come in shore until the fall of the year, the earliest fish I ever took of any size being off Hastings, or rather midway between that port and the newer Bexhill, on the last day but one in September. That is, however, in the ordinary course, quite three weeks too soon, and the third week in October right on to the end of the year will be found the best time. There is not much to be said in the way of special instructions for this cod-fishing, for, truth to tell, it is all a matter of the fish passing your boat; and I have more than once seen a new recruit catch the finest cod of the week on his first outing, scarcely knowing what bait was on his hook. This does not, however, detract much from the undoubted enjoyment of a day off Deal on a fine crisp November morning, when fish of twelve or fifteen pounds are taking the sprat or lugworm freely. On a stiff rod, such fish give good, though brief, sport, and they may for a few moments tax the angler's cunning to bring them to gaff. The bag is usually varied on such occasions by a few good-sized whiting and pout, both of which are capable of taking the largest baits used for cod. The smaller cod, or codlings, are caught inshore throughout the year, especially in May and June, and one of the best spots for them that I can call to mind is, or was, the particoloured buoy outside Ramsgate harbour. They are, like the majority of sea-fish, most capricious in their comings and goings, more particularly in certain sheltered bays that lie somewhat outside their course. Thus, one July morning in 1896, I caught a score of fine codling on the Pier Rocks, Bournemouth, in the course of half an hour, few running under a pound. With one small exception, in August, these were the only codling I saw at Bournemouth that summer; while in the present year, I have seen not a single one. Bournemouth Bay is, however, rather subject to sudden and unlooked for incursions on the part of capricious migrants; thus, the present summer witnessed an almost unprecedented July arrival of small scads, or horse-mackerel, numbers of which were taken in the sean-nets, and a few even from the pier. In the course of an acquaintance extending over a number of years, I only once before saw these fish in any quantity at Bournemouth, and that was close on ten years ago.

Conger-fishing is the same all the world over; and, though it entails night-fishing, with all its attendant discomforts, cold, darkness, and the rest, there are few who do not desire at one time or other the novel experience of a night's congering, or, having once tried it, are satisfied with one taste only. For, in truth, it is most exciting, and differs in every respect from the methods

Congering.

described in the foregoing pages. A few small conger are, it is true, taken by day—the largest I ever remember hooking in this way weighed but 6 lbs. 11 oz., though I have been told of conger of three times that weight being taken in the full glare of day. These I cannot regard, however, as other than exceptions, and those who embark for conger-fishing pure and simple will not need to leave the shore until the last rays of the sun are on the water. I suppose the very darkness—conger-fishers resent even the pale light of the moon—lends a spirit of adventure to the outing; and the rest of one's enjoyment consists in hand-to-hand fights with enormously strong fish, that are all over the boat at once, knocking over lanterns, dashing between your legs, barking and grunting, and altogether entering into the fun.

The tackle figured for whiting (p. 197) serves admirably for conger, only the hook may be anything up to three times the size, and should be lashed to a strong snood of new gimp or soft flax, served with copper wire. I have used the snooding that is said by those who supply it to be *too* soft for the conger to bite through; but my faith in it has been somewhat shaken of late years by one or two accidents, though I believe it varies much in quality, as I have certainly had excellent results with it in former seasons. On the whole, however, the flax snood served with copper wire takes some beating. The conger does not as a rule take the bait very far down, so that it is unnecessary for more than a yard at the most to be served with copper. I tried for the first time, last year, a tarpon-hook on a snood of raw hide, which was supplied to me by Farlow, and it certainly proved efficient, although I took no large conger that season. This summer I had better opportunities for testing it, and, as it stood the strain and teeth of conger of very fair size, its excellence cannot be questioned. Only, it is larger than it need be for conger.

The professionals use enormous hooks for this fish; but these are quite unnecessary, and the amateur will find one of the size figured (p. 55) ample for every purpose. On such a hook, I have killed conger weighing 40 lbs.

The conger come alongshore about June, but August is, on the whole, the best month for them. Down at Mevagissey, there are excellent conger-grounds within a couple of hundred yards of the shore, both to the eastward off the Gribbin; and, in the opposite direction, down by the Deadman, or Dodman. We used to glide out of the little harbour with the pilchard-boats, about six in the evening, and make straight for the ground nearest their pitch for the night, commencing operations with fresh mackerel or squid for bait, and, towards nine, at the first haul, running alongside one of them for half-a-dozen pilchards, just removed from the strangling meshes. I have brought a few conger to book with the rod in those waters, one weighing $24\frac{1}{2}$ lbs.; but, candidly, I don't enjoy the fun. In the proper sense of the word, the conger gives no play; and the strain on the rod, no matter how stiff, is such as to render it unfit in a very short time. The loss of time is prodigious; in the time it took me to kill that particular fish on the rod, I should probably have accounted for three or four on the hand-line. And, lastly, in a conger of anything over a dozen pounds, there is just enough of the element of resistance to make the capture of it, even on a hand-line, fairly attractive. The procedure is simple, given fresh bait and strong tackle. The hook is passed two or three times through the bait, and is lowered with as little disturbance as possible. If the hook is a fathom below the lead, let the latter just touch the bottom, and draw in about 5 ft. of line, so that the bait hangs undisturbed on the rocks, hitching the line round the rowlocks. Leave about three fathoms of slack coiled in the boat; after which make fast to the thwart. The line is thus made doubly fast; the fisherman then grasps it very lightly just over the side, and without moving the bait in the slightest, as conger are easily alarmed. The bite comes in the form of a picking at the bait, the largest fish often picking quite lightly; this, when followed up by a steady pull, must be answered with a sharp strike; and, as soon as the fish is fairly hooked, the line is released with a turn from the rowlock, and the fisherman hauls his eel as soon as the circumstances of the case allow. With really reliable tackle, no quarter need be given, unconditional surrender being insisted upon at once, before the fish has got its shoulder to the line and learnt its own strength. It is wonderful how effective is bluffing with these big fish; on the rod, it is the correct thing to give law and let the fish have a run for its life; but with the conger on a hand-line, no such etiquette is observed, and the eel is smuggled over the gunwale before it quite realises the situation. A sharp tap with the bludgeon, already advocated, or with any other handy weapon, on the snout (or, better still, on the vent, "where its life lies," as the fishermen say), reduces the fish to order, when the hook can be freed with a twist and the eel stowed away for'ard out of the way, so that it gives no trouble when, as is presently the case, it comes to its senses. Large eels are better killed, which is easiest effected by stabbing them in the back of the neck with a long pointed knife, and thus severing the spinal cord.

Like the pollack, and some other fish, the conger will occasionally blow the bait, apparently untouched, a foot or two up the line ; but this should be removed after each fish is unhooked, and a fresh bait cut for the next. It should be unnecessary to give any warning against the conger's teeth, for the great mouth will be forbidding enough for most tastes, and a "gag," such as the Jardine pattern mentioned on a previous page, should always be employed in extracting the hook from all but the smallest ; a conger of but 3 or 4 lbs., than which it is unusual to hook smaller, can bite very smartly.

Small congers of this weight can, however, in the absence of any handy weapon, be quieted by inserting the forefinger and thumb of the right hand in the gills, and, having got a firm grip, dashing the tail once or twice against the thwart or gunwale. Anything is preferable to the use of a blunt knife, as the blood of the conger, though lacking the nauseous smell of that in sharks, is yet sufficiently copious and sticky to be exceedingly unpleasant in the boat. In addition to this, a slime, thicker even than that from the fresh-water eel, adheres in thick films to everything with which the conger comes in contact. The necessity for having conger-baits perfectly fresh has already been stated ; and there is every reason to believe that, its large eyes notwithstanding, the sea-eel seeks its food by scent rather than with their aid.

An occasional conger is taken on the drift-line when there is sufficient out for it to reach the bottom; but on the whole, the boat-shaped sinker with two large hooks on the snooding above mentioned, will be found the most reliable gear for this work.

The conger is not held in much esteem for the table, but there is a continental method of stewing a slice from the neck of one weighing 5 or 6 lbs., which makes a more agreeable dish than the majority of those that figure in the second course at most English restaurants.

On the capture of flat-fish, some remarks have been offered incidentally under the head of pier-fishing; and it only remains to note the modifications in tackle called for in seeking them with the aid of a boat on the outer grounds. The throw-out tackle there referred to is obviously not the correct thing in boat-fishing, and even the ordinary form of leger loses its sensitiveness when used vertically. I have, therefore, used, what I advocated ten years ago, the conical plummet, in place of the coffin-shaped leger-lead or bullet, stopping its progress towards the hook in the same way, with a fragment of match on the line. The friction between line and lead is thus even less than in the leger thrown from shore, and the slightest bite can be

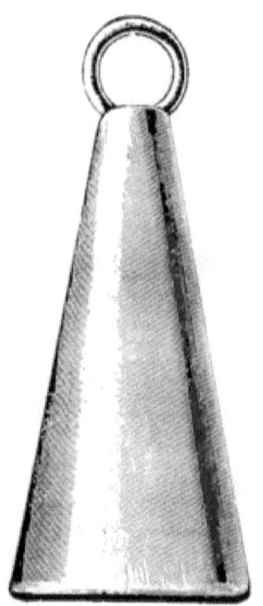

Conical Lead.

Flat-fish

felt, the strike acting moreover directly on the fish without raising the lead from the ground.

The baits for flat-fish are, as already intimated, many, among the most effective being mussel, which sometimes requires tying on, especially when the fish are biting so shyly as to require half a mussel only on the hook. It is easy enough to bait with a whole mussel, fixing it securely on the hook without the aid of thread; but a portion of the mollusc, necessarily deficient in some of the more gristly parts that help to fix the whole on the hook, offers no such facilities, and a few turns of brown thread will be found most useful.

Other baits for these fish are lugworm, not more than half an inch of which should be allowed to hang from the hook, raw shrimps, and fragments of mackerel, fresh herring, squid, or sand-smelt, the last being, as already mentioned, one of the most killing baits for turbot. Owing to their shape, these fish offer considerably more resistance to the water than others of like weight and size, and a landing-net should always be handy to relieve the strain on the rod-top and gut trace. Not only indeed are they rarely of a size to require the gaff, but, save on those of very large size, that implement would be very difficult to use. It is not unusual out in the deeper water to hook a heavy skate or ray of some kind while fishing for flat-fish, and some patience must be exercised in hauling this odious-looking creature very slowly, otherwise the strain will break the gut. A gaff is easily used on these gristly scavengers, and care should be taken to avoid a blow from the whip-like tail, armed in some with sharp spikes.

It would take too many pages to give a tithe of

the marks for flat-fish that occur to memory, because these are, plaice and dabs more particularly, among the most abundant fish within five miles of the coast. It may be borne in mind that, although they affect sand, or even mud, the finest plaice are often caught on the edge of rocks, and I have even taken them well on the reef, as evidenced by my hooking sponges and weeds at the same time.

Among the best plaicing-grounds that I can call to mind at the moment are those off Bopeep (St. Leonard's), September being the best month. Lugworm can be dug with ease at half ebb on the shore abreast of the ground, which is known to all the local fishermen, and there is no better bait locally. There is another good ground just east of Beachy Head, where you also stand a good chance of a catch of whiting.

Bopeep and Eastbourne

At Bournemouth, quantities of small plaice and dabs are caught throughout the summer on what is known as the dabbing-ground, less agreeably as the outfall (a name not remotely connected with the corporation sewage department: *see* Appendix); but by far the largest catches of flat fish at Bournemouth, in point of both numbers and individual size, are made on the "hard grounds," two or three miles out, found by getting the cabmen's shelter by the pier under the tall steeple of St. Peter's church, and opening the outer edge of Branksea Island (Poole Harbour) over the first sandbank. This "hard" is out and away the best all-round ground for summer fishing; and I have taken on it in an afternoon conger, pollack, mackerel, whiting, plaice, dab, gurnard and codling, not to men-

Bournemouth

tion dog-fish of 12 lbs. and over. It is advisable, however, to be tolerably sure of your weather before venturing so far in a very small rowing-boat, as there are some awkward winds in Bournemouth Bay, for all its apparently snug position, with the Island on one side and the protecting bluffs of the Isle of Purbeck on the other; and I have known more than one case in which small boats were compelled to run into Poole Harbour, or worse still, make a wearisome bid for shelter further up the Solent, rather than face the terrific rollers on the Bournemouth beach.

It is somewhat less easy to find good inshore grounds for flat-fish on the rocky coasts of Cornwall; but there is an excellent dabbing-ground at Mevagissey, to give a single example, just west of the Gribbin, off Pentewan. The depth does not exceed five fathoms, the beach being less than two hundred yards distant, and the bag is usually a mixed one, small skate being at times common, while, late in August, such mackerel as have gone to the bottom are found feeding along with the flat-fish. *[Mevagissey]*

It is not probable that any one would set out expressly to catch gurnard. There are certain fish that we catch rather accidentally than by design; and the gurnard, as the dory, garfish and horse-mackerel, must be reckoned among these. Assuming that any one were really anxious to make a catch of these unprepossessing ground-feeders, I should say that the best plan would be to moor the boat over the edge of the rocks in not less than four fathoms, to bait the hooks with small pieces of fresh herring (or, if in Cornwall, pilchard), and leave them to their own *[Gurnard]* devices just on the bottom. The gurnard will hook themselves; indeed, with their enormous mouths, they cannot do otherwise, and may be added to the bag while you are at lunch. It cannot be called sport; but this fish rarely furnishes sport, unless a large one is accidentally caught on the lightest of gut tackle. Besides taking almost any fresh bait that is allowed to linger within reach —the gurnard is a lazy fish, rarely exerting itself in procuring food—this fish will generally seize a very slow spinning bait, and many a time is the disgusted pollack-fisher compelled to reel in perhaps fifty yards of line to unhook a miserable gurnard, weighing under a pound, which fastened on to the spinner as the boat turned and the line slackened for a moment.

The pleasures of mackerel fishing have already been alluded to in connection with the chief methods by which this fish is captured, namely whiffing, or "plummeting," and drift-lining. At the end of the summer, however, some time in August as a rule, the mackerel go to the bottom, feeding along with the flat-fish and whiting. There is then no better tackle for them than the paternoster, for they may feed at any distance from the bottom, usually between 2 and 10 feet, and the paternoster searches different depths as does no other combination. When the exact depth at which they are feeding has been ascertained, I have, it is true, improved matters by substituting the chopstick tackle, but as a rule, the paternoster of single gut will kill against anything.

Mackerel

Mackerel are among the few fish in pursuit of which it is, owing to their roving habits, unnecessary to take any account of "marks." With pouting

—otherwise whiting-pout, or "bibs"—the case is very different, and, although it is not uncommon to make large catches of the smallest size from piers, like that at Hastings, not actually on the rocks, it is essential for good pout-fishing to take a boat and anchor exactly over some reef of rocks or wreck. Old wrecks are famous pout-grounds, and there are several in the Spithead. Pout-fishing is rarely much use in a strong tide, as the fish then seem to go off the feed. As silver whiting and flat-fish show no such fastidiousness, it is usual to anchor over the sand and fish for these and kindred spirits until the tide is slack enough to make it worth while bringing up on the rocks for the pout and small conger, the latter also objecting to strong currents almost as much as to very clear water. Occasionally, however, pout are found to feed throughout the day, and the great thing is to use just enough lead to "keep" the bottom without making the constant hauling too tiring.

Pouting

The continual shifting of leads in this and whiting-fishing in the tideway entails much unavoidable loss of time, and several devices more or less ingenious have appeared of late years to reduce this, among the best being a lead devised by Mr. Campbell Macpherson of Southampton, to whom I am indebted for the accompanying cut, the only improvement I can suggest being to invert the whole and use it with the pointed end downwards, in which position it will be less likely to get foul in the rocks. This lead makes a number of combinations, the only objection, as in others constructed on similar lines, being that when only one or two of the sections are in use, the extra brass wire exposed is too bright and conspicuous for

O

clear-water fishing. Possibly, however, it could be stained, or better still, the connecting link made of thick line. Similar leads were shown in Chapter III.; and if another objection is wanted, though

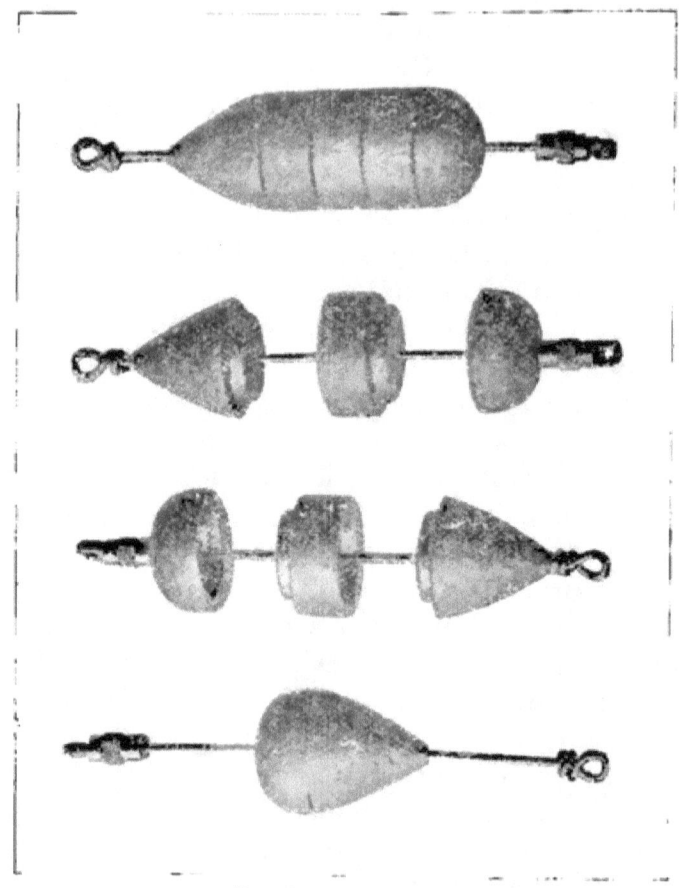

NEW ADJUSTABLE LEAD.

under certain conditions these patent arrangements answer admirably, it is that the gradations are not small enough; one often wants to add lead by the half ounce, not, as in most of these, two or three ounces at a time.

Pouting-fishing is at once the most and least difficult of all inshore sport. The capture of small pouting, creatures going six or eight to the pound, and gorging without demur baits the size of their own head, is child's play, and needs no discrimination in the matter of tackle and baits, and very little skill in hooking the fish. When, however, the fish run about three quarters of a pound, a fair proportion indeed topping the pound—such as one may fall in with any fine September day in the Downs—it is no longer a case of All Fools' Day, but the prizes fall to the best tackle and the most skilful fisher.

The first thing is to be perfectly sure of the bearings; for in pouting-fishing, above almost all other, the exact spot is of first importance. Having hit on the spot—and nothing but local knowledge will determine it—the next thing is to determine the depth at which the fish are feeding at the time, which is best learnt with the aid of a long paternoster, as previously described, having the lowest hook on the ground and three or four others strung above it at intervals of four feet. Baiting these with lugworm, mussel, squid (an excellent bait), or mackerel, it will soon be found that the pouting, if there are any in the neighbourhood, are taken on one, perhaps even on two adjoining, of the hooks. It is then an easy matter, by noting the exact distance between the lead and the hook in question, to dangle your baits at, or near, that depth. When feeding madly, as is often the case, pouting will practically hook themselves; but it is usually necessary to strike smartly while the fish is *wriggling* on the hook. This striking is particularly necessary with the hand-line; the springiness of rod is as a rule sufficient to hook the fish alone.

When fairly hooked, these little fish should be hauled into the boat without slacking the line for a moment, as they are somewhat clever at getting off the hook. They present no difficulties in the way of spines, and may be handled with impunity, the worst that can be said of them being that they are slimy and given to shedding their bronze-tinted scales. Two distinct races will be noted; one with, the other without, black bars on the sides—a difference due, I fancy, to surroundings. Few fish are quicker to unbait the hooks, and if there is a lull after two or three bites, the line should be hauled, when the hooks will generally be found to be without bait. It is not necessary to cover the hook, so long as the bait has a fair chance of keeping on.

Whiting. The whiting proper, otherwise silver whiting, is a more elegant and tapering fish than the last-named, which has in many districts usurped its name. Unlike the pouting, the present species is taken on the sand, particularly on hard sand flats in the tideway, for the whiting does not, as mentioned above, mind a little tide.

As in most forms of angling in salt water, there is whiting-fishing and whiting-fishing. There is the modest pursuit of small whiting in a few feet of water—I recollect seeing an unpatriotic Hampshireman on board the same boat as myself at the Naval Review hauling up numerous small whiting the whole time the royal yacht was passing through the smoke of the big guns—and there is the heavier, more enjoyable work out in the offing, where the water is over 100 feet deep, the leads a

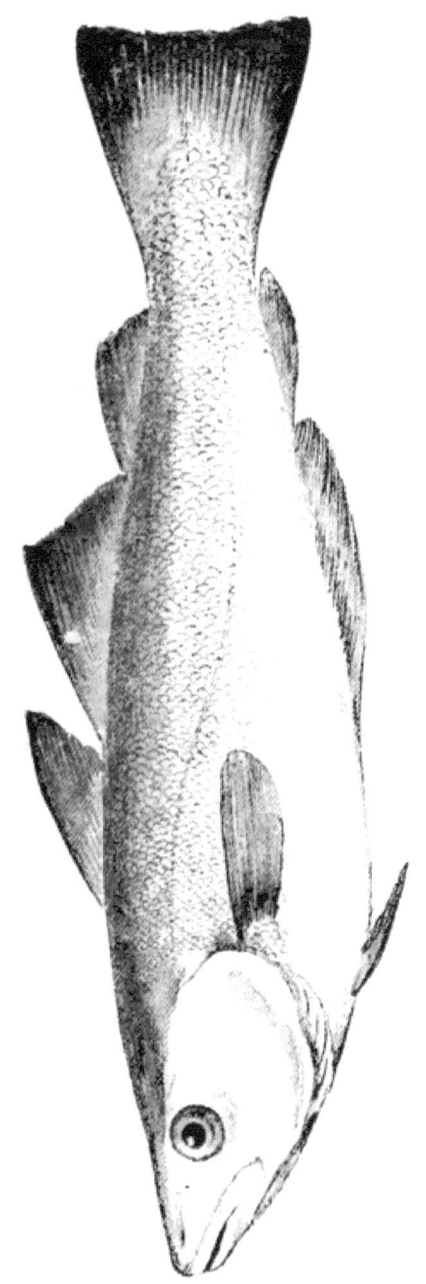

WHITING.

couple of pounds in weight, the tide running like a mill-race while the fish, averaging a couple of pounds or more, come up two at a time. That is fishing indeed, and is to be enjoyed throughout July and August on the south-west coast, or somewhat later in the year, say October, further up the Channel, off Deal and Ramsgate. My friend "John Bickerdyke" recommends above all other tackle the paternoster for whiting; but personally, I have found nothing beat, especially when after the large deep-water fish, the shearing tackle used by the Cornishmen, and described as a "sid-strap," whatever that may convey.

The accompanying figure will give the general idea of the gear in question; and the correct method of throwing out the boat-shaped sinker so as to avoid a foul was given in the chapter on hand-lining. As bait, we used in Cornwall pieces of pilchard, or, when that was too soft, strips of mackerel that had been caught on the plummet-lines on the way out. (For size of hook, *see* p. 55).

Lugworm, sprat, herring, or mussel, these are the baits commonly used on the Kentish coast, and I have had extraordinary luck with squid, only it is not always to be had in the autumn, when one gets the whiting-fishing so near shore.

WHITING-TACKLE.

Striking in deep water is, as was also explained in Chapter III., no finicking turn of the wrist; and, although whiting have a habit, when in biting mood, of hooking themselves, a great many more will be caught by careful attention to the lines, sharp striking and rapid hauling. It is when hauling whiting a few miles off the Cornish cliffs, that the sharks mostly come round and levy toll, usually biting off the tail and body, but rarely, to my knowledge, getting foul of the small hook.

Should these scavengers prove too troublesome, the proper course is to get all light tackle aboard and put out a strong line with a whole pilchard on a conger hook. No lead is wanted on this line, the pilchard being allowed to drift freely with the tide. It must be confessed that the sharks, ready enough in all conscience to take half the fish from the light lines, have usually the wit to keep clear of the stronger hook; but the withdrawal of the other lines has often the desired effect, and they go prowling elsewhere, after which fishing can be resumed. The advent of sharks anywhere in the neighbourhood of midday is as good a time as any for tiffin, the lines being meanwhile taken aboard.

Some little discrimination is needed, where several whiting-lines are in use from a boat, in distributing the heavier and lighter leads from fore and aft respectively in order to obviate a foul, just as in whiffing, or plummeting, the stern line is far lighter than the rest. The heaviest lead and line should always be for'ard if the boat rides head to the tide. As in pouting-fishing, "marks" are all important, and these being as a rule several miles from the coast, only the local fishermen are able to pick them up with any certainty. Although they predominate, it is rare to take only whiting on these grounds, large mackerel, gurnard and flat-fish of various kinds, not to mention rays and dog-fish, usually helping to fill the bag. At the same time, I have sometimes found it possible to adjust the depth of a couple of hooks on the tackle above mentioned so accurately as to take only whiting, the baits being too high for the gurnard and flat-fish, too low for the mackerel.

The whiting should be split and cleaned by your boatman almost as soon as removed from the water; although few fish are more delicate eating when perfectly fresh—and doctors are fond of ordering them for convalescents, even in the half stale condition in which alone they are to be had in London—few, as I have had occasion to say on a previous page, lose their freshness more rapidly, and they are in fact less adapted than most fish to the purposes of gifts to absent friends. The will is, in such case, better than the deed.

On the subject of the remaining fish that are likely to be caught in small boats within a few miles of the coast, I have thought it unnecessary to offer, save incidentally, any remarks. Wrasse and rocklings of more than one species will often seize the bait meant for pouting; while weevers, bull-heads, snake-fish and other monstrosities, interesting to the naturalist if not to the sportsman, will likewise die on hooks intended for dab or whiting. These are, however, to be regarded in the light of chance catches, and, like most things undesired, come without the seeking. Instructions are therefore superfluous.

* * * * * *

This, I find, concludes my remarks on the practical aspects of modern sea-fishing for sport, in writing which I have endeavoured, in view of the fact that more than one book has appeared on the subject in recent times, to bring my account of tackle and methods up to date. The topographical portions of the subject, the whereabouts of grounds and other items of local interest that bear on sport, are dealt with at some length in the Appendix. All said and done, sea-fish are caught, allowing for the difference of existing conditions, by methods closely resembling those followed in fresh water, an analogy more than ever apparent since light gut tackle and ground-baiting have come in vogue in salt water. Our paternoster is but an exaggeration of that used for pike and perch ; our leger and float-tackle are powerful counterparts of those used for bream or barbel ; our whiffing is no more than the trailing that was formerly legitimate in the Thames and other waters in which it is now tabooed, a prohibition that by the way casts no aspersion on its practice in the sea, where the conditions are so different. Spinning, fly-fishing and live-baiting are ruled by the same general principles in sea and river, and only one tackle, less used by amateurs than any other, the chopstick, fails to find its counterpart inland.

It will not escape notice that I have throughout the foregoing pages given the preference to bait-fishing, devoting little or no space to the "artistic" use of spinners and flies. These are doubtless admirable in their way, but a good deal has been written of them elsewhere, and as I have not undertaken anything beyond giving some practical instructions for the capture of sea fish, it seems quite admissible to confine my remarks to those methods by which, for the most part, I kill some hundreds of fish each summer.

WHIFFING FOR MACKEREL.
(*From a Kodak snap by the Author.*)

APPENDIX.

INTRODUCTORY.—ON "MARKS."

WHEN I proposed last winter, as a direct outcome of a suggestion made by "Red Spinner" to the *British Sea Anglers*, the compilation of a sea-fishing guide with the joint aid of a number of amateurs, the "Anglers' Library" was not even contemplated, and I little thought how soon I should be allowed an opportunity of putting my proposal to the test. The assistance I have received, both from Mr. R. B. Marston (*Fishing Gazette*) and Mr. W. Senior (*Field*) in reaching the different gentlemen in possession of the requisite information, and subsequently from the latter themselves, has been most encouraging; and I think and hope that the joint result of their contributions, in which my own share is very trifling, will be most valuable to the amateur who wishes to try a new resort, or revisit an old after a lapse of years, in the course of which maybe new piers have sprung into existence, old harbours silted up, old "marks" vanished, old grounds got fished out. These and many other contingencies are ever at hand to render the very latest information essential.

"Marks" are, as has been already explained, the means of rediscovering certain submerged patches of rock or sand, themselves invisible, which are known to harbour fish; and consist in four objects ashore, selected on certain principles easy to grasp, through which pass two imaginary lines, if possible at an angle of 90°, to the eye of the observer seated in a boat moored exactly over the right spot.

The aforementioned principles, on which all "marks" should be chosen, are four in number: they should be conspicuous from the fishing-ground; they should be of a permanent nature, buildings being less suitable than more natural "marks," such as headlands, old trees and the like; they should be available at all seasons, temporary bathing shelters or green fields being of use during no more than a very small portion of the year; and they should be at some considerable distance apart, both as regards the distance of each pair, the one behind the other, and the distance between the two pairs and consequent angle between the imaginary lines, which, as recommended above, should be not less than 90°. The last of these conditions alone requires explanation, and it will easily be seen that if the objects in a line are close together, the boat might easily shift a few yards off the ground without shifting the line from both; whereas with the objects far apart, the least shift throws them out of line. This, if not indeed apparent, can be tested on the first opportunity. The same advantage attaches to keeping the lines as nearly at right angles as possible. The necessity for the greatest accuracy, even allowing for the play of the tide on the painter, has received notice. It will be seen that "marks," pure and simple, form by no means the bulk of the information in the following pages, and for this two reasons may be assigned. In the first place, as a well-known sea-angler wrote me on a recent occasion, many of these grounds have been discovered after a deal of experimenting (though more often by chance), and are known only to a few amateurs, or professionals, or both; and it is hardly to be expected that they can be regarded as other than confidential. Indeed, a sharp look-out has usually to be kept for smart "locals," who are fond of sailing by with a far-away expression on their honest sunburnt faces, merely, it is perhaps unnecessary to point out, with the express object of filching the bearings. Greek meets Greek, I regret to say, in the most perfidious manner; and the order, as soon as these gentry are sighted, is to let out the whole of the painter, which has the effect, needless to say, of taking the boat right off the mark. This is accomplished without fuss, and the occupants of the boat continue their sham fishing, in which they are absorbed until the intruders have taken what they imagine to be the bearings and sail off again. Then the ground is picked up once more, and the wily ones resume operations in good earnest. Another factor bearing on the publication of such "marks" in a work like the present is the difficulty of indicating the exact spot to a stranger. Thus, I might advise getting the steeple of a certain church over a windmill; but churches are many, and so for the matter of that, though too often idle nowadays, are windmills, especially on the West Sussex coast

A hill with a quaint name, often hard to pronounce for the ear of residents from whom the visitor would learn its whereabouts, would not be easy to identify, and there are in fact but few objects that may, without further explanation, be set down in a book. If there is but one pier and but one flagstaff at its extremity, there can of course be no risk of confusion if I give that flagstaff as a bearing. If there is but one fish-market, the clock-face on its entrance will also serve the purpose. So too would the opening of the only tunnel visible from the sea, or a certain chimney on the coast-guard station. It will be seen that the following notes make no pretence to furnish a complete guide to the sea-fishing obtainable on the English, Scotch and Irish coasts. Those who know anything about the matter will, I think, agree with me that such an undertaking would require to itself a volume twice the size of the present, and years of original labour supplemented by at least a hundred other contributors. I have not at my disposal either the space, the time, or the collaborators. All that has been attempted, —and not, I venture to think, without some success,—has been the selection of a couple of dozen stations on widely different parts of the coast, and some notes are given on these that were kindly furnished by sportsmen who have fished there comparatively recently. So careful have I been, believing this to be the crucial point, not to hash up old information, that many spots that I fished but three or four years back are either altogether omitted, or referred to only incidentally. As for the notes on sea-fishing in foreign and colonial waters, no more than a very short selection could be made; but I have, supplementing my own notes with those of Mr. H. A. Bryden, been able to offer some idea of the sport that may be expected on the coasts of South Africa and Australia, as well as at several ports of call on the route to the Antipodes. As the fishing does not alter so rapidly in those seas, it is not of consequence that these foreign notes are not quite of yesterday, though they are in no case out-of-date.

At Home.

Aberdeen I am indebted to Mr. G. Mackay, who has already been quoted in connection with rock-fishing, for a few particulars of the sport at Aberdeen; and I am only sorry that the Scotch coast-fishing (and Irish as well) should be so meagrely represented in these pages, as I am assured that these localities give such sport as fully compensates the angler for the long and somewhat tedious journey. It is a question, however, of the correspondents available, and I have spared no pains to importune as many as I could lay hands on for notes!

From the mouth of the Dee, says Mr. Mackay, the natural boundary between the counties of Aberdeen and Kincardine, south to the confines of Forfar, stretches one of the most picturesque and accessible tracts of coast that the rock-fisher could find anywhere in the north. From Aberdeen to the "Foulshooch," half-a-dozen miles south of Stonehaven, there must be twenty miles of fishful voes and bays, any and all of which may be got at either by alighting at side stations, or, more comfortably, by easy drives from Aberdeen, Cove, Muchalls, Portlethen, or Stonehaven. Green cod and saithe, or coal fish, ranging in weight from 1 to 16 lbs., with occasional heavy fish of near 30, are the fish most sought. The tackle and baits for the sport have been given in Chapter IV. Most rock-fishers on that coast give the preference to bait fishing with the long rods aforementioned. Having selected their favourite spot, or approached as near as the state of the tide will allow, they fish until their seat becomes risky from a rising tide, or the height too great for safely hauling the fish by reason of a falling tide, when they shift to a more conveniently placed ledge and resume operations. Shelled mussel, the bait most in use, is sold in almost every hamlet thereabouts. Herring is preferred for the flat fish, but these are only taken in numbers in the sandy bays near Newburgh, Collieston and Cruden. The "holes" are in some cases by no means easy to reach, and a certain amount of careful climbing may be the first consideration. On the whole, however, very few accidents have occurred, strangers being as a rule taken round at low tide and brought back at the next fall. The fish are not as a rule as keenly on the feed on the ebbing tide as they are on the flood. There is, besides this more characteristic rock-fishing, a considerable amount of off-shore fishing at and near Aberdeen. Mr. Ritchie, of Newburgh, has a large boat for those people staying at the hotel who wish for sea-fishing, in addition to a number of smaller craft for the tidal anglers after finnock and sea trout in the estuary.

Mr. W. Laing, tackle-maker, of Sterling Street, Aberdeen, makes, says Mr. Mackay, a speciality of this rock-tackle, and among his goods are, besides the aforementioned "bay set," a number of flies and artificial baits, as well as special sinkers for both bait- and fly-fishing.

Mr. Gerald Geoghegan has kindly given me some particulars of the winter beach-fishing at this Suffolk watering-place. Most of the fishing, he says, is done from the shore; indeed, with the exception of the netting of sprat and herring, a certain amount of long lining, locally called "tipple-towing," and a little boat-fishing for cod over some rocks opposite the village of Thorpe, the fishing may be said to be confined to this method. The throw-out lines, known as "butt-lines," may be obtained in the town; but still better sport may be had from the beach with a stout pike rod, plaited hemp line and twisted gut paternoster. *The* bait for this fishing is the lugworm; but herring, whelk, and sprat are all regarded as fair substitutes. The season for this sport lasts from October to Christmas, and the most likely days are those on which, after a spell of south-westerly wind, there is still a heavy ground-swell. It is important not to throw out too far, as the fish feed quite close inshore.

Aldeburgh-on-Sea

As to the best spots, Mr. Geoghegan says there is no fishing north of the town. Going south, however, towards Slaughden Quay, the first "pitch" is what is known as the "Miller's Hole," situate opposite the windmill at the end of Brudenell Terrace. There is a second good place south of Slaughden, over the ruins of an old battery opposite the martello tower; but it is necessary to fish well to the south, otherwise the tackle is certain to get foul of the bricks and other *débris*, or is likely to roll from the battery into the sea. Still further on are the "Shepherd's House" and the Volunteer rifle range; and some fifty yards south of the target is another favourite spot, the "Point." Yet a mile further south are the "Dirty Wall Stakes"; and Mr. Geoghegan considers that the very best fishing of all is to be had about 150 yards north of these stakes, though the sport is at times good from the stakes themselves as far as Orford lighthouse along the bight of the bay. In very rough weather, some sport is obtained by shooting a line in the river, which is, however, too weedy for rod-fishing.

Bexhill-on-Sea, see *Hastings*.

Bognor (Sussex) The sea-fishing off Bognor is practically confined to the three months August to October. In August there is some pollack-railing, with an occasional bass, off the rough ground east of the pier-head, and so, intermittently, to Littlehampton (*q.v.*). The fish run larger, however, though less numerous outside on the rocks about a mile and a half beyond the pier-head. From the pier itself, the fishing is worse than useless, very small flat fish and whiting being about the only fish caught there nowadays. In September, the railing falls off, but the ground-fishing (boats anchor within five hundred yards of the pier) improves. In October, there is good boat-fishing for cod and whiting. There are so many lobster-pots out throughout the summer months that extreme care is necessary in railing in order to avoid smashing tackle among the corks. At Selsea, a few miles to the westward, there is in the summer months very fair boat-fishing for pollack with live prawn, but the wind should be off shore.

Bournemouth In devoting considerable space to the Bournemouth grounds, I do not wish to claim for the place any fishing better than that obtainable at many other spots not treated of in these pages at half the length. I have fished at Bournemouth, however, at intervals during the past sixteen years, have watched the red bricks gradually encroach on the pine trees ashore, and corresponding changes in the fishing afloat; and I give an account of the present state of affairs there more as an example of the completeness with which, had there been material, I would gladly have treated all the rest. Some mention has already been made of Bournemouth in the foregoing pages, but I shall recapitulate here most of what has been said before.

The fishing from the pier may be dismissed in few words. It is of four kinds: smelt-fishing with very light tackle and a fragment of mussel for bait; bass-fishing in rough August weather with a heavily leaded line pitched into the surf, the bait being mackerel or fresh herring; the afore-mentioned mackerel-fishing with rod and float; and, lastly, the ordinary throw-out fishing for flat-fish, chiefly dabs and turbot, and all lamentably small. During the present summer (1897) I have seen perhaps half-a-dozen flat fish, out of several hundreds, that should have been retained. As in all sheltered bays, exceptional visitors occasionally take the hook here in the warm weather, and there have been one or two cases of red mullet, small scad and skate; dory, too, are not uncommon in the latter days of August, and they feed well on the launce and sand-smelts that swarm beneath the piles from the beginning of June until the end of September. Altogether, the pier-fishing is poorer than at most places; the bass are in all years few and far between, in some absent altogether; the mackerel only hang about the pier during a few of the hottest days in August; the smelts are, it is true, as inexhaustible as the mussels that cover the piles to high-water mark, but one soon tires of catching fish so small; and the flat-fish are, as already mentioned, undersized almost without exception.

Nor, it must be confessed, is the fishing from boats other than disappointing during nine months of the year. From the middle of July, however, until the middle, sometimes the end, of October, there are fair quantities of fish in the bay; though it is absolutely necessary, except when railing or drift-lining for mackerel, which travel all over the bay, to pick up the "marks" with great care.

The following will be found the best grounds off Bournemouth :—

(1) The *Outfall*—A sand-ground for flat fish, small whiting, gurnard, and occasional large mackerel (local, "race-horses"). Row out from the beach about 100 yards east of the pier until the flagstaff on the end of the latter is exactly on the red steeple of the Presbyterian church at the further end of the Exeter Road (and to the left of the gardens) and the white patch on the further side of Durley Chine (the first, westward from the pier) is just open. The fish shift slightly on this ground according to tide and wind, but a boat anchored according to these bearings is over the centre of it. I think it, however, fair to mention, for the benefit of those who may have pronounced views on such matters, that this Outfall is named from the two sewers that terminate in the immediate vicinity! Instead of opening the white patch in the first Chine, some open the road in the third (Alum).

(2) The *Pier Rocks*—An excellent, but small, reef for pout, with an occasional good conger. On one occasion only, in the first week of July, 1896, I took a large number of fine codling, averaging a pound, in a very short time, but have not heard of any there before or since. This ground is in dead line with the pier, so that the boat has to be rowed out with the flagstaff dead on the clock at the other end, and the other mark is either Branksea Castle (it can be seen as a grey patch behind the trees on Branksea Island, Poole Harbour) just clear of the end of the cliffs beyond Branksome (the westmost) Chine; or—an excellent bearing on very clear days—"Old Harry Rock," out to the south-west, beneath the apex of a light triangular field on the hillside beyond Swanage. It is well to bear in mind that, if really good sport is expected, the boat should be anchored right on the single high rock, and that any carelessness in picking up the "marks" may have fatal results. This ground is not profitable when a strong tide is running, an objection that applies to all pout- and conger-grounds.

(3) The *Inner Durley*—As Bridle, the only local lobster-man, keeps his pots on this reef throughout the summer, the ground is often to be picked up by his corks. Still, even Bridles are ephemeral; and the bearings of this reef, which is not more than a couple of hundred yards from the beach, and immediately off the Durley

Chine, are as follows :—Get the boat-steps on the pier landing stage immediately under a conspicuous red-tiled house on the East Cliff, and row out until right off the sand-heap in the middle of the Chine.

(4) The *Outer Durley*—About the best, as it is certainly the most frequented, of the more easily reached rocks in the bay, this is picked up as follows :—The pier flagstaff is brought right in the centre of the patch of trees between the above-mentioned red-tiled house and the white house immediately above it, and the boat follows that line in a south-westerly course until "Old Harry" just shuts out the extreme point of St. Alban's Head, the headland beyond Swanage. On somewhat hazy days, this is a little difficult to make out, and it will then be found to answer the purpose if you open what appears to be about a yard of Branksea Island. The former mark is, however, the more accurate.

(5) The *Westmost Rocks*—This is an outer ground, and will not as a rule be visited by a stranger, or without the means of sailing out and back, as the row would on a hot day be a tiring way of getting one's fishing. This is quite the best ground in the bay for conger, of which I have here caught fair-sized examples early in the afternoon. It is three parts of the way to Swanage, and the bearings are :—"Old Harry" just outside Swanage Castle, and a tall chimney stack in Poole over the east cottage on the sandbanks.

(6) The *Woodbury Rocks*—Another outer ground, of which it would be useless to give the bearings, as they are comprehensible only to the professionals, or to those who know the shore well.

(7) The *Hard Ground*—For August, this is certainly the best all-round ground in this part of the bay; and I have taken in the course of a couple of hours several large mackerel, conger up to 7 lbs., whiting of good size, bream and flat fish up to 2 lbs. Unfortunately, it is also well known to the dog-fish of the neighbourhood, and the catch generally includes a "nurse" of 10 or 12 lbs. The ground, which is a couple of miles from shore, is reached by getting the small Cabmen's Shelter next the pier under the steeple of St. Peter's Church (seen over the Gardens), and rowing S.S.W. until the outer end of Branksea Island comes over the first (eastmost) sand bank.

I have now given the bearings of half-a-dozen of the best grounds for Bournemouth fishing. There are others, no doubt. There is an old wreck, for instance, which, laden with railway-metal, has lain many a year on the bottom about three miles east from "Old Harry," and which, known only to one or two Poole trawlers who have left £20 of gear apiece as the price of their knowledge, would be a famous swim for pollack and conger, if we could but find it. There are also the "Herbert Home Rocks" and a patch off Boscombe. But the foregoing grounds all contain fish of some kind or other during the summer months.

Two subjects of local interest remain—baits and boatmen. As to baits, the pier supplies endless mussels, which should *not* be scalded, and squid may occasionally be got from White, the diver, or from the Poole boats. Lugworms are not much used locally, though anglers possessing bicycles sometimes ride out to Poole harbour, and dig them on the ebb tide. The Poole lug are, however, for the most part, of small size. The sand-smelts, caught in numbers on the pier, are acceptable to most fish, particularly to turbot and other flat fish; and the sand-eels, less frequently hooked, are still more deadly.

The boatmen are many, and I prefer not making any invidious comparisons. They mostly know the grounds; and, whether the visitor employs Davis, Dyer, Kettle, Lucas, Maynard, Munday, or any other, he may reckon, so long as he has no objection to paying half-a-crown an hour, on being properly waited on. Without a man, the recognised charge for small rowing boats is 1s. per hour, and it is usual to pay a small sum extra for bait and lines, as well as a not exorbitant tip should any but the owner of the boat lend a hand in hauling her up on returning from the grounds.

With regard to the sea-fishing at neighbouring places, there is a good reef about a mile off the salmon-run at Mudeford (Christchurch); a few bass are occasionally hooked from the stunted pier at Southborne; and a few of good size are taken from the Hamworthy Bridge, Poole (so Mr. Beckford of Parkestone informs me), as well as large numbers at various grounds in the harbour, the fishing of which is, however, ruined by indiscriminate netting. From Swanage, one of the best grounds is that known as Chapman's Pool, to the westward round the next headland.

As for the fresh-water fishing to be had in the neighbourhood, I may mention that there is at times very excellent pike-fishing at a place not far distant, known as Redhill, for which the charge is 2s. 6d. per day, but live bait is most difficult to procure. Lightwood, of Christchurch Road, is, I believe, the agent. At Christchurch, only a few miles distant, is the joint estuary of the Stour and Avon, the former famous for its pike, the latter for its salmon; though the fishery for the latter, at Mudeford, has been worse during the present summer than for years past. A considerable stretch of the Stour is now rented by Alderman Newlyn, of Bournemouth, who has, within the last twelvemonth, turned upwards of five thousand fish of all kinds into the water. I had the pleasure on a recent occasion of punting with him over the whole stretch down to below Iford Bridge; and he pointed out, having known the water for forty years, many a historic salmon-pool or backwater famed for the capture of some monster pike. Most of these rivers are strictly preserved, and the aforementioned stretch near Redhill (about a mile beyond the terminus of the omnibus that runs from the top of the Richmond Hill) is about the only one I know of where fishing can be had by day-ticket.

Without ranking among the better sea-angling resorts near town, there was, until within the last few years, fair sport to be had at Brighton. The old Chain Pier, now a thing of the past, gave bass in summer, while there was first-rate conger- and pout-fishing off such grounds, now for the most part fished out, as the "Wreck," "Town Hall Rocks," and others.

Brighton

As at so many other spots, however, the Brighton sea-fishing has gone from bad to worse, until, as Mr. H. S. Harland, who has watched it for many years, writes me quite recently, it is now only *poor* and *very uncertain*.

The following epitome of the months, for which I am indebted to the same correspondent, will be of use :—

January to March: Chiefly deep water fishing, five or six miles from land.

April: Fish draw closer inshore, but not in numbers.

May: A few pout and flat fish are taken.

June and July: Pout and a few early silver whiting, plaice, and a few bream. Towards the middle of July, bass come along with roughish weather, and two were taken this year on the beach at the Kemptown end. Mackerel also come inshore, but will not yet take the hook.

August: Chief sport, mackerel-railing.

September and October: Silver whiting.

November and December: Silver whiting and cod.

I have given Mr. Harland's summary because, with some little variation, it applies to the entire coast between the Foreland and the Land's End. With regard to the fishing-grounds off Brighton, Mr. Harland recommends two, the "New Found Out" rocks, about a mile from shore, and opposite Sussex Square, Kemptown, bearing slightly to the eastward; and a sand ground, the best for plaice, also off Sussex Square, but not more than half a mile out.

Seaford, to the east of Brighton, is rather famous in the annals of conger-fishing, and I have had better conger there than anywhere in the Channel east of Exmouth.

Brixham. For some information as to the fishing to be presently obtained off this picturesque Devon village with the famous trawling fleet, I am indebted to Mr. A. Collingwood Lee, of Waltham Abbey, an enthusiastic supporter of the B.S.A.S. since its inception, who has also been good enough to send me notes on half-a-dozen places besides. I have fished a great deal off Brixham myself, but not during the last few years, so that I shall give only Mr. Lee's more recent experiences. The fishing, he says, is still as good as ever: pollack, bream and conger are the chief fish. Pollack of good size can be caught inshore, and there is deep water round the "Cod Rock," a short distance from the harbour, near which is excellent broken ground for large bream. As all the able-bodied men of the place are engaged aboard the trawlers, it is necessary to get hold of one of the old hands, past active work, to take you out to the grounds. The harbour is safe, the fishing-ground is close at hand; and in rough weather there is even fishing of a kind in the harbour itself, the baits being squid, mussel, and worms, all easily obtainable. Mr. Lee caught one small bass there on a mackerel-spinner, and was told that earlier in the summer there were many about the harbour. A "gentleman," the fishermen complained, had ruined the bass-fishing by taking enormous quantities in a specially-constructed silk trammel, selling them subsequently for his own profit.[1] The whiting-grounds, on which the sport is first-rate, are only about three miles out.

This little fishing village, within easy reach of Exmouth, is a capital place for mackerel-railing and pollack-fishing, the former fish being found everywhere, the latter residing among the rocky ledges off the mouth of the Otter. There are also large bass off Ottermouth, but they are said to take some catching. **Budleigh Salterton**

Cowes, see *Southampton*.

With its autumn cod and whiting, this place has, particularly since the arrival of the B.S.A.S. on the scene, achieved considerable notoriety among London, and even provincial, sea-anglers. **Deal**

Though knowing it well, I have preferred to get these notes from one who visits the place regularly, and Mr. G. Read Clarke, of the B.S.A.S., has kindly come to the rescue. Besides the cod- and whiting-fishing aforementioned, there is, he says, an earlier season (roughly, May to September) for pollack and ground-fish.

There is fishing, of a sort, from the pier throughout the season, and in the autumn some really good cod and whiting are taken here. For boat-fishing, the grounds are many, particularly in the form of wrecks, terribly common on this coast, and small patches of rock. Thus, there is a wreck off Walmer Castle, to find which it is necessary to get the flag-staff alongside the Walmer lifeboat house in line with the land side of the steeple on the house, and the windmill just clear of the Walmer Castle woods. Another wreck off Sandown Castle, an excellent pout-ground, is found by getting the land end of the pier-pavilion in line with the edge of Deal Castle and the first chimney (counting from the centre to the

---

[1] This "gentleman" is not unknown to me, and I once narrowly missed the pleasure of dragging an anchor through his trammels off Portland. The manner in which he has for years been permitted to deplete the Devonshire and Dorset estuaries of their bass, once famous, reflects little credit on the winking foreshore Conservancies.

Margate side) of the coastguard-station on the flag-staff in front of the station.

The grounds for flat-fish are not so many, but up to about a couple of years ago very large plaice were caught on a mussel-bank which had formed in line with the pier, some two hundred yards from the shore. There swooped down, however, a couple of Folkestone trawlers, who not only caught all the fish, but also destroyed the bank. Consolation was, however, derived from the knowledge that the raid cost them their nets! Another bank is now forming on the south side of the pier, from which, in the course of a season or two, good sport should be obtained. The baits for Deal fishing are lugworm, sprat, herring, and mackerel; and pollack are also taken on the pier on ragworm, which has to be got from Dover (*q.v.*). The fishermen charge about 6*s.* per day for their services, and know all the best grounds. It is noticeable at Deal, more perhaps than elsewhere, that the rod has all but superseded the hand-line in sea-fishing.

Dover — Almost immediately west of Deal, separated only by its continuation, Walmer, by St. Margaret's, once famous for its prawns, and the Foreland, the famous port of Dover offers somewhat different fishing. The ground generally is rougher, so that we have on summer evenings an amount of pollack-railing close to the beach that is unknown at Deal. From the piers, there is not perhaps very much sport to be had; the new Promenade Pier has been ruined by the insensate scraping ("cleaning," I believe it is called locally) of the piles of all the weeds and mussels that render them so attractive to the different fish; and the Admiralty Pier is too lofty to be a convenient spot for angling, not to mention the continual arrival and departure of mail steamers. There is nevertheless a certain amount of hand-lining in the autumn for codling and whiting over the west parapet, whence also radiate the "weavers' beams," on which local anglers, baiting with ragworm, are said, though I never witnessed their triumph, to catch fine grey mullet in August.

For the following useful notes I am indebted to my friend Surgeon-General Paske, who resides at Dover, and has consequently opportunities of watching every change of grounds.

One of the best all-round grounds is on the west side of the Admiralty, anchoring the boat opposite the first horizontal ventilator of the tunnel and in line with the staff on which they hoist the weather-signals—*i.e.*, about half-way up the Admiralty. On this rough ground, as well as on a more sandy one fringed with rocks, and situated somewhat further west, just before you come opposite the spot at which they are now boring, you may catch large pollack on the drift-line, and, in autumn, cod on the paternoster. There is yet a third good ground still further on, beyond "Gatehouse's Den," and just off the spot at which the fresh-water spring empties itself on the beach.

To the eastward, and at intervals as far as the South Foreland, there are several grounds, two of the best being that opposite the caves, a little beyond the jetty; and another, somewhat better as a rule, in a line with the outer end of the jetty and just beneath the coastguard station, where the zig-zag pathway up the face of the cliffs just comes in view. Bait, never easy to obtain at Dover, is becoming an increasing difficulty with every succeeding year. Rockworms were hard to procure last season, even at the very fair price of 1$s.$ a score, whereas three or four years ago they could generally be bought for one-third of that sum. Ragworms, good bait at times, though always inferior to the last, are plentiful in the mud of the harbour, though it is not always easy to find any one to dig them. Squid is brought ashore, *if bespoken*, by the smacks from the Varne grounds outside; otherwise, not being in any demand among local professionals, it is thrown overboard with appropriate language. Mussels of good quality and large size are imported by Drincqbier, the fishmonger (Snargate Street), and cost about 10$d.$ per gallon.

To these notes of Mr. Paske, I may add that some hand-lining is done from the wooden jetty off what is known as the "Mole Rock," soft crab being a first-rate, though not always procurable, bait; and pollack of fair size are sometimes landed on summer evenings from the breakwaters at the east end of the town.

Eastbourne, see *Hastings and district*.

One of the best spots for bass before the trammel and trawl had swept the coast clean of these fish, Exmouth can now be regarded only as a second-

Exmouth

rate station for sea-fishing, though the whiting-fishing is excellent in the fairway throughout the autumn months. There is the usual July mackerel-railing in the bay, and good pout-fishing on the rough ground towards Salterton. Mr. Hare informs me that he used to get good sport with the bass here a few years ago—best fish 10¼lb.—mooring the boat off the jetty at the flood tide, and baiting with the living sand-eel, which he had to sean at low water on the bar.

Fowey I have practically fished most of the best grounds outside Fowey from the neighbouring village of Mevagissey (*q.v.*), but Mr. Collingwood Lee sends me some notes of the inshore-fishing. There is the great variety characteristic of Cornish fishing, pollack, sharks, dog-fish of all kinds, conger, mackerel, garfish ("longnoses"), large gurnard ("tubs"), bream, whiting, pout, flat-fish, and the chance of a bass. There was formerly—it is somewhat deteriorated, but not altogether a thing of the past—good general fishing at the mouth of the harbour, a convenience in rough weather. Mr. Lee caught on one occasion a quantity of small conger there, running up to 5 lbs., with rod and gut line and in hot sunshine; on another, he was so fortunate as to catch a 9 lb. bass on a hand-line half way up the harbour, and at night. Bait—squid, mussels, pilchard, &c.—is easily obtained. Boats cost from 30*s*. to 35*s*. per week, according to size. Tomlin, either of the Pills of Polruan, or "Captain" Rice can be recommended. There is good whiffing-ground for pollack right along the coast to Polperro or westward to Par Bay, and the bream- and whiting-grounds are some way out.

Hastings and district At one time I knew Hastings and all the coast for half-a-dozen miles either way like a book, as I fished there for part of at least a dozen summers in succession. It is now three years, however, since I fished there, and I have therefore supplemented my recollections of the place with some hints by a resident. There are two piers at Hastings, or, more correctly, one there and another about a mile to the westward, at St. Leonard's. From the former, I have taken a few, a very few, bass, conger up to 6 or 7 lbs. weight, and pout by the thousand, but of small size. The stone groynes at the east end of the town, beyond the fish-market, yield innumerable "fresh-water" eels, as well as an occasional bass, which surprises no one more than its captor. As the ground off these breakwaters is very rough, consisting of parallel reefs of rock uncovered at low water and typical of this part of the coast, float-tackle and a rod are the best method here, though hand-lines with heavy throw-out leads continue, in spite of breakages without number, the favourite local gear. As bait, a slice of fresh herring, bloater, or squid is as good as anything. The "marks" for boat-fishing are many, but the following will suffice :—

(1) A good ground for plaice and ground-fish generally lies off Bopeep, and is found by rowing straight out opposite the east end of the cutting behind which the Eastbourne trains disappear, until the entrance to the old pier is just under the Castle.

(2) The Castle Rocks, good for pout and conger, are found by rowing straight out from the Albert Memorial until you get the brewery chimney (in the old town) half way along High Wickham.

(3) Another good patch of rock was found by getting the head of the old pier in line with the inner end of the largest stone breakwater, and rowing south-west until off the west side of Warrior Square, when the course was altered, and the boat taken about fifty yards nearer the land.

(4) Mr. Henry Dowsett, of Hastings, sends me the bearings of a famous ground for summer flat-fish and autumn whiting. It is found by rowing straight out from the dust destructor, under the East Hill, until Fairlight Church stands well out over the hill.

(5) I am indebted to the same correspondent for the "marks" of the "Castle Hard," for dabs and whiting, viz., straight offshore from the fish-market till Fairlight Church stands out clear.

(6) The "Hooks Hard" is reached by rowing straight out from Fairlight until you open the barn on the opposite side of the glen.

Mr. Dowsett suggests that Mr. Ball, of Wall's End, Pevensey, would give all information about the Bopeep fishing, the grounds for which vary according to season.

The fishing at Bexhill is practically the same; but in

October and November there is an inshoring of cod, which are then caught from boats moored over the rocks, not more than a couple of hundred yards from the beach. The bait most used is the whelk; and King has, or had, all that is necessary in the way of boats. Off Eastbourne, especially towards Beachy Head, there is a good deal of rough ground on which at times fairly good fishing is had for pollack and bream, as well as pout by day and conger of an evening. There has always been much spinning for pollack from the pier here; but I never caught much myself, nor, indeed, saw any one else do so. It seemed, in fact, as if much of the fictitious excellence of this pier depended on the fact that a charge was made for the right of fishing; and that folks imagined, as they so often do, that it must be warranted by something particular in the sport to be obtained. I believe that the fishing has, curiously enough, somewhat improved of late years. If so, this is indeed exceptional!

For the following notes on Irish coast fishing I have **Irish** to thank Sir H. W. Gore-Booth and the Rev. W. **Coast** S. Green. All around the rocky shores of the west there is good summer pollack-fishing, a large white-winged fly with red body generally giving good results. The mouth of the Kenmare River is good water. As it is often, however, a question in Ireland of hotel accommodation, the sea-angler will not do much better than Waterville, where there are first-rate accommodation and great variety of fish.

Another place that both correspondents recommend is Valentia, and, as at all other points on the Irish coast where there is a regular mackerel fishery, bait is not, as a rule, difficult to procure. East of these places, at Carthtownshend and Baltimore, the fishing is good, but the hotels cannot compare with those at Waterville.

The india-rubber eel is coming into use among the coast-fishermen, who are also taking to gut snooding for their mackerel-railing.

Mr. Green says that there is much excitement in a good night among the hake, but the fisherman must not mind anchoring well outside the headlands in the ocean swell.

Good sport could also be obtained at Mullaghmore,

co. Sligo, where there are some lodges (belonging to the Hon. Evelyn Ashley) that can be taken by the month.

The port of Arundel, without offering anything exactly brilliant in the way of sea-fishing, has at least this advantage, that in rough weather there is at times something to be done with the grey mullet from the quays. The grey mullet is, in fact, *the* fish hereabouts, at any rate between May and September (October, in warm years), and the correct way of taking it is to moor your boat out by the east beacon during the neap tides at daybreak, that is, on the flood, and fish with a light paternoster of four hooks, baiting with the ragworm. The boat is anchored at the bow and made fast aft to a tree between the last two posts. This worm may almost without fail be procured from Carpenter, one of the railway porters, who gets it from Ford. When the water is much disturbed, so as to prevent the mooring of the boat in the right way, anglers climb on the beacon itself, making the boat fast alongside, and using a long-handled landing-net. Many fish from the Beacon by preference in all weathers. Other spots for this mullet-fishing are the railway-quay, just above the higher ferry, the slaughter-house, just below this and also on the left bank, and the old hulk on the other side of the river.

Littlehampton

Next to the mullet, the bass is the most coveted fish of the Arun estuary, and it is angled for in a variety of ways, one of the most novel being that practised above Arundel when the spring floods have sent plenty of salt water into those reaches, the bait being a live roach or dace. E. Slaughter, of Market Square, Arundel, knows all about this fishing, and provides boat and baits for the day for 15s., which includes his own attendance. There are several Slaughters at Arundel, so be sure you ask for Edward. For the mullet-fishing in the harbour, I can thoroughly recommend G. Pelham, who owns several boats.

The deep-sea fishing at Littlehampton is of no high order, the Kingmere Rocks, six or seven miles to the south-east being about the only ground; and even on these, sport is anything but certain.

There is more than one tackle shop in the town, and at Arundel there are two, Pain's and Tisdall's.

Not far east of Fowey lies the little Cornish harbour

Looe of Looe, one of the best stations on that coast for pollack-fishing. Mr. Collingwood Lee recommends as boatmen Pengelly or either of the Toms, boats costing about 6s. per day, or 30s. per week. The pollack run to at least 12 lbs., and one of the best grounds is eastward from the Bell Buoy off Downderry, or on the "Black hedge" to the westward. In the stormy days of late autumn, large pollack are taken in quite shallow water between the island and mainland. Pilchard bait for drift-lining is easily obtainable; while for whiffing, they use very large black or dark green artificial eels, which, although twice the size of those met with elsewhere, seem to answer capitally with the large pollack hereabouts. Occasionally, small lampreys, a very killing bait in these waters, can be had. To the west of the island generally, the water is deep and excellent for whiffing. Polperro, between Looe and Fowey, has also a small harbour, and is an equally good station, the fishing being to all intents and purposes the same as that obtained off the neighbouring ports.

There is perhaps no more remarkable fact in the scenery of our south coast, though compara- **Lulworth** tively little known even to passing yachtsmen, than the sudden change of character in the outline of the coast between Swanage and Weymouth. It is a sudden corner of Devon transported, side by side with the tamer Hampshire sandstone. It is isolated; for there is none of the grandeur of the cliffs round Durdle Door a mile or so further west, and the heights round Weymouth Bay are mild to a degree. In the very centre of this brief spell of lofty precipice breaks the little cove of Lulworth. The whole population, which consists, East Lulworth included, of a few hundreds, is devoted to the lobster industry, the men catching, the women boiling and packing. In the beautiful little cove itself, where the water is usually clear as in the tank of an aquarium, there is no fishing, though I have been told there of bass hooked at the entrance. Outside, however, and without much need of exact marks, there is good pollack fishing right up to the cliffs, one favourite anchorage being about 200 yards off Durdle Door, the finest natural archway on the south coast. Another good ground is to the eastward, where you open the top of

Lulworth Castle. Of so little account were "marks" when I was last there, that we used to let the boat drift alongshore and pick up pollack here, there, and everywhere. Bait is the great difficulty at Lulworth, far more so than at Dover. The worm from the shell of the hermit-crab is about the best, but it is not easy to get the men to set enough pots on the right ground (*not* the best lobster-ground). Ragworms are also got by post from Weymouth, but they are not cheap, and arrive as often as not dying or dead, in which condition they are useless.

Lulworth lies, like the Cornish hamlets, off the railroad, the station being Wool (pronounced 'Ool), six miles distant, if I remember rightly. The most pleasant way, however, of reaching the place, save for those who desire a dusty and unpicturesque drive through Hardy's country, is by steamer from Bournemouth or Weymouth. Steamers run most frequently from the latter port. There is a good ground two or three miles out known as the "Shell Beach," where bream are many and large. A good boat, with two men, is necessary for this, and a whole day is usually given up to it. Boatmen are almost more of a problem at Lulworth than even bait; for the men seem to prefer their regular occupation among the crabs and lobsters to the casual patronage of visitors from town, nor can it be said that they know very much about hook fishing; 30*s.* a week satisfies them, however, though bait will be found an item, especially if it has to be got daily from Weymouth. I have seen small eels, rather above the elver stage, in the ditch that runs down the only street; these might possibly be caught in a small trap, and should make excellent pollack-baits for whiffing.

About midway between Fowey and Falmouth is the harbour town of Mevagissey, at which are important sardine-factories, under the management of that keen observer of fish life, Mr. Matthias Dunn, to whom Buckland, Couch, and Day, not to mention almost every living ichthyologist in this country, have acknowledged frequent indebtedness. Knowing Mevagissey well myself (I was fishing there a month ago) I shall describe one or two matters in detail as characteristic of Cornish sea-fishing (than which it may be doubted whether these islands offer any better) generally. The coast here-

Meva-
gissey

abouts, as throughout the Duchy, is bold and rocky, the Deadman, or Dodman, being the most magnificent bluff for miles either way. Off this Dodman, which is, in a good breeze, twenty minutes' sail west from Chapel Point, is some first-rate rough ground for pollack close inshore; but it is uncertain some years, and the chad and squid are at all times a greater nuisance than on the outer grounds. The former may, it is true, be hooked, and a slab of tough chad is no bad bait for pollack. The squid, however, worry the hooks with impunity. Time after time the angler, feeling the sharp backward jerks that betray the presence of one of these cephalopods, thinks that he has at length hooked the intruder; but, though he may coax it almost within reach of the landing-net, only a proper "jigger," made by filing the barbs off three conger-hooks and lashing the latter in a triangle, will hold them. Mevagissey Bay, properly speaking, lies within Chapel Point to the west and Penaer Point to the eastward, where it adjoins St. Austell Bay. This inshore water, which is usually calm, affords in the summer plenty of whiffing for mackerel and small pollack, and there is a good "sand" off Penaer for flat fish and gurnard. The best grounds, however, lie outside, and the following are the principal :—

For bass—moored off the Gwingeas, or close to Chapel Point. For pollack—Tom Ash (off Fowey); Australia (west of the Gribbin); Martin Vane and Point of the Zone (off the Turbot Head, three miles out); Moldeser; the Deadman, etc. For Whiting—Martin Vane (off the rocks). For Conger—just off the Blackhead, or about a mile off Chapel Point, opening a certain tree behind the Turbot Head. It would be useless to give bearings, as a fisherman is always employed.

There was once on a time very good bass-fishing round the Gwingeas, anchoring about 100 yards east of them on a flowing tide, or whiffing on all sides; and I recollect when I was fishing at Mevagissey for a couple of months in 1894, "Sarcelle," keenest of sea-fishers, who is, I understand, soon to cast his hooks once more in the Channel, sending me glowing accounts of the bass he once caught there. His "Mogador dodge," which he exhorted me to try, is so good that I give a cut of it. It consists merely of two hooks four inches apart, the gut surmounted by a "baby," and from the bend of each hook trails a strip of fresh herring or other fish. He particularly recommended strips from the belly of a bass, but, alas! there were few bass when I was there last.

SARCELLE S "MOGADOR" BAIT.

Dynamite and other poaching methods had already done their work. I hooked but one—and lost it!—off Chapel Point.

Bait for ordinary fishing presents, as throughout Cornwall, no difficulty. Fresh pilchards enough for a day's fishing can be bought for a few pence, and mackerel may be taken by "plummeting" (p. 62) on the way out to the grounds. It is unusual indeed to run short of bait, but it is only necessary to up anchor and sail round for another mackerel or two; or if there are any chad abroad —they generally put in an appearance early in the day— a slice from one of them, silvery and far tougher than the freshest pilchard (if pilchard is not absolutely fresh, it is as flabby as sodden paper), makes a first-rate bait for the pollack, though not always appreciated by the ground-fish.

As to boats and men, they are still to be had in the Duchy at a moderate cost, 35$s.$ a week being considered fair. When the proper spirit of piracy has, as it inevitably must do with the development of Cornish railways, found its way west of Plymouth, I shall go abroad for my sea-fishing, or at any rate to the north of Scotland or west of Ireland. My own man is George Marshall, but I have also heard well of Bob Blight (of Port Mellon) and Mills.

In concluding these remarks upon the subject of Cornwall as a fishing resort, I give one hint which will, I think, if acted upon, save a deal of unpleasantness and misunderstanding on both sides. Treat your boatman and everyone else with whom you come in contact as thoroughly honest folk. Do not suspect them of being up to the cockney tricks and impositions that are rife at seaside places nearer town. Do not be afraid of leaving your purse or watch at your lodgings : I would leave mine almost in the streets without fear. If these simple and unsophisticated folk think themselves suspected of instincts foreign to their nature, they will, not unreasonably, make themselves unpleasant at the very times when your sport and comfort depend on their willingness to oblige.

Above all do not, whatever you do, "put on side" with them. It will not impress them, and the only result is to place these freer children of nature in a very favourable light beside the more stilted manners of cities.

For the following very useful notes I am indebted to Dr. W. J. Simpson Ladell, of the Gresham and British Sea Anglers' Societies.

Mounts Bay and the Scillies "There is such a variety of fish to be caught, as well as so many methods of catching them, at these spots, that the angler finds a long holiday all too short and a short holiday is reckoned with the past almost before it seems to have commenced.

The angler with a long holiday and deep purse can find plenty of men to take him out, at from 15s. to £1 a day, but you can get an equally good man for 6s. or 7s. a day and his food. The Great Western Railway Company runs excursions to Penzance and Scilly during the summer months for 26s. and 31s. respectively. The trains leave at 10 P.M. every Friday and at 7.55 A.M. every Saturday during July, August and September, the journey occupying about twelve hours. But a word to the wise: be at Paddington quite an hour before the train starts, for a corner seat is very desirable on so long a journey. Arrived at Penzance, the angler cannot do better than call on Mr. Rowe, 78 Market Jew Street, about four minutes' walk from the station. He will be able to supply the necessary tackle, will also willingly give every information about boats, baits and fishermen, and may even be able to name suitable lodgings. If able to obtain lodgings with Mrs. Phillips, 1 Regent Square, Penzance, the angler will, I am sure, be comfortable at a reasonable price.

"Captain James, a retired sailor, knows a good many of the marks, is an enthusiastic fisherman, and has a good boat with plenty of beam, rather a consideration when at anchor in a rough sea. Mr. Rowe will be able to give the names and charges of other equally good men.

"But as there are no dangerous tides in Mounts Bay between Cuddan Point and St. Clement's Island, off Mousehole, the angler may prefer to go by himself. He can then hire a small boat from Mr. Nichols, eastern end of Promenade, for 6d. an hour; if baits and lines are supplied, 1s. an hour; and if a lad is sent as well, 1s. 6d. an hour.

"If the angler wishes to go whiffing or railing, he can do so in any part of the bay, but early morning and evening are the best times; with neap tides and light westerly wind, he is sure to have good sport among the mackerel, pollack, and, during July and August, bass. The best places to whiff or rail are from Rayman to Cuddan Point; round the Gear Pole, and from Newlyn Lighthouse to Low Lee Buoy; also (but this is further afield) from Mousehole to Lamorna Cove. Still further west, there is good whiffing inside the Runnel Stone Buoy, but the tide here runs at times so strong, one should never venture to fish without an experienced boatman. A method of fishing for bass at this point is called "Kentling," the hook is baited, thrown over without a sinker, and carried out by the tide. The Sennen fishermen use the same method in bream-fishing, only they have crab instead of pilchard as bait.

"When tired of whiffing and railing, the angler can turn his attention to bottom-fishing. To do this with advantage he must either know something of the marks or have some one with him who does. Mr. J. B. Cornish, to whom I am indebted for some of the marks given below, tells me there are more than forty recognised marks in Mounts Bay. The principal are: Tower and Long Hedge, twelve fathoms at high water; the Coath, twelve fathoms at high water; the Burntships, sixteen fathoms at high water; tail of the Island, thirteen fathoms at high water; White Houses, fifteen fathoms at high water; Low Lee, nine fathoms at high water; Gaddy Madden, twenty fathoms at high water; Boscowen, eleven fathoms at high water; south-east Gear, nine fathoms at high water.

"There is good conger ground one mile south-east of Penzance called *The Coynes*; the marks are Madron

Union over middle hummock of Battery Rocks and Tower on Long Hedge.

"*The Ebble*, for pollack and conger; marks, two houses south of Pentee Point just peeping and Captain Carew's (white house) over Penzance Lighthouse.

"*Gaddy Madden*, $3\frac{1}{2}$ miles south from Penzance; marks, Paul Tower over old pier-head of Mousehole with Logan Rock over Bucks Point; fish: conger, pollack, ling, cod, hake; neap tide and rounding of either ebb or flood, best times.

"*Gazzan*, $1\frac{1}{2}$ miles south-east from Lamorna Point; marks, Owen's house over Carn Dhu and St. Mary's Tower over height of Mousehole Island; good whiting.

"*Outer Stennack*, within half-a-mile of Lamorna Cove; marks, Logan Rock on Bucks Point and Mousehole Island peeping with Kimiel Point; big fish generally; easily reached from Lamorna, where boats can be hired from 2s. a day, but they are few in number.

"*Porthgwana* has good fishing, especially for bream. Kentling should be practised here. Get into an eddy and let bait go with tide. Tides here run very strongly. It is unsafe to go out unless accompanied by one who knows the neighbourhood.

"*Sennen:* grand fishing for pollack, bream, conger, but dangerous to go out without fisherman. To reach it, take 'bus from market-place, Penzance, at 9 A.M., this goes fairly direct; or brakes run through the summer, but stop at places of interest for the benefit of tourists, and take three times as long. Peter George, Villa Cottage, Sennen, charges 6s. a day, and can also accommodate lodgers. He is a very good fellow and knows the marks.

"At *Porth Curno*, good flat fish can be caught as the bottom is sandy, also large plaice, turbot, ray, skate, &c. Having tested these places, the angler can continue his trip to Scilly, his ticket allowing him to break his journey at Penzance. Embarking from the pier at Penzance, he lands in about three hours at St. Mary's. There are two hotels in the place, but I know nothing of their charges; there should, however, be no difficulty in finding lodgings. Matthew Nichols, who works for Mr. Frank Watts of Old Town, and is better known as the only barber on the island, will be able to give particulars of boats, boatmen and their charges. Perhaps some of the boatmen may be willing to take in lodgers.

"There are so many rocks, reefs and ledges round the coast, and the tide runs so strongly, that it would be very unwise for the angler to go far from shore without a companion who knows the neighbourhood, for the sea has a nasty knack of suddenly becoming very rough and turbulent, apparently without reason; but with a good boat and careful boatman there is no cause for anxiety.

"Whiffing and railing, one catches mackerel and pollack, the latter up to 15 or 20 lbs. I also caught a gurnard whiffing. Bottom-fishing is good; anywhere in Crow Sound bream, chad, pollack, gurnard, wrasse, and dogfish can be caught on the bottom. About $1\frac{1}{2}$ to 5 miles from Old Town Bay is good conger ground; this summer I caught ling to 26 lbs., ray 14 lbs., sharks and dogfish on this ground. Round the Eastern Islands one is sure to get good pollack. Off Seven Stones is good pollacking, while to the westward, from St. Agnes round Annett, especially round the Ruddy Rock and the Renneys, good pollack are found. The angler should spare a few minutes when so near Annett to pay it a visit, for it is the breeding-ground of gulls, puffins, and other fowl, and the burrows of the puffin are well worth examining. But the great desire of every angler is to go to Pol, about ten miles west from St. Mary's and three from the Bishop Lighthouse. With a good boat, a good crew, and a stomach able to bear the swell, and the tide dead neap, you are sure to have sport—conger of 60 lbs., cod 30 lbs. ling 40 lbs., turbot 14 lbs., sharks and dogfish innumerable; no small fish, the hooks and baits being too large for them. Fishing in fifty fathoms with a sinker of from 4 to 7 lbs. and a line as thick as a lead pencil, you feel after a day at Pol that you never knew what fishing was until then, and long after the fish have gone the way of their kind your aching limbs and back and blistered hands will remind you of that red-letter day.

"I do not give any marks for the fishing off the Scillies, as you must have a boatman and he will know them. In conclusion, I must again express my thanks to Mr. J. B. Cornish and Phil Nichols, Trinity Pilot of Penzance, for giving me particulars of the fishing marks in Mounts Bay, most of which I have used when fishing there. One last word, beware of the gentlemen in blue jerseys who haunt the quay. They will take you out in their boats for an exorbitant price, will cast anchor just where they think, and will, after a few hours, take you home again fishless and disgusted with the place. The only fishing they understand is connected with your purse, and if they can get a good haul they are quite satisfied with their day's sport."

Plymouth. At all times a favourite and important station, it must be admitted that the fishing at Plymouth has fallen off sadly of late years, and grounds that were long famous have now got quite worthless. Mr. Hearder has been compiling a list of up-to-date "marks" for local fishing, and I have persuaded him to let me have the use of them for this volume. They are certainly, if all correct (and there is no reason whatever to doubt their being so), about the most thorough collection of local fishing-grounds I have ever seen together. I give them *seriatim*:—

(1) The *Flat Rock*, just inside the Mallard Buoy (good for pollack-whiffing on the ebb tide): Teats Hill House, in line with flagstaff on the corner of the emigration depot, and the coastguard flagstaff at Batten over the second chimney of the coastguard cottages.

(2) *Diamonds* (pollack): The centre chimney in clump of five on citadel over white patch by the ladies' bathing place, and the flagstaff at Batten over centre chimney of coastguard station.

(3) *Cobbler Deeps* (pollack, or three or four boats' lengths east or west for pout and whiting): Red patch of sand under coastguard station at Batten in line with white house at Turnchapel, and flagstaff on the citadel in line with large clump of chimneys on citadel.

(4) *Black Ball* (good on flood-tide for whiting on the bottom, or pollack on drift-lines, and lies off Withy Hedge): Get the chimney of a solitary house on Staddon Hills over the gap at Withy Hedge, and Sherwell chapel in line with the new church.

(5) *Leek Beds* (pollack): Get the corner of Bovisand Fort in line with the clump of furze in Bovisand field, and the tower of Norrington's manure works in line with Gibbs's chimney. The outer end of these beds is marked by the white buoy on what is known as the Duke Rock.

APPENDIX.

(6) A good spot for pollack on the ebb is found by getting the two lamps on the lifeboat pier at the Great Western Docks in line with the spire of the Catholic Cathedral, and the Smeaton Tower on the Hoe over the west end of West Hoe Terrace.

(7) Another excellent ground for large pollack and pouting a couple of hours before high water: Get the clock of the Victualling Yard between the two pillars at the entrance of the coastguard station at Devil's Point, and the flagstaff on the Hoe in the centre of West Hoe Terrace.

(8) The *Mewstone*: There is good whiffing for pollack, with occasional bass, all round this rock throughout the summer, early morning being the best time. Beyond the Mewstone to the eastward is a group of rocks known as the "Slimers," and just south of these is one of the best spots in the neighbourhood for large bream; best time, half tide.

(9) The *Shagstone*: A rock standing by itself between the breakwater and the Mewstone, easily found by the beacon on it.

(9) The *Breakwater*: There is some fishing from a boat anchored just outside the east end of the breakwater on the flood tide, rather heavy leads being necessary. At the west end of the breakwater is a good spot for large pollack and sometimes bass, also outside on the rocky shoal between the Knap and Panther buoys.

(10) The *Knap Deep*: This consists of a bed of rocks bordering the Horn Channel, and rising a fathom or two above the bottom. It lies about 600 yards eastward of the Knap Buoy, which should be brought in line with Kingsand, and the edge of the platform of the breakwater lighthouse against the casement of the Stonehouse battery. This is also a first-rate night ground for conger. Unfortunately, this ground lies right in the way of vessels entering and leaving the Sound, so that a conspicuous mast-head light must be used.

(11) The *Tinker Shoal*, another pollack ground: It is marked by a buoy at either end, known respectively as the East and West Tinker, outside east end of Breakwater.

(12) The *Horn Channel*, on which the ground-fishing

is at times good, though uncertain, the bottom consisting of coarse gravel and shell. It runs from near the breakwater seawards for about three-quarters of a mile: Get the clump of trees above the ladies' bathing-place underneath the Hoe in line with the spire of the new church.

(13) *Penlee Point*: Good sport is often had off here in the summer months with pollack and bass, artificial bait often killing well. Fishing is carried on both from boats and the rocks.

(14) The *Quinnows*: A ledge of rocks round the Rame Head, where there are at times large pollack and bass. The weed hereabouts is very long, and plays havoc with tackle of every description, and the gear must be fine and strong.

(15) There is a good spot for *ground-fishing* between Redding Point and the west end of the breakwater. A paternoster baited with mussel and worm, squid, or herring is the best method of fishing here, and skate are rather common.

(16) For *conger* fishing at night, one of the best grounds lies about a mile south-west of the Rame Head.

(17) For *whiting*, the following are three of the best grounds:—

(*a*) Get Maker Tower on the heights above Mount Edgcumbe just to the left of Penlee Point, and the Moor Hills over the point of the rocks at the mouth of the Yealm.

(*b*) Get Mount Batten Castle in a line with Penlee Point, and the solitary clump of trees on Wembury Hill over the summit of the Mewstone.

(*c*) Get the eastern battery on Maker Heights in line with Penlee Point, and the point of Moor, to the eastward, over the centre of the field above Yealm Gut.

The Plymouth whiting-ground may be said to be reached when you get far enough down the western channel to look well up Yealm Gut.

Porth-leven
Another station of which I have received some account from Mr. Collingwood Lee is the little hamlet of Porthleven, between the Lizard and Land's End, where, he says, the pollack run larger than at most other Cornish grounds. The weather is, however, most uncertain, and the seas run high. Besides a quantity of pollack, Mr. Lee got plenty of mackerel and

a cod of 11 lbs. The pollack-grounds appear to lie closer inshore than at most places. Accommodation is not costly, as there is a comfortable inn, charging only £2 a week, and 6s. was the daily charge for a large boat and two men. Amateurs rarely visit the place, and the aborigines were much surprised to find what large pollack could be killed on the rod and "capstan," as they insisted on calling the winch. The harbour is sufficient for the requirements of trawlers, but is said to be unsafe at times. The sea breaks with great force on the ledge of rocks on either side. Those who care about the experience of going out with the long liners, and seeing them kill tons of conger, ling, and the like, cannot choose a better place than Porthleven.

Very different in character from the fishing on the Cornish and Devon coasts is that obtainable at Ramsgate, where the conditions closely resemble those already given for Deal and Dover. I know no sea-angler with a longer and more varied experience of this place than Captain Lambton Young, who so often presides, unless prevented by ill health, at the B.S.A.S. meetings. He writes me that the best time for the fishing is August to October. As to "marks," almost anywhere about three miles off the coast, or even off the red buoy just west of the harbour, where you may get a good catch of whiting or flat-fish. Also, off Sandwich, in the small Downs, and right up to the North Foreland, is all good ground. Boats usually keep inside the Goodwins, one favourite ground being about three to four miles due north of Deal pier and two to two and a half miles off Sandwich. Lug, dug in the mud of Pegwell Bay, or bought of the bait-dealers in the town, is considered the best bait, but squid, obtained from the trawlers, is also much used. Boats cost about 2s. an hour, but an arrangement can usually be made by the week.

Ramsgate

Mr. Lee, to whom I have been indebted for so many useful notes in the foregoing pages, sends me a few lines on the sea-fishing obtainable in the Channel Islands, and more particularly at Sark. Though it is much vaunted—and I have had some first-rate sport myself yachting off Guernsey—Mr. Lee does not consider the fishing in these islands any better than that

Sark

in Cornwall, if indeed as good. Turbot are a feature of the bag in these parts; my correspondent killed one of 12 lbs. on the rod, and found it much like hauling a deal table through the water. The local bait is sand-eel; and Mr. Lee is very rightly of opinion that, if we could but get this bait in Cornwall, it would not be difficult, if desired, to sink a boat with fish. The coast is very dangerous, and the tides run close inshore with such terrific force that at times when only about a quarter of a mile from the harbour, it is necessary to sail or row right round the island and make the harbour from the other direction. Thus a large boat and two men are necessary, the charge being 25s. a week for their boat and services and 18s. a week to the hotel for their lunch. This includes a small bottle of Bass each; they will not drink draught ale! Driot, Guille, and Pierre Hamon are all good men. The hotel (Bel Air) is comfortable, and charges only £2 a week.

Scarborough

Among the many places at which sea-fishing has not altered for the better of late years is that somewhat over-popular resort Scarborough. Ten or fifteen years ago the sport was excellent, but it is now described by a resident as "not good." Mr. Clarke sends me the following "marks" of modern grounds, and points out that the best fishing is that with the rod for rock-cod (up to 28 lbs.) in the winter months. The best ground for general ground-fishing throughout the year is got by sailing due east from the harbour a couple of miles out to sea until the light can be seen shining through the windows of the Castle. Then Scalby Mills should be visible on the north and Cayton waterworks on the south. Mackerel are hooked in summer in the tideway a couple of hundred yards from the east pier, the best plan being to anchor the boat and "stream" with unleaded lines, practically drift-lining.

For winter cod-fishing the following are two good grounds :—

(1) A deep hole directly beneath the South Steel Battery and a couple of hundred yards from the pier.

(2) The Ramsdale Scar, opposite the Grand Hotel.

There is also much rock-fishing, particularly from the White Nab, two miles south of the town; Knipe Point, about one and a half miles beyond; and Redcliffe, two

APPENDIX. 235

miles further still. To the north, the Castle foot is all good ground, and there are favourite spots at Scalby Ness, one mile out of the town; Colam Hole, two and a half miles; Cloughton Wyke, five miles; and Peak, ten and a half miles, the last two being reached by the Scarborough and Whitby Railway.

The fishing is rough work, and much tackle is lost, but the fish are often of large size. A Scarborough reel of seven inches diameter is used, and the hemp line in local favour costs no more than 6*d*. for about seventy yards, so that breakages do not entail much expense. The best rod is ten feet in length, and must be very strong, as it is often necessary to hold the head of a large fish up, else it will sulk under the rocks.

Mr. Wilcocks has written so much of the bass-fishing at Shoreham with the drift-line and living sand-eel, that it is unnecessary to give the subject more than brief mention in this place. In four seasons, Mr. Wilcocks took at this place a total of 150 bass, which is more than most of us see in ten. His best season's score was 62, and he got the *only* bait from the Brighton seaners, who were after whitebait in the harbour.   *Shoreham*

The best grounds outside are the Kingmere Rocks, six miles off Littlehampton, ten from Shoreham; and the "Billy Boy," otherwise a wreck of a ship that was conveying Portland stone to the harbour for the building of Lancing College. One huge stone burst through her, so heavily did she ride at her anchors, and she foundered immediately with all hands except one boy. It is not always easy to pick up, in consequence of which one of the local fishermen generally leaves a buoy and line to mark it; the north, or shore, mark being a certain barn over another indescribable building; the other mark, which is often obscured in certain winds by the Brighton smoke, involving the use of a steeple in Brighton and a building somewhat nearer.

This ground is good for pollack; but the former, which I have fished from Littlehampton, is better.

For the following list of grounds and spots in repute among local anglers at Southampton, I am indebted to Mr. Campbell Macpherson, of that town. I have now and again had excellent sport   *Southampton* from a yacht anchored close to the moorings of the German Lloyd steamers, the whiting in October running much larger than those which I had taken on the more open grounds out in the Solent. The local baits are soft crab and mudworms, and these are indeed the characteristics of most harbour and estuary towns.

Mr. Macpherson's list is as follows :—

Marchwood : for bass trolling.

Coal-hulk off pier : paternostering for bass.

Gymp : smaller bass and ground fish.

Pier : mostly eels ; some mullet and bass.

Town Quay : small mullet and bass.

Inner Dock, Lock Pit, Deals Jetty, Empress Dock, and Dublin Jetty : all mullet.

Extension Jetty : pout, eels, and flat fish.

Medea Buoy : whiting and flat fish.

Bell Buoy (off mouth of the Itchen): plenty of small bass.

A good whiting-ground about 300 yards south of Hythe Pier.

From the Guard-ship, Netley, down to Calshot is fair all-round fishing.

Mr. Larbalestier, who has fished much at Southampton, tells me that there is a short spell of bass-railing at the end of May, in which the bait is a bunch of ragworms on two salmon hooks dressed on double gut. This arrangement is trailed in the ordinary way behind small boats, the ground being, however, limited to a channel of 200 or 300 yards, and the best time being just before low water. The water off Cowes is much fished from Southampton. I have never caught very much off that favourite yachting station, except a fair quantity of whiting in the autumn ; and, as for "marks," "John Bickerdyke" writes me that there are practically no hard and fast marks, boats being anchored 200 or 300 yards off shore, and constantly shifted according to the tide. I understand that anglers caught over 2 cwt. of grey mullet from the quays and piers during one week this August.

Weymouth A good deal of fishing may be had at one season or another in Weymouth Bay, and the best catch I ever made personally was a bag of over 100 whiting, mostly of good size, from the deck of a yacht anchored about 300 yards off the pier, and in not more than a couple of hours. The most character-

APPENDIX

istic sport at this port is the fishing for bass and grey mullet from the piers and bridges. Of the mullet-fishing with macaroni for bait something has already been said; and for the following notes on the bass-fishing at Passage Bridge I have to thank Mr. C. H. Wheeley.

Passage Bridge, he says, spans the inlet between Weymouth and Portland; and although the fishing was perhaps better before the building of the iron bridge, sport is still fairly good if you hit on the right tide.

August and September are the months for this sport, and strong tackle must be used, as the best fish are taken on the spring tides, which run swift in these parts. The largest bass are usually taken at night, at the half flood, the bait being strips of mackerel, soft crab, live shrimp, squid (locally, "quiddle"), or, when procurable, living sand-eel. The "Wagtail," trimmed on wire, is a good artificial bait. Most of Mr. Wheeley's bass were caught here on strips of mackerel; and an angler fishing near him caught on one occasion a bass weighing near 13 lbs., using for bait the head of a mackerel. There is an inn at the Weymouth end of the bridge, giving shelter in dirty weather and refreshment at all times; and the best spot for the bass was alongside this inn, where the point of the wall formed an eddy with the flowing tide. Large fish have to be played to the Portland end of the bridge, where the bank slopes gradually to the water and a long-handled gaff can be used.

Whitstable

Mr. G. R. Clarke sends me a note on the fishing at this place, which one is more apt to associate with the lately ostracised oyster. The fish, he says, are mainly flat-fish (soles, dabs, and plaice, the last-named up to 2 lbs.) and "silver" eels, the bait most used being lugworm. Prince's Channel, 11 miles run from the Nore, seems to be one of the principal waters, and Thomas Knight (charge, 6s. per day) of 45, Albert Street, is recommended as fisherman.

ABROAD.

EUROPE.

North Sea fishing is all practically the same as that obtained on our East Coast, while the sport that offers on the less exposed portions of the west coasts of France and Portugal cannot be said to differ materially from that previously described under the various Channel ports.

There are, however, a number of seas in Europe that are more or less shut off from the outer ocean, differing from it more particularly in their percentage of salt and feeble tides, both of which are important factors in their indigenous fish life. On the fishing that may be had in two of the principal, the Baltic and Mediterranean, I propose offering a few notes from my own log.

Baltic The more northern sea I have not visited since the year 1890, but I then spent nearly a year fishing on the north German coast, and it is unlikely that the conditions should have greatly altered in water so under-fished. It cannot be said that the sport was of a very varied nature, as, for the greater part of the year, plaice, ranging in weight from a few ounces up to 3 lbs., formed the bulk of one's catch. So abundant were these fish, however, and so innocent of the wiles of fine tackle, that it was no feat, baiting with fresh herring, to land three or four score in the course of a couple of hours' fishing from the Warnemünde pier.

The great feature of this Baltic fishing, one which may be ascribed to the low percentage of salt and the considerable number of large rivers that empty themselves into this enclosed sea, is that river fish are, in the summer months at any rate, caught in every estuary within a hundred yards of the open sea in the company of the said plaice and other marine species. Bream of good weight, perch up to 1 lb., bleak in any quantity, all swell the day's catch. I have even heard of jack being caught in this way at the very end of the pier in the salt water, but was not so fortunate as to get one myself, though I had some out of the broad, or Breitling, close by.

The boat-fishing was, owing to the absence of properly known grounds, nothing more than a game of chance, the best catch being an occasional garfish that had accompanied the small mackerel in from the German Ocean.

It is as well to know that the fishing in most of these German rivers is very strictly guarded by the professional fishermen; and to such an absurdity was this carried in the Warnow, the river alluded to, that even the professionals of Warnemünde, the little watering-place at the

APPENDIX.

mouth of the river, were prohibited from angling in the river, all rights being vested in the fishermen of the more important town of Rostock, nine miles higher up.

In the Mediterranean, the sport, though uncertain, is as much bolder as is the accompanying scenery. It is in fact an almost unvarying relation this; the bolder the scenery, the better the sea-fishing. In the more southern sea, it is true, we have far different conditions; the percentage of salt is much greater, the tides are of considerably more account, and, in some inshore places, the water is, if anything, over-fished. Yet the variety of the fish, more especially of breams, gurnards and wrasses, is certain to delight the naturalist, even if the individuals are often too small to give much sport.

Mediterranean

The fact is, the best chance of a good bag, whether of grey mullet in the docks, or of large bream and allied fishes without any English name from the open water outside, is at night, and to accompany a really skilful Italian on a night's expedition and watch his cunning manipulation of groundbaits and horsehair lines and gut traces is an education for any sea-fisherman. The Germans, the Mecklenburgers at any rate, have but the crudest notions of fine tackle, and indeed as long as their fish remain unsophisticated and learn no better from intruding Englishmen, there is little need for them to improve their tackle or vary their methods. The universal worm, unscoured and half dead, impaled on a blunt hook will do all that is necessary.

But with the Italians it is another matter, and there are few of the secrets of angling that are not, in one form or other, known to them. Rods and reels, fine lines of spun black horsehair, gut traces, swivels to lessen friction, different baits and groundbaits to suit certain conditions of wind and weather, all these find a place in the lore of the humblest angler on the rocky shores of the Mediter-ranean, and indeed most of the fraternity belong to the poorer class, so far at least as Italy is concerned.

There are few of the methods alluded to in the fore-going pages that might not with more or less prospect of success be practised in the Mediterranean, though I should from experience be inclined to counsel as little waste of time as possible with artificial baits. Much of the water off Leghorn and Naples looks the very thing, for instance for railing, yet have I rowed and sailed with all manner of rubber eels and various metal delusions without any result whatever. The exception to this, however, is the successful use of a couple of white feathers lashed to a hook and used at night in connection with a torch hung over the bow of the boat, by which means a fine fish known as *dorata* is caught. Gurnards and sea-scorpions are very common in all the deep rock-pools; and grey mullet may often be caught at daybreak in the docks (my best mullet water at Leghorn was at the private quays of the *Ingenio civile* of the Government) with a paste made of arrowroot biscuit and pounded sardines or anchovies. No yachting man should go on a Mediterranean cruise without laying in a few sovereigns' worth of tackle, a stout rod or two and an assortment of hand-lines, leads and hooks, for he will have great opportunities for first-class sea-fishing. Were it not indeed for indiscriminate netting and not a little dynamiting, the fishing of this sea would probably be second to none in the Old World.

AFRICA.

Morocco   "Sarcelle" has told us from time to time in the columns of the *Field* of the excellent sport he enjoyed during his official residence on the Mogador coast, and more than one correspondent has assured me of the mighty fish that may there be hooked, only lamenting that the coast is so exposed that it is often impossible to get out for days, even weeks, together. There is also a little fishing at times outside Tangier Bay, but the fish run small as a rule.

Suez   I have fished in passing at various spots on the Suez Canal, though of course such chance wetting of hooks is of little value in determining the actual sporting value of that waterway. A few small bass off the mole at Port Said and several garfish one daybreak off Ismailia, hooked but lost, three or four small ground-sharks resembling rowhounds, though not identical, and a good catch of black sea bream, none over half a pound in weight, off Suez, these represent my angling acquaintance with the Canal.

APPENDIX.

I nearly had a bit of excitement one evening, however, off Aden, where our steamer had brought up temporarily rather close to the African shore. **Aden** It was only a couple of weeks after the last shark accident had befallen the small divers who immediately surround each boat as soon as the anchor is down. On a stout line and hook snooded on wire-served hemp I lowered a whole mullet of about a pound in weight straight from the ice-chest, and, as fishing was out of the question with so much disturbance on deck, I let the tempting morsel down through the port-hole of my cabin and made the line fast to the bunk. The bait lay at the bottom untouched for several minutes, after which I left the cabin for a moment, returning to find the line straining and stretched to the utmost it would bear. I got my head and arms out of the port and put a steady pressure on the gentleman below, who was boring like a pollack, only a pollack the size of a full-grown giraffe. I think my notion was to summon my cabin steward and get him to pass the line clear on to the deck overhead, when I should possibly be able to haul the shark. I could not, however, get at the electric bell without leaving hold of the line, which, fearing a sudden rush, I dared not think of. To cut the story short, I held on to that fish for nearly ten minutes and at last began to gain steadily, hauling in quite three fathoms without much resistance. From the weight, however, I knew it was a shark of large size; and there was something so unutterably disgusting in the notion of bringing it face to face with me in the gathering darkness and at such close quarters that—I have regretted it ever since—I let the line run out again, which so encouraged the brute at the other end that it wrenched itself free.

The African fishing, however, that is most likely to interest Englishmen is the sea-fishing, deservedly famous, at the Cape. For the following notes **Cape of Good** I am indebted to Mr. H. A. Bryden, whose **Hope** writings on all kinds of African sport are so widely appreciated. He writes:—

"There is probably no part of the world where better or more abundant sea-fishing is to be obtained than at the Cape of Good Hope. The seas there absolutely swarm with fish of many kinds, not a few of which afford very excellent sport to the amateur. Table Bay, Kamps Bay, Fish Hook Bay, and Simon's Bay all offer capital fishing for rod and line. So great are the teeming numbers of Cape fish, that the docks have periodically to be disencumbered of them. At a single clearance of one dock, tons of fish are taken out and thrown away. The best places for the amateur fisherman are certainly Simon's Bay, Kalk Bay, and Muizenberg. These places all lie in the great False Bay, to the east of the Cape Peninsula, and can be reached from Cape Town, of which they are practically suburbs, in an hour or a little over. Good accommodation can be obtained at all these places, especially at Muizenberg and Kalk Bay, which lie close together.

"Sea fishing at the Cape is, as a business, almost entirely in the hands of the Malays. These people are expert fishermen and, whether with sail or oars, handle the long whale-boats, sharp pointed at both ends, in which they ply their trade, extremely well. The best known fish are snoek, kabeljouw, Roman, rooi steenbras, blaauw steenbras, rooi stompneus, seventy four, Hottentot, poeskop, silver fish, Jacob Evertsen, katunker, stokvisch, springer (mullet), klipvisch, king klip visch, hangeberger, windtoy, gurnard, geelbek, sancord, baardmannatje, and paempelmoesje. It will be observed that these are all, or almost all, old-fashioned Dutch names, for, at the Cape, people are essentially conservative.

"Among the rocks at Green Point, Kamps Bay, and Kalk Bay, the angler with rod and line may expect to obtain fair sport with some of the smaller rock fish, such as Hottentots, klip fish, poempelmoesje, king klip fish, and others. The king klip fish (king rock fish) is deservedly esteemed as one of the most delicious of Cape table fish. Speaking generally, it is not to be denied that our northern fishes afford far better eating than most tropical or subtropical kinds. But the Cape fish, although they cannot vie with the best of north European fish in this respect, belong mainly to the south temperate zone, and many of them are really excellent at table. Especially to be singled out are the king klip fish, Roman, sancord, Jacob Evertsen, baardmannatje (little bearded man), poeskop, and rooi stompneus. Many of the larger fish, such as snoek, steenbras, kabeljouw, geelbek, and others are salted for export or pickled for the use of the country people. In fishing from the rocks for the smaller fish I have mentioned, the usual bait is a piece of the tail of a crawfish. These crustaceans, locally known as *kreef*, swarm in Cape waters and are a positive nuisance to the rock-angler. Time after time the fisherman pulls up one of them instead of the Hottentot, or klip fish, or poempelmoesje, for which he is trying. There is a canning factory for crawfish at the Cape, and as many as 16,000 have been landed in a single day.

"If the angler wishes for more exciting sport than fishing from the rocks, he should betake himself to Kalk Bay, and unless he has friends who possess a private boat, hire a boat and crew from the Malay fishermen. Two or three of these men accompany the party and perform the rowing, work the sail, and provide lines and bait. The cost is somewhat extravagant, and is usually from 25s. to 30s. for the day for the whole outfit. Three or four anglers can find room, however, in the long Cape whale-boats, and the divided cost is, after all, not so great. The naval officers at Simon's Bay, who often enjoy first-rate sport, of course employ their own boats.

"Baiting as often as not with a piece of steenje (stone fish), the lines are presently, when the boat is well into the bay, put out and sport begins. Romans, magnificent fish of the most brilliant vermilion, running from two to four or five pounds in weight, are often encountered and give excellent sport. Rooi stompneus (red stumpnose), big, heavy-shouldered fellows, striped in pink and silver, often weighing well over 10 lbs., afford still better runs, and silver fish, katunker, poeskop, geelbek, and many others will probably be encountered. Sometimes a huge steenbras, a grand fish running up to 70 lbs. weight and even more, may be hooked, and the angler has then his hands as full as he cares about. These monsters fight desperately and often break away. Fishing is of late becoming more scientific at the Cape, and some of these heavy fish, such as steenbras, geelbek, kabeljouw, and others are now played and successfully landed with rod and line.

"After an average day's sport off one of the numerous small inlets of False Bay, the hook and line fishermen may usually expect to come in with the bottom of the boat loaded with magnificent fish. In these days, when anglers go so far afield for their sport, fishermen may be well advised to try the Cape seas. The voyage now lasts no more than a trifle over a fortnight, and, as I have hinted, some of the finest sea-fishing in the world lies awaiting the traveller at Cape Town and in its vicinity. The pleasures of this magnificent fishing are greatly enhanced by the fine climate and some of the most beautiful scenery to be found south of the equator."

AUSTRALIA.

There are three principal kinds of amateur sea-fishing practised by Australians: there is the famous schnapper-fishing on the outer reefs; then there is the more restful hand-lining for black bream in the creeks and so-called "harbours"; and, lastly, there is the rock-fishing for groper and other large fish.

I had, during my stay in the colonies, several enjoyable schnapper outings, and belonged, indeed, to two schnapper clubs, admirable institutions, by which the expense of hiring the necessary steam tug and crew for the day is shared by a party of from six to twenty.

Schnapper-fishing. The grounds, otherwise reefs of rocks, lie, as a rule, about two miles from the coast, and there is a constant succession of these reefs along the coasts of New South Wales and Queensland, from Port Jackson northwards past Broken Bay and Moreton Island. The correct thing for really good schnapper fishing is to leave the Circular Quay, Sydney (or any other quay anywhere else), about midnight and steam away to sea so as to drift over the grounds as it is getting light next morning. No anchor is used in this fishing, the tide, which is usually considerable, being allowed to carry the boat broadside on over the reef, so that all the party must necessarily fish from the same side of the boat. As soon as the boat has drifted to the edge of the reef, which is usually announced by the capture of one or two "flatheads," allies of our gurnard that dwell mostly on the sand, lines are hauled aboard, the tug steams back to the other end of the reef and fishing is resumed. It would be useless for any one visiting the colonies to attempt to take his tackle with him, as there are several tackle shops in all the capitals where everything necessary, including special heavy leads and strong hooks with a peculiar twist mounted on very stout snooding, are supplied at low cost. The line—rods would, as I have pointed out, be out of the question— is a hundred yards in length and is usually wound on a cork bung. Two hooks are attached at intervals of a foot above the end to which is fastened the lead. The bait consists of squid and various small fish known as yellowtails, trevally, old wives, etc., and each fisherman of the party is allotted a small heap of assorted baits which one of the crew cuts up and places on the deck opposite the member's number (drawn by ticket) chalked on the gunwale. Besides the schnapper, which is nothing more than a large and powerful red bream, caught of a weight of 30 lbs. (but far more commonly of 3 lbs.) other fish of greater interest to the visiting naturalist than to the resident fishermen (who always curse them as "wrong colour") come to the hook, notably, "leather jackets, a grotesque type of trigger-fish, traglin, morwongs of considerable size, "sergeant bakers," pig fishes, and groupers, as well as the aforementioned flatheads, as soon as the baits lie on the sand. In addition to all these and more, sharks are often a great nuisance, not the small sharks that give trouble on the Cornish coast, but monsters of anything up to 20 feet in length that think nothing of biting off three-quarters of every fish that is being hauled. So fiercely do they swarm round one's boat at times, that there is nothing for it but to steam away to another ground.

For those who cannot stomach the motion of the Pacific, which is at all times considerable, often next door to distressing, there is the quieter pursuit of black bream in the sheltered creeks of Middle Harbour and similar still waters; and this "black brimming" is without a doubt the highest form of sport practised in the colonies.

Black bream

The fisher expert with black bream takes his place with our roachers, and there is certainly no other form of sea-fishing with which I am acquainted, if this inland sport can strictly be called sea-fishing, that involves such delicate handling of the finest of tackle and such careful manipulation of complicated ground-baits. The latter, known as "berley," is no unimportant factor in a day's sport with these fish, and among its ingredients are bran, cheese and tinned salmon, the last-named usually condemned. The line and single hook-snood are of the finest, and some care is taken to moor the boat fore and aft in the right spot with as little disturbance as possible. The best sport is, as with so many other fish, usually obtained at daybreak and sunset, and the summer months (September to March) are the right season.

Of rock-fishing I need say little, as it does not differ materially from the same kind of sport on our own coast. The enthusiast in those parts is certainly not deterred by any amount of dangerous climbing, and some of the favourite grounds round by the North Head, outside Sydney harbour, are only to be reached by clambering down escarpments that might well frighten an ibex.

Rock-fishing

The principal fish sought by these rock-sportsmen is the groper, or grouper, an enormous wrasse that grows to a weight of, I believe, sixty or eighty pounds, though the largest taken quite near Sydney would probably not reach half that weight. In addition to this, the ostensible object of their sport, they sometimes get schnapper of good weight, traglin and flatheads, while leather-jackets and small sharks furnish the "vermin" of the venture.

The chief bait of this rock-fishing is, as indeed all the world over, green crab, and it is thrown out on an unleaded hand-line, the fish when hooked being given little law, but hauled as quickly as possible to the ledge where sits their captor.

The other branches of sea-fishing practised in Australia are of secondary importance. There is the fishing for their so-called "whiting" in the shallows of the Brisbane and other rivers, the angler wading out to meet the rising tide and using a light rod. There

"Whiting"

is also a certain amount of fishing off the sandy beaches, much as on our east coast, but I never saw the beach-fishers catch more than sharks or an occasional foul-hooked "salmon." *Beach-fishing*

The black-fish of Port Jackson and other inlets is caught with a peculiar green weed for bait, a rod being generally used. *Black-fish*

Lastly, there is the great perch of the Fitzroy and other Queensland rivers, wrongly styled "barramunda," which gives great sport on a short stout rod, the bait being a live "skip-jack." *Barramunda*

INDEX.

INDEX.

A

ABERDEEN, 94, 206
Aden, 4, 241
Africa, Sea-fishing in South, 240
Aldeburgh-on-Sea, 207
"Amateur Rock-Fishers' Association," 94, 95
Anchor, 170
    Casting, 171
Anchovy, 178
Anemone, 25
Appendix, 203
April fishing, 213
Artificial baits, 64, 150
Arun, 29, 113, 114, 116, 221
Arundel, 113, 115, 221
Atherine, 13, 103, 138
August fishing, 14, 17 (*f.n.*), 28, 37, 99, 103, 105, 106, 107, 109, 117, 124, 135, 136, 183, 185, 191, 192, 209, 211, 216, 226, 232
Australian fishing, 3, 7, 17, 43, 44, 71, 93, 97, 98, 128, 178, 181, 244
Automatic Striker, 88
    Winch, 51
Autumn fishing, 18, 109, 197
Avon, Hampshire, 104, 213

B

"Baby spinner," 64, 66
"Ballard," 17
Baltic, 24, 51, 110, 132, 238
Baltimore, 220
Barramunda, 247
Basket, 68
Bass, 7 (*f.n.*), 13, 19, 35, 40, 46, 99, 103, 105, 106, 109, 112, 113, 114, 121, 155, 163, 179
"Bay-set," 131, 207
Beachy Head, 190, 220
Beckford, Mr. (quoted), 212
"Berley," 178
Bexhill, 182
"Bib," 33, 193
"Bickerdyke" end-ring, 48
    Line-guard, 50
Black-fish, 247
Boat-fishing, 44, 70, 144
Boat-shaped lead, 63, 83, 150, 181, 188, 197
Boats, Management of, 144
Bognor, 112, 113, 159
Boom, Revolving, 56
Boscombe, 121, 212
Bottle to carry out line, 91
Bottom-tackle, 54
Bournemouth, 6, 7, 19, 22, 28, 29, 31, 37, 51, 64, 80, 102, 103, 107, 118, 120, 122, 124, 135, 138, 146, 159, 174, 183, 190
Bream, 16, 110, 181, 182
    Black, 16, 245
    Red, 16
    Spanish, 17 (*f.n.*),
Brighton, 213
Brill, 103
"Briming," 5
"British Sea Anglers' Society,"

1, 42, 95, 203, 214, 215, 226, 233
Brixham, 214
"Broodiness" of the sea, 5
Bryden, Mr. H. A. (quoted), 205, 241
Budleigh Salterton, 215
Bullheads, 199
Buoy, cork, 158, 166

C

Cane spreader or outrigger, 156
Cape of Good Hope, 241
Care of tackle, 53, 76
Ceylon, 10
Chad, 17
Channel fishing, 4, 8, 13, 14, 21, 44, 147, 197, 238
  Islands, 109, 233
Chapman spinner, 64
Cheese, 179
Chopstick, 56, 112, 131, 148, 170 200
Christchurch, 212, 213
Christmas fishing, 139, 207
Chub, 177
Clarke, Mr. G. R. (quoted), 215, 237
Clearing Ring, 142
Clothing, 10
Coal-fish, 9, 17, 96, 206
Cockle, 18
Cod, 10, 11, 13, 18, 96, 99, 100, 139, 163, 180, 182, 206
Codling, 18, 103, 139, 183, 190
Colour of the sea, 5
Compass, 147
Conger, 18, 20, 36, 74, 80, 92, 103, 107, 118, 135, 179, 183, 190, 193
Conway, 30
Cornish fishing, 5, 15, 17, 20, 32, 33, 37, 53, 61, 62, 72, 81, 82, 83, 85, 92, 109, 145, 149, 160, 162, 167, 169, 176, 178, 181, 191, 197, 198, 222, 223
Cosmopolitan range of sea-fishing, 4
Courge, 119, 166, 180
Cowes, 134, 173 (*f.n.*), 236

Crab, 19, 97, 115, 177, 178, 179, 181
  , Hermit, 25, 127
  pots, 15, 34, 179
  worm, 20, 160
Creel, 68, 119
Cunningham, Mr. (quoted), 9, 23, 28
Cuttle, 20

D

Dab, 21, 31, 109, 129, 190
Dawlish, 161
Day, Dr., 17 (*f.n.*)
Deal, 5, 18, 102, 126, 139, 140, 182, 197
Depth in whiffing, 153
Devon, 214, 215 (*f.n.*)
Disgorger, 73, 74
Diving Bell for groundbait, 177
Dogfish, 21, 72, 74, 81, 191, 199
Dorset, 160, 215 (*f.n.*)
Dory, 8, 22, 102, 103, 105, 106, 139, 191
Double tides, 107 (*f.n.*)
Dover, 26, 34, 44, 126, 127, 134, 160, 216
Driftlining, 67, 118, 129, 148, 149, 162, 167, 192, 209
Dunn, Mr. Matthias, 223

E

Eastbourne, 126, 135, 140, 220
East wind, 7
Eel, 22, 118
Elvers, 22
Exe, 114
Exemouth, 114, 138, 161, 217

F

False Bay, 244
Field, the (quoted), 134, 203
Fine gear with handlines, 83
Finnock, 207
Fishing Gazette (quoted), 30, 43, 95, 203

Flatfish, 10, 21, 23, 31, 35, 39, 70, 75, 103, 108, 129, 132, 163, 179, 188, 191, 192, 193, 206
Float-fishing, 66, 97, 108, 111, 115, 116, 117, 121, 181, 200
Floating trot, 67
Flounder, 23, 109, 129
Fly fishing, 97, 112, 120
Foreland, 33
Forfar, 206
Fowey, 167, 218

G

Gaff, 70, 189
Gag, 73, 187
Garfish, 8, 23, 191
Geoghegan, Mr. Gerald (quoted), 100, 207
German anglers, 110, 239
Gibraltar, 44
Gimp, 164, 184
Gore-Booth, Sir H. W. (quoted), 220
Gorleston, 100
Green, Rev. W. (quoted), 220
"Greenbone," 23
"Gresham" bag, the, 69
Grey mullet, 179
Groper, 94, 128
Groundbait, 168, 177
Guernsey, 30, 233
"Guffin," 168, 178
Guillemots, 102
Gulls, 14, 40
Gurnard, 24, 103, 180, 190, 191
Gut, 163, 189

H

Haddock, 24
Hake, 24
Hand-lines, 42, 54, 79, 96, 112, 128, 181, 185
Harbours, 102
Hare, Mr. (quoted), 30, 218
Harland, Mr. (quoted),
Harmsworth, Mr. A. (quoted), 50
Hastings, 6, 21, 23, 107, 109, 116, 117, 135, 136, 182, 193, 218
Heacham, 100
"Hercules" gimp, 164
Hermit crab, 25
Herring, 25, 97, 121, 132, 139, 181, 191, 197, 206, 207
Hooks, 54, 96
Horse-mackerel, 37, 191

I

Indian Ocean, 4, 51
Irish fishing, 109, 161, 205, 206, 220
Isle of Wight, see Wight, I. of
Italian anglers, 178, 239

J

January fishing, 213
Jardine's float, 66
 ,, lead, 63
Java, 4
John Bickerdyke (quoted) 64, 161, 173 (*f.n.*), 197, 236
"John Dory," 22
July fishing, 103, 125, 209, 226
June fishing, 14, 28, 183, 185, 209

K

Kentish coast, 197
Killick, 170
Kincardine, 206
Kirby, Mr. (quoted), 134
Knife, 75

L

Ladell, Dr. W. J. S. (quoted), 226
Landing-net, 70, 71, 125, 169
Land's End, 33, 161, 232
Larbalestier, Mr. W. R. (quoted), 236
Launce, 22, 36, 106, 128
Leads, 46, 62, 67, 89, 150, 164, 193

INDEX.

Leather-jacket, 94
  see Mr. Collingwood (quoted), 214, 218, 222, 232, 233
Leger tackle, 30, 56, 108, 112, 129, 148, 170, 181, 188
Leghorn, 103, 133, 240
"Lemon sole," 38, 103, 129
Limpet, 26
Line-drier, 77
Lines, 52
Ling, 26
Littlehampton, 112, 113, 114, 115, 133 (*f.n.*), 134, 221, 235
Live-baiting, 200
Livornese, 178
Lobster-pots, 149, 154
Long line, 67
Long rough dab, 21
Looe, 222
Lugworm, 5, 26, 28, 29, 30, 36, 38, 97, 99, 105, 132, 190, 194, 197, 207
Lulworth Cove, 104, 160, 161, 222
Lythe, 109

M

Macaroni, 29, 133
Mackay, Mr. G. (quoted), 95, 206
McIntosh, Prof. (quoted), 9
Mackerel, 5, 7 (*f.n.*), 10, 13, 27, 31, 37, 52, 62, 64, 70, 72, 79, 80, 81, 102, 103, 105, 121, 122, 149, 161, 163, 166, 168, 180, 181, 185, 189, 191, 192, 194, 197, 199, 209
Mackerel-midge, 14, 28, 36
MacPherson, Mr. C. (quoted), 235
Mahseb sprool, 89
Maples, Mr. (quoted), 29
March fishing, 213
Marks, 173, 198, 203
Marston, Mr. R. B. (quoted), 26, 203
Mavis, 55
May fishing, 28, 105, 183, 221
Mecklenburg, 132
Mediterranean fishing, 4, 28, 51, 178, 239
Mevagissey, 7 (*f.n.*), 17 (*f.n.*), 85, 159, 176, 185, 191, 223

Morocco, 240
Mounts Bay, 226
Mullaghmore, 220
Mullet, Grey, 28, 70, 72, 103, 107, 109, 133, 216
  Red, 9, 29, 103, 107
Multiplying winch, 51
Mussel, 26, 29, 30, 36, 64, 96, 104, 119, 124, 132, 137, 139, 166, 178, 189, 194, 197, 206, 209

N

Naples, 44, 240
Natural History, 12
Needles, The, 108, 161
Newburgh, 207
Newlyn, Mr. (on the automatic winch), 51
New South Wales, 244
Night-fishing, 38, 92, 135
North Sea, 237
Norwegian fjords, 109
"Nottingham" style, 98, 123
  winch, 50, 51, 115, 130, 133
November fishing, 182, 220
Nurse, 21, 31, 81

O

October fishing, 18, 105, 109, 139, 182, 197, 207, 209, 220, 221

P

Pacific Ocean, 43, 51
Packing fish for carriage, 70
Par, 218
Paske, Surgeon-General C. T. (quoted), 216
Paternoster, 56, 121, 127, 148, 170, 194, 200
Pegwell Bay, 233
Pentewan, 5, 191
Perch, 109
Picked (or piked) dog, 21
Piers, 102
Pilchard, 17, 24, 133, 167, 185, 191, 197

INDEX

Pipe-lead, 63, 150
Pith, 177
Plaice, 27, 31, 38, 103, 129, 190
Plumb-lining, 61
Plummetting, 61, 62, 81, 148, 149, 161, 192, 197
Plymouth, 64, 85, 87, 161, 166, 230
Pollack, 9, 13, 17, 21, 31, 34, 36, 40, 46, 52, 70, 74, 79, 83, 102, 103, 105, 106, 107, 118, 121, 126, 128, 149, 152, 154, 161, 163, 165, 166, 168, 187, 190
   Reel, 87
Polperro, 222
Poole, 28, 104, 107 (*f.n.*), 180, 190, 191, 211, 212
Porbeagle, *see* Shark
Porthleven, 232
Port Jackson, 98, 247
Portland, 134, 215 (*f.n.*)
Port Said, 240
Pout, 10, 33, 40, 103, 108, 136, 183
Pouting, 33, 132, 136, 180, 198, 199
"Power-cods," 33
Prawns, 33, 37, 116
Presents of fish, 70
"Priest," 75
Pulley-block, 48

Q

Queensland, 244, 247

R

Ragworm, 34, 127, 133, 150, 167
Railing, 61, 62, 81, 148, 149, 150, 209
Ramsgate, 74, 183, 197, 232
Rays, 19, 35, 189, 199
Razor-fish, 39
Red Sea, 51
"Red Spinner," suggestions of, 42, 203
Reel, 50
Reeling, 61

Revolving hand winder, 86
Rings, 47
Rock-fishers, 94, 96, 246
Rockling, 36, 199
Rockworm, 127, 167
Rods, 44, 96, 110, 114, 149
Rostock, 239
Rough hound, 21
Rowhound, 21, 22, 31
Rubber knob for rods, 46
Rye, 23, 118

S

Sachs, Mr., 139
St. Albans Head, 211
St. Leonards, 190, 218
Saithe, 17, 96, 206
Salmon, 37
Salt, effects of, 77
Salter's Guide, 30
Sand-dab, 21, 38, 103
   -eel, 14, 36, 64, 97, 103, 105, 106, 118, 119, 120, 125, 150, 165, 180
   -smelt, 13, 22, 36, 105, 132, 138, 189
Sardines, 134
"Sarcelle," 224, 240
Sark, 233
Scad, 37, 103, 109
Scarborough, 234
Schwapper, 17, 94, 181, 244
Scillies, 226
Scotch-fishing, 17, 25, 37, 96, 109, 161, 205, 206
"Sea-Angler," 42
Sea-trout, 207
Seine, or Sean, 120
Sennen, 228
Sensitive pipe-lead, 63
September fishing, 106, 182, 190, 221, 226
Shark, Blue, 14, 32
   Porbeagle, 32, 85
Sharks, 43, 94, 198
Shoreham, 29, 180, 235
Shrimp, 37, 116, 132, 137, 166
Sid-strap tackle, 197
Skate, 35, 80, 103, 189, 191, 209
Slider float, 98, 123

www.ingramcontent.com/pod-product-compliance
Lightning Source LLC
Chambersburg PA
CBHW032105220426
43664CB00008B/1134